A Century of Russian Foreign Policy

1814–1914

THE LIPPINCOTT HISTORY SERIES

General Editor: Robert F. Byrnes,
Indiana University

A Century of
Russian Foreign Policy
1814–1914

Barbara Jelavich

INDIANA UNIVERSITY

J. B. Lippincott Company
Philadelphia and New York

For Charles

Preface

The purpose of this book is to explain and describe how Russia, who became a European great power in the eighteenth century, was able to maintain that position and to extend her borders in the nineteenth century, particularly in the Far East and Middle East, although possessing a social, political, and economic system not up to the level reached by her neighbors and competitors to the west. The emphasis will thus be on the tracing of lines of continuous policy to show that despite internal weakness the Russian government in foreign affairs usually demonstrated an instinctive understanding and a remarkably consistent recognition of the realities of the Russian diplomatic situation. This condition, combined with a great deal of plain good luck, brought a degree of success greater than that achieved by states with a more highly developed technology and civilization. The history of a successful foreign policy has in no way been to the unmitigated advantage of the Russian people. The sacrifices demanded of them have perhaps been greater than those asked of any other European nation; they have paid for state power with the sacrifice of the comforts of western Europe and personal freedom. They have, in return, maintained their independence from foreign control, gained dominance over one of the greatest stretches of territory on the globe, and are perhaps on the verge of surpassing their opponents in certain branches of technological achievement, an accomplishment that has been a major Russian objective since the time of Peter the Great.

It must also be remembered that although the following pages record a steady slackening of Russian power and prestige from the height of March, 1814 to the catastrophe of 1914, this decline was relative. The task of Russian diplomacy in the nineteenth century was to protect the boundaries reached by 1815; it succeeded well in its basic undertaking and, in addition, brought into the empire great areas of territory in Asia. In 1945, after almost thirty years of devastating war and revolution, Soviet Russia emerged as one of two world powers from a conflict that shattered forever an international situation in which four European states, in a relative power equilibrium, decided diplomatic policy for the world. The century of relative peace enjoyed by Russia in the nineteenth century, an age that at no time demanded that her full national strength be devoted to foreign enterprises, whether offensive or defensive in direction, allowed her to withstand later disasters. This theme should be followed in the reading of the subsequent account.

This survey is designed primarily for the reader with an interest in eastern Europe or in diplomatic history; it is therefore in form and content not written for the specialist in the subject. The attempt has been made to follow major issues and the main lines of development in the policies adopted by Russia toward her neighbors with the hope that this description will provide a clear picture of Russian intentions, which were usually simple and logical in design. It should also be of assistance in the study of Soviet policy today, which has many points in common with its predecessor.

In the organization of the material the reigns of the five tsars have been taken as the lines of division because of the predominant role played by the ruler in Russia in the final determination of policy. In each succeeding period it was the tsar who gave the pattern and direction to Russian actions; he held the final responsibility for the successes or failures. Throughout these pages it will be noted that the tsars were served by foreign ministers who functioned in fact as secretaries and advisors; the counsel of those outside the ministry was often followed against the express wishes of the officials concerned with foreign policy. This condition was natural to the Russian system, although, of course, many similar examples can be found in the history of other governments.

The narrative of this survey is based primarily on research and reading which the author and her husband have done in connection with the preparation of more detailed studies. These are: *The Education of a Russian Statesman: the Memoirs of Nicholas Karlovich Giers* (Berkeley, 1962); *Russia and Greece during the Regency of King Othon, 1832-1835: Russian Documents on the First Years of Greek Independence* (Thessaloniki, 1962); *Russia and the Rumanian National Cause, 1858-1859* (Bloomington, 1959); *Russia in the East, 1876-1880; the Russo-Turkish War and the Kuldja Crisis as seen through the Letters of A. G. Jomini to N. K. Giers* (Leiden, 1959); *Russland 1852-1871: aus den Berichten der bayerischen Gesandtschaft in St. Petersburg* (Wiesbaden, 1963) and *Tsarist Russia and Balkan Nationalism; Russian Influence in the Internal Affairs of Bulgaria and Serbia, 1879-1886* (Berkeley, 1958). Therefore in certain questions, notably on Russian policy in the Balkans, the book rests on a base of documentary evidence and research in the archives of London, Vienna, and Munich, and on the unpublished correspondence of N. K. Giers. In other fields, selected monographs and general histories have been used, with no attempt being made to cover all of the literature of the subject. For the entire period the author found of particular value: Michael T. Florinsky, *Russia: a History and an Interpretation* (Macmillan, 1960), two volumes; Hugh Seton-Watson, *The Decline of Imperial Russia, 1855-1914* (Praeger, 1961); R. W. Seton-Watson, *Britain in Europe, 1789-1914* (Cambridge, 1955); Karl Stählin, *Geschichte Russlands* (Graz, 1961), four volumes in five; L. S. Stavrianos, *The Balkans since 1453* (New York, 1959) and A. J. P. Taylor, *The Struggle for Mastery in Europe: 1848-1918* (Oxford, 1957). Selected monographs for the different periods are listed in the bibliography. Particular mention should, however, be made of T. Schiemann, *Geschichte Russlands unter Kaiser Nikolaus I* (Berlin, 1904-1919), four volumes; W. E. Mosse, *The European Powers and the German Question, 1848-1871* (Cambridge, 1958), and volumes one and two of V. P. Potemkin, editor, *Istoriia diplomatii* (Moscow, 1945) for a Soviet interpretation. Since this survey is for the general reader, the bibliography contains only works in the English language. The books by Stavrianos and Taylor, listed above, provide additional references in other languages.

In the transcription of Russian names the spelling most familiar in the West has, in general, been adopted. In most cases this form is equivalent to a simple transliteration of the Cyrillic according to the Library of Congress system. Although in the nineteenth century the Russian calendar ran twelve days behind that of the West, only the European, or new style, form will be given. The Russian date can be determined by subtraction. In the twentieth century the number must be increased to thirteen.

The author wishes to express her great appreciation to Professors R. F. Byrnes, F. T. Epstein, and J. M. Thompson of Indiana University, and to Professor P. Scheibert of the University of Marburg, who read and commented upon the entire manuscript; to Professor S. Y. Teng of Indiana University for his assistance with the chapters on the Far East; and to Professor R. A. Pierce of Queens College for his comments on the sections on Central Asia. As in the case of previous publications, this study is in fact the product of joint research and writing which the author has done with her husband, Charles Jelavich, to whom this book is dedicated. The preparation of the manuscript was also immensely aided by the co-operation of Mark and Peter Jelavich and by their enjoyment of traveling in the countries dealt with in these pages.

October, 1963

BARBARA JELAVICH

Contents

Maps

I

The Eighteenth Century Background

Although the major portion of this study will be devoted to the politics of the nineteenth century, a brief account of the developments of the previous period is necessary, chiefly because the major task of Russian diplomacy after 1815 was the protection of the empire whose construction was completed during the earlier years. With the conclusion of the Vienna treaties the Russian boundaries reached their maximum extension in the west, the culmination of three centuries of almost constant expansion. The eighteenth century was also of particular significance since it brought Russia into the European state system and thereafter linked her history primarily with that of the west. During that century the design for much of Russian policy for the succeeding decades was set, and diplomatic patterns were formed that were to remain constant until the outbreak of the First World War.

At the end of the seventeenth century, Europe, organized into a system of independent states usually under the rule of an absolute monarch, had as its guiding principle in international relations the idea of the balance of power, a concept designed to prevent one nation from dominating the continent. After the Thirty Years' War, which wrought great devastation in central Europe, France was clearly the strongest power and the state that threatened to achieve continental hegemony. In 1643 one of the most remarkable of European monarchs, Louis XIV, came to the throne of France and adopted a frankly expansionist program, aiming at the acquisition of France's "natural frontiers." The diplomatic pattern for western Europe was thereafter largely determined by the moves of the French king and the efforts made to block them. All of the other major powers of the age, Britain, Spain, the Habsburg Empire, the Ottoman Empire, Poland, Sweden, and Holland, were influenced by French activity.

The first area under attack from France was that of the Spanish Netherlands. Spain under the rule of a weak and mentally deficient monarch held but a shadow of her former glory. Although in possession of a great empire in America and of lands in Italy that gave her domination over that peninsula, the nation as a whole was in a process of economic and political decay. In contrast, Holland, the second state under pressure from France, presented a glowing picture of wealth and prosperity. This former Spanish possession had raised itself to a height of mercantile and commercial achievement despite the obvious fact that the country itself was too weak to be able to withstand the attack of a major power. Across the channel, Britain, the major beneficiary of the balance of power principle, like Holland, had built its position on seapower as well as on widespread commercial and colonial ventures. At first primarily concerned with Dutch competition, Britain entered the ranks against France when the victories of Louis XIV threatened to result in a tremendous increase in French power.

In central Europe the traditional rival of the French Bourbon kings, the Habsburg Empire, found itself in a difficult strategic position, which, when combined with its internal divisions, limited its power. Pressed on the one side by France and by problems arising from the Habsburg position in Italy, Spain, and the Germanies, this state was also threatened on its other front by the Ottoman Empire. After 1355, when the first conquests on the European continent were made, this Moslem power had successfully extended its control over the Balkans and threatened to expand into central Europe. The end of the seventeenth century brought the last great attack; in 1683 the Ottoman armies again approached the gates of Vienna. With their failure to capture this city, the force of Turkish power thereafter waned. In 1699, in the Treaty of Karlowitz, the Habsburg Monarchy made the first victorious peace with Turkey and the menace to Europe was ended. Thereafter the situation reversed itself; the Christian powers now turned to the conquest of Turkish territories.

Despite its successes against the Turks, the Habsburg state as a power complex was not equivalent to France. By 1720 Austria had also gained the former Spanish territories of Naples, Sicily, and Milan and thereby the control of Italy. The addition of new lands did not, however, contribute to Habsburg strength. The basic problem of the empire remained what it was to be until its collapse in 1918—that of how to organize and administer as an effective unit lands of varying national composition, historical development, and past tradition. Success in foreign relations in the next two centuries was to lie more in the hands of those with strong national centers, such as France, Britain, and even Russia, and to be denied to loosely organized empires such as Austria and Turkey.

Habsburg influence also remained strong in Germany, although this land was little more than a geographic expression. Economically devastated by the Thirty Years' War and politically fragmented into over 300 competitive entities, this area could play no part as a unit in international politics. Certain individual states, nevertheless, such as Prussia, Saxony, and Bavaria, did compete for great power status and for a stronger position in relation to their other German rivals.

To the ranks of the major powers two other states, Poland and Sweden, must also be added. The fate of the first, Poland, who held an area the size of France, will be discussed in detail in the following pages. Sweden, whose conflict with Russia in the Great Northern War dominated the reign of Peter the Great, had, under the leadership of the able house of Vasa, expanded in the Baltic region until it in fact controlled that sea. Swedish domination was naturally contested by the powers with Baltic interests— the independent kingdom of Denmark (at this time united with Norway), Prussia, and Russia, who were naturally interested in limiting or breaking Swedish power.

The diplomatic pattern confronting Russia at the accession of Peter the Great was, therefore, one dominated by France and Louis XIV. It must also be noted that France traditionally had followed the policy of the eastern barrier in central Europe. In an effort to outflank the Habsburgs she had maintained close relationships with Sweden, Poland, and Turkey. This combination was also to prove useful against Russia. Because her attention was focused primarily upon these states, Russia thus usually found herself in the opposite camp to France. She did not, however, directly participate in the great allied campaigns against Louis XIV that ended in his defeat and in the settlement of Utrecht of 1713.

PETER THE GREAT

The diplomatic history of Russia as a European great power commences with the reign of Peter the Great in 1682. Prior to that date the Russian rulers had devoted their energies to the great task of re-assembling the Russian lands after the Mongol conquest, establishing a state that could protect itself against renewed foreign invasion, and extending their dominion across Siberia to the Pacific. Peter the Great not only brought Russia into the politics of western Europe, in the manner to be discussed on the following pages, but he also laid the lines of Russian foreign policy

EUROPE AROUND 1700

for the next century. His program and his methods of action were followed by his successors, and his aims were largely achieved by Catherine II by the 1790's. His reign saw the inauguration of a plan of active expansion toward the Black Sea at the expense of the Ottoman Empire, of conquest and annexation along the Baltic coast, and of intervention in Poland and to a lesser extent in the affairs of the small German states.

In his direction of foreign policy Peter I demonstrated the same ruthless energy and ambition with which he achieved his internal reforms. He had also the imagination and daring to embark upon courses of action which, although dangerous in conception, ultimately brought great rewards. Without the driving force of his leadership, it is probable that although Russia might inevitably have followed the direction which she now took, it would not have been with such precipitation and, perhaps as far as external affairs are concerned, with such a degree of success. The career of Peter I is the best demonstration of the statement made previously of the importance in Russia of the tsar in the formulation and conduct of foreign policy.

Peter I inaugurated his career in 1695 with an expedition directed against the khan of the Crimea, his intention being to take the Black Sea port of Azov. In this, his first military undertaking, he took personal charge of the operations and thus shared in the blame for the failure of the undertaking. However, from his initial defeat he learned valuable lessons. Since he now saw clearly the necessity of developing Russian sea power, he immediately embarked upon the construction of what was to be the forerunner of the Russian navy. A year later, with his crudely constructed ships, he succeeded in capturing Azov. Thereafter, with his attention primarily directed toward the seizing of lands from the Ottoman Empire, he devoted a great deal of personal attention to naval problems. He sent many of his subjects abroad to study shipbuilding, and in 1697 he himself visited European shipyards and docks. There he worked as a carpenter in order to become thoroughly acquainted with the details of the craft.

Peter's journeys through Europe, although they did not include France, the leading nation of western Europe, brought the tsar into close contact with the civilization of the west. What fascinated him in his travels was not so much the culture and refinements of European life as its technological superiority. Therefore he sought first to bring into Russia those aspects of western life that would contribute to the ultimate power of his state. The manners and customs, the frills and decorations of aristocratic life were also admired and desired, but the concentration remained on the elements that would eventually contribute to Russian military power.

Since his chief interest at this time lay in expansion southward, Peter I used his European trip to lay the groundwork for a campaign against the Turks in which he proposed to join with the two nations with similar interests, Austria and Venice. Although the alliance concluded with Austria in 1697 marks the beginning of Russo-Austrian collaboration in the Balkans against the Ottoman Empire, the Habsburg Monarchy at this time was not ready for ambitious undertakings. In 1698, at the Congress of Karlowitz, Russia joined with Austria, Poland, and Venice in negotiations with Turkey. This assembly gave Austria a great victory; Russia, who received only a two year armistice, felt betrayed by her ally. In 1700 Peter I was able to conclude a further treaty with the Porte, providing for a thirty year truce, the possession of the port of Azov, the right to keep a resident minister at Constantinople, and permission for the Orthodox to make pilgrimages to the Holy Places, which were under Ottoman control. Despite the fact that this agreement was not long kept, its provisions had a tremendous significance for the relations of the two countries, and they set a pattern for future treaties. The settlement with Turkey now permitted Peter to turn his attention northward toward the Baltic.

The Great Northern War, which commenced for Russia in 1700, dominated the entire period of Peter's reign and lasted for twenty-one years. None of the major participants, Russia, Saxony, or Denmark, anticipated such a protracted struggle when in 1698 they determined to attack Sweden. In fact, on the surface the situation appeared ideal for a joint assault. Although Sweden at the time ranked among the great powers and dominated the Baltic Sea, her position was steadily deteriorating. Moreover, she was ruled by a new king, Charles XII, who ascended the throne at the age of fifteen. In 1699 an alliance was concluded between the three Swedish opponents under the sponsorship and on the initiative of the Saxon ruler, Augustus II, who was also King of Poland. Since Peter I was still involved in hostilities with the Porte, Saxony and Denmark commenced the war alone. To the immense surprise of the allies, it soon became apparent that in the person of her king Sweden had a military genius of the first order. Even before Peter I had made peace with the Porte, Denmark had been defeated and forced to leave the war. The first Russian major engagement resulted in one of the most crushing defeats in Russian military history—that of the battle of Narva in November, 1700. Here a force of about 8,000 Swedish soldiers completely routed 35,000 Russians. The battle clearly showed Peter the poor quality of his army.

The disaster at Narva, however, forced Peter I to inaugurate a thoroughgoing program of military reform. He immediately embarked upon a complete reorganization of the army, and he sought in particular to improve the training methods and discipline of the soldiers and the quality of the armaments. He clearly recognized the danger that threatened Russia from a probable Swedish invasion; the question was whether his opponent would allow him time to prepare. Fortunately for the tsar, the rout of the Russian army at Narva had left Charles XII with little more than contempt for Russian power. Instead of following up his victory against Russia, he turned instead toward Saxony and for six years campaigned in Poland. Peter I thus won the necessary time to recover his strength and reorganize his armies. By 1701 he was able to begin action against the Swedish forces in the Baltic provinces. In 1703 he took the mouth of the Neva river where he began the construction of the city of St. Petersburg.

The chief field of battle in the meantime remained Poland. Here Augustus II was unable to withstand his brilliant opponent. In 1704 Charles XII chose a puppet ruler, Stanislas Lesczynski, for the Polish throne. Although Peter despatched an army to his aid in 1705, the Saxon king was forced in the next year to make peace with Sweden, thereby renouncing both the Polish crown and the Russian alliance. With the status of Poland, Saxony, and Denmark now settled in his favor, Charles XII could turn to Russia. Peter I, without allies and still unprepared for a major war, sought to make peace by every means possible. Charles XII, however, in January, 1708 with a well-equipped and experienced army of around 46,000 crossed the Russian border and began to march toward Moscow.

To meet this attack by the technically superior Swedish forces, Peter I adopted the tactics that were to be repeated in 1812 and 1941 when once again Russia faced invasion by stronger armies —the scorched earth policy. Peter I withdrew his forces toward the interior of the country and avoided any direct encounter with the Swedish army that could result in the annihilation of his forces. He simultaneously destroyed along his line of retreat all supplies that could be used by the enemy. The Swedish armies had first embarked upon a direct route to Moscow; in September it was decided that they should march southward where supplies were believed more plentiful and that then they should attack Moscow from the southwest rather than from the west. Charles XII was hopeful of receiving aid from malcontent Ukrainian groups, particularly because he was assured of the support of the hetman, Mazeppa. The Swedish hopes were not fulfilled; the winter proved severe and sufficient supplies could not be procured from the hostile countryside. Charles XII also did not receive reinforcements from outside, and no great Ukrainian uprising assisted the Swedish invasion. The Ukrainians feared that a Swedish victory would bring not national freedom, but renewed Polish domination by Sweden's puppet king, Stanislas Leszcynski.

The ravages of a bitter winter, the failure to obtain sufficient provisions, and an ever-decreasing army provided the background for the Swedish defeat at the battle of Poltava in July, 1709. Even though the Russian victory was gained over an exhausted and greatly weakened opponent, Russia had nevertheless successfully met an invasion by one of the most formidable military powers of the day. Charles XII, accompanied by Mazeppa, fled to Turkish territory. Once in Constantinople and supported by the French diplomats stationed there, the Swedish king worked assiduously to involve the Porte in renewed hostilities against Russia.

In 1710 the Swedish endeavors met with success and the Ottoman Empire declared war on Russia. To meet this new threat Peter determined upon a campaign in the Balkans where he hoped to enlist the support of the governors (*hospodars*) of the Turkish-controlled principalities of Moldavia and Wallachia. The Russian government also issued an appeal to the subject Christians of the Ottoman Empire to rise and fight with Russia to throw off Moslem rule. Although these initial efforts met with no response, the issue of Russian interest in and Russian responsibility toward the Orthodox Balkan peoples had been raised. Russia had also found a weapon that could be used most effectively as a threat against the Porte, but one that inevitably aroused the suspicion and hostility of the other powers.

The failure of Peter to win the co-operation of the Wallachian *hospodar* despite the fact that his counterpart in Moldavia, Cantemir, did render assistance, contributed to the Russian defeat. In July, 1711 on the Prut river Peter I suffered the most crushing personal defeat of his career. His forces were surrounded, and he was forced to seek peace. In this seemingly desperate situation Peter was prepared to make great sacrifices, including even the abandonment of his Baltic conquests. The Porte, however, perhaps as a result of a judicious distribution of bribes, demanded only the surrender of Azov and the destruction of the Russian Black Sea fleet. Although these terms signified that Peter I abandoned all of the gains which he had made in his wars with Tur-

ACQUISITIONS OF PETER THE GREAT

SWEDEN

Nystadt

Petersburg

Volga River

Baltic Sea

Niemen

PRUSSIA

River

Moscow

Oka River

Vistula

Bug River

River

POLAND

Dnieper River

Warsaw

RUSSIA

Don River

Kiev

Dniester

River

KINGDOM
OF HUNGARY

Prut River

Azov

Danube

CRIMEA

River

Kuchuk Kainarji

Black Sea

OTTOMAN

EMPIRE

key, they were nevertheless moderate under the circumstances. The victory of Poltava had not only freed Russia from the Swedish threat, but it had also allowed the Russian allies, Denmark and Saxony, to re-enter the conflict. They were later joined by Prussia and Hanover. Augustus II was able to take back the Polish throne, and operations were launched against the Swedish positions in the Baltic. In 1714, after quarreling with his Turkish hosts, Charles XII returned to Sweden. Despite the relative weakness of the Swedish forces, the war continued, largely because a lack of co-operation between the allies precluded any decisive victories. In 1718 Charles XII was killed on the field of battle, and with the loss of its greatest military leader Sweden gave up any hope of regaining its former domination of the Baltic.

The long war between Sweden and Russia was ended with the signing of the Peace of Nystadt in September, 1721. In this agreement Russia received extensive gains on the Baltic coast: Livonia, including Riga, Ingria and a part of Karelia. The new lands not only gave Russia ports on the Baltic Sea, providing far better communications with western Europe, but they also brought into the state a population that was to play a most significant role in the future history of Russia, particularly in the administration of foreign policy and in the army. The Baltic lands Russia now acquired were inhabited by a Lettish and Estonian population ruled over by a predominantly German nobility. The Baltic Germans, who came from an area more highly developed than Russia proper, entered in large numbers into state service and in the course of the next century they came to dominate the highest positions in the army, navy, and civil administration. The use made by the tsars of this element of their population, which was in general diligent and talented in administrative work, was a great advantage to the Russian autocracy. Russia had no great middle class from which to draw state servants and bureaucrats. The fact that the Baltic nobility was non-Russian made them more reliable servants of the monarch and mitigated the danger that they would join with their Russian counterparts to form a strong center of opposition to the central power.

FROM PETER TO CATHERINE

Between the death of Peter the Great in 1725 and the beginning of the reign of his true successor, Catherine the Great, Russia was ruled by six sovereigns of widely varying abilities. Although, as could be expected, Russian foreign relations in this period did not show the great successes of the years of Peter's rule, it is to be noted that Russia suffered no major losses despite the comparative weakness of her government. Following in the path set by Peter I the Russian government continued to remain intensely concerned with the international balance in Europe, and an active policy was pursued in regard to Swedish, Polish, and Turkish affairs. The Russian position in these years was most deeply and permanently influenced by the chief diplomatic event of the mid-century—the emergence of Prussia under Frederick the Great as a great power. The other major struggle of the time, the colonial rivalry between Britain and France, affected Russia only indirectly in that it could be assumed that these two powers would always be on opposite sides in any diplomatic or military conflict. Policy could thus not be based on alliance or co-operation with both at once. As a result of the French policy of the eastern barrier, that is of the diplomatic support of Sweden, Poland, and the Ottoman Empire, Russia was usually hostile to France and, because of increasing commercial ties, friendly to Britain. Poland, Sweden, and the Ottoman Empire remained the centers of Russian diplomatic activity.

Because of her unique internal conditions, Poland after the death of Peter became and remained little more than a pawn in the power conflict of her stronger neighbors, Russia and Austria against France. Well before the death of Augustus II in 1733 the rival states prepared for the event. France supported the candidacy of Stanislas Lesczynski, who was the son-in-law of the French monarch, Louis XV. When Lesczynski was elected by a majority of the Polish diet, a pro-Russian minority of the Polish nobility appealed to Russia, who replied by sending troops to assist her friends. Although France was thus deeply engaged in Polish affairs, she gave her partisans only token support in the form of men and money. The War of Polish Succession of 1733, in which Russia and Austria were allied against France, Spain, and Sardinia, was concluded in 1735 with an Austro-French armistice. Subsequently under the rule of the Austro-Russian candidate, Augustus III, Poland was under the practical domination of Russia.

The Russian expansionist policy toward the Ottoman Empire was continued by the launching of another campaign in 1736. Austria joined in 1737, but the entire undertaking was not successful. When this ally withdrew, Russia was forced to conclude the Peace of Belgrade in 1739. Here Russia received Azov, but on the condition that the fortifications be destroyed. Russian commercial shipping also continued to be excluded from the Black Sea. Shortly after the conclusion of this agreement, Russia became involved in another war with Sweden, who had never accepted as final the terms of the Treaty of Nystadt. Russian military victories forced Sweden in 1743 to accept a peace that gave the victor some Finnish territories and brought the Russian candidate, Adolphus Frederick of Holstein, to the Swedish throne. The Russo-Swedish War had meanwhile merged with the far more significant War of Austrian Succession.

In 1740 Frederick II of Prussia, in agreement with France and other German states, used the occasion of the succession of Maria Theresa to seize the Austrian province of Silesia. The acquisition of this territory was to enable Prussia henceforth to play a major diplomatic role in European history. Although in theory Russia was allied to Austria and Britain in this conflict, her participation in the actual hostilities remained limited. The first part of the duel over Silesia between Austria and Prussia was ended in 1748 by the Treaty of Aix-la-Chapelle, which confirmed the Prussian conquest. It was however to be only the prelude to a major diplomatic realignment of the great powers.

Until the middle of the century, as we have seen, the major Russian opponent had been France, who in turn had supported Sweden, Poland, and the Ottoman Empire against their eastern neighbor. Despite disagreements over Balkan policy, Russia had been in alliance with Austria and had also worked with Britain and Prussia. In general, Russia, Austria, and Prussia had together opposed France, the strongest single power on the continent. The increase in Prussian strength under Frederick II introduced a change in the European balance. Once this state was raised out of the category of the German states of second rank, such as Saxony and Bavaria, the question of her potential danger to Russia arose. The signing of the Treaty of Westminster in 1756 between Prussia and Britain also increased Russian apprehensions since it appeared to be in contradiction to the existing Russo-British agreements.

Meanwhile, in a complete reversal of their previous policies, Austria and France now patched up their quarrels and formed an alliance against Prussia. This diplomatic revolution was accomplished chiefly through the activities of the Austrian minister, Prince Kaunitz. Fearing the gathering coalition, Frederick in August, 1756 attacked Saxony and thereby precipitated the Seven Years' War. In December Russia joined Austria and France and sent her armies into central Europe. Although Frederick II, like Charles XII, was a military commander of the highest caliber, the Prussian state, like the Swedish, did not have the manpower or resources to support a war of indefinite duration against a coalition. Aid from Britain came chiefly in the form of subsidies, which, although valuable, could not overcome the great disadvantages under which Prussia fought. Although Frederick was assisted by the divisions among his allies, his final victory came largely from a stroke of luck. In 1761 Empress Elizabeth, who had favored strongly Russian participation in the war against Prussia, died and was succeeded by her nephew Peter III, who had a deep admiration for Frederick. He not only immediately ended the war against Prussia, but he also formed a military alliance with the former enemy. Russian troops now marched to the aid of Prussia, and Elizabeth's policy was nullified.

Despite the fears of the empress, the Prussian state that now emerged as a major power proved an element of strength and not a threat to Russia. Henceforth, until the breaking of the Reinsurance Treaty in 1890, Prussia (united Germany after 1870) became the most enduring and reliable of Russia's allies. Joined by dynastic ties in the succeeding years and with similar interests in Europe, Russia and Prussia co-operated closely in international affairs, in most instances to the advantage of both powers.

CATHERINE THE GREAT

The true heir to the tradition of Peter the Great was the wife of Peter III, who came to the throne in 1762 after the assassination of her husband. A German princess from the minor principality of Anhalt-Zerbst, Catherine II identified herself with the interests of her adopted country and extended the Russian boundaries as had few other rulers in Russian history. Like Peter I she favored a policy of close participation in the life and politics of western Europe. The first question she faced was that of the liquidation of the war with Prussia. Although she did not return to the policy of Elizabeth, she did recall the troops which had been sent to the aid of Frederick II. Subsequently, the two belligerents, Prussia and Austria, now both without effective allies, came to terms, and the Prussian conquest of Silesia was again confirmed.

With the conclusion of the Seven Years' War the situation in Europe was favorable for the commencement of an expansionist policy by Russia. France and Britain had been and were to be preoccupied with colonial problems. Austria, exhausted by the past years of warfare, had little desire to contribute to the aggrandizement of Russian power, but she could be tempted into territorial divisions. Prussia was about to become a Russian ally.

Catherine could thus without the fear of the formation of a hostile coalition turn her attention to the Polish and Turkish problems.

By the 1770's the internal political conditions in Poland had rendered that enormous state virtually helpless before her neighbors. The third largest in territory and the fourth in population among the nations of Europe, she had fallen into a state of internal anarchy and could no longer defend her independence against foreign intrusions. The power in the government lay in the hands of the landowning aristocracy, which formed about 8 per cent of the population. In a series of measures introduced over the preceding years this group had rendered the central organs of the administration powerless. In the Diet of Lublin in 1569 they succeeded in making the kingship elective; through the institution of the Liberum Veto, by which one vote could negate all action, the Polish diet was prevented from becoming an effective and constructive instrument of government. Because of the right of the nobility to form confederations, or armed associations, civil war and civil turmoil were legalized. Although these measures in theory guaranteed the liberties of one class, they in fact made the Polish state a free field for foreign intrigue and intervention.

Poland, as has been mentioned, was part of the French eastern barrier, which had as its objective, first, the confinement of the Habsburg Empire and, second, the walling off of Russia from Europe. French interests, therefore, called for the maintenance of a militarily strong Poland in alliance with France. Certainly, strong natural connections existed between the two states apart from their common interests in international relations. Both were predominantly Catholic and the high level of French civilization exerted a strong attraction over the Polish gentry. In contrast to France, Russia had no interest in the existence of a strong Poland, particularly in alliance with France, Sweden, or the Ottoman Empire. The entire area was vital for Russian defense. In the hands of a hostile power it could be, and had been, the launching point for an invasion. Moreover, the religious conflict in the state, particularly in the areas where a Catholic Polish nobility ruled over an Orthodox Russian peasantry, was continually a source of irritation and discord. Thus in her national interest and in her position as the defender of Orthodoxy, Russia had convincing reasons for her intervention in Polish internal affairs. Throughout the eighteenth century the Russian government kept a strict watch on events in Poland and tried to control the state without actual annexation.

Prussia and Austria had similar interests in the fate of Poland. Prussia desired to annex the Polish territories that separated her East Prussian territories and prevented the consolidation of her lands. Austria, although with less at stake than her neighbors, had seen Poland used against her by her Bourbon enemies. However, perhaps the greatest concern of the two German powers was that Russia would simply annex the territory she in fact controlled already and that she would do this without compensating Berlin or Vienna. This disturbance of the balance of power in eastern Europe would have been dangerous for both powers.

The death of Augustus III in 1763 again reopened the question of the Polish kingship. Catherine II at once produced a candidate in the person of her former lover, Stanislas Poniatowski, a Polish nobleman. The support of Prussia for the Russian choice was assured through the alliance of 1764. In this treaty, both powers agreed to aid Poniatowski, to guarantee the religious rights of the non-Catholic people of Poland, and to assist each other in case of attack. The agreement, which remained in effect until 1780, joined the two powers together in a common front in international affairs. Thereafter Catherine II embarked on a policy in Poland that led to far more active interference in the internal affairs of the country than had hitherto been the case. In 1767 Russian troops entered the country, and the diet was forced to pass measures in the interest of the Lutheran and Orthodox elements of the population. Russian intervention led to the formation of the Confederation of Bar in 1768 and to four years of guerilla warfare. Both France and Austria, in an attempt to prevent absolute Russian domination, sent the rebels arms, men, and money. The Russian troops, however, were led by one of the greatest of all Russian generals, Alexander Suvorov.

Meanwhile, the Polish revolt merged with a renewed Russo-Turkish conflict. French diplomats worked actively in Constantinople to gain the support of the Porte for the Polish Confederation. In October, 1768 a border incident led to a Turkish declaration of war on Russia. Thereafter the principal attention of the Russian government once again shifted southward toward the Black Sea and the Balkans. With great energy and resourcefulness Catherine II and her advisors began the campaign against Turkey. An army was despatched along the now familiar route to the Danube. Of greater interest, however, was the Russian naval expedition that was sent to the Mediterranean from the Baltic. The aim of this move was to challenge the Turkish navy in its home waters and, if possible, to raise in revolt the Christian populations of the empire. In this endeavor Russia received encouragement and naval supplies from Britain, who at this time considered France the principal threat to her commercial and imperial supremacy. Britain thus welcomed Russian victories over the French allies—Sweden, Poland, and the Ottoman Empire.

Once in the Mediterranean the Russian fleet, although in poor fighting condition and without experience, defeated an even weaker Turkish navy off the island of Chios in July, 1770. The subsequent destruction of Turkish naval power opened the possibility of an attack on Constantinople. The Russian commander, Orlov, was reluctant to take the risk, and, certainly, the Russian forces available were not adequate for grand military manoeuvres. Moreover, the Christian populations had not risen to support the Russian attack. The Greeks, who had expected large scale Russian aid, were reluctant to move when only token assistance arrived. The minor rebellion that did occur was easily crushed by the Ottoman forces.

The Russian naval victories and the success of the armies operating in the Danubian Principalities had an alarming effect upon the other powers, particularly Prussia. Frederick II recognized that no advantages could be gained for his state from the collapse of the Ottoman Empire since this was an area in which he could not claim compensation. He also saw that the situation in the east could in the end lead to an Austro-Russian conflict, which he feared in view of his alliance with St. Petersburg. He, therefore, approached both powers with the suggestion of a partition of Poland with the understanding that Russia would make a moderate peace with Turkey. On August 5, 1772 the three powers signed the first of the partition treaties. Here Poland lost a third of her territory and almost half of her population. Russia received as her share a large part of White Russia; Austria took Galicia and southern Podolia; and Prussia annexed Polish Prussia.

The war with Turkey continued two more years, but, finally on July 21, 1774, the most important treaty in the entire history of Russo-Turkish relations, that of Kuchuk Kainarji, was signed. In this agreement Russia gained an increase of territory in the Black Sea region and the port of Azov; the Khanate of the Crimea was recognized as an independent state. The Principalities of Moldavia and Wallachia, which had been occupied by Russian troops, were returned to the control of the Porte on condition that religious freedom and good government be maintained. Russia reserved the right to intervene and speak in behalf of the Christian population. Wide commercial privileges in the Ottoman territories were also gained. Russia was allowed to appoint consuls in the principal cities of the empire; her subjects were permitted to trade and navigate in the Black Sea and the Danube. She also was to receive most friendly nation privileges in her trade with Turkey.

Although these gains were certainly considerable, the section of the treaty bearing most significantly on the future was that which concerned the position of the Orthodox in the Ottoman Empire. Russia was to be allowed to construct a church in Constantinople and to have jurisdiction over it. Even more important, however, was the clause: "The Sublime Porte promises to protect constantly the Christian religion and its churches, and it also allows the Ministers of the Imperial Court of Russia to make representa-

tions . . ." The exact meaning of this statement was never clari-
fied. Later Russian representatives were to use it as a justification
of a policy of interference in the internal affairs of the empire.
Quite obviously the sentence permitted Russia to complain officially of any measures Turkey might take to the detriment of
her subject Christian populations, but it was not clear whether
the Ottoman government was obligated to listen to or to accept
Russian advice. The interpretation to be given this clause, and,
for that matter, those in relation to Russia's special position in the
Principalities, remained a point of dispute until after the Crimean
War when Russia was forced to abandon her claim to the sole
protectorship of the Balkan Christians.

The Treaty of Kuchuk Kainarji was thus a notable defeat for
the Ottoman Empire. It lost its attempt to maintain control over
the Black Sea; the Russian right of intervention in the Principalities obtained official recognition. Russia also gained certain ill-
defined rights to speak in behalf of the Balkan Orthodox. If the
terms of the treaty were to be interpreted in the sense most
favorable to Russia and if they were backed by predominant
military power in the Balkan Peninsula, Russian control could be
established over the Ottoman Empire.

The division of Poland and the peace with Turkey raised
Russian prestige to a new height. In 1778 Catherine II mediated
a dispute between Prussia and Austria concerning Bavaria. In 1780
she organized the League of Armed Neutrality between Denmark, Sweden, Prussia, and other states in protest against the
British treatment of neutral shipping in the American War of
Independence. The chief concern of Russian policy, nevertheless,
remained the fate of Poland and the Ottoman Empire. Despite the
great gains of Kuchuk Kainarji, Catherine II, with the collaboration of her advisor, Gregory Potemkin, drew up further plans for
even greater conquests in the east.

The death of Maria Theresa in 1780 and the removal of her
restraining hand opened the way for closer co-operation between
Austria and Russia. Joseph II, who like Catherine II was a student
of the Enlightenment, had long been in correspondence with the

Russian empress. Although with less enthusiasm, Joseph II was won over to Catherine's wide plans for the destruction of the Ottoman Empire. In 1780 the Prusso-Russian pact lapsed; Austria and Russia then joined in the next year in a defensive alliance whose main aim was the ultimate partition of Turkey. Catherine II now proposed that in the division of Ottoman lands Russia should receive the western Caucasus, the Crimea, and territory to the Dniester river. Moldavia and Wallachia were to be joined to form the independent state of Dacia. Joseph II, for his share, was to have parts of Wallachia, Serbia, Bosnia, Hercegovina, Istria, and Dalmatia. What was left of Turkey-in-Europe, the Bulgarian and Greek lands, was to be formed into a new Greek Empire, with Constantinople as the capital and with Catherine's second grandson, Constantine, as emperor. The provision was also made that the new state should never become a part of Russia proper.

Conflict with Turkey was provoked through Russian interference in the affairs of the theoretically independent Khanate of the Crimea. Since it could obtain the support of no other state, the Porte was forced in 1783 to cede the territory to Russia. Thereafter under the able direction of Potemkin, a policy of the rapid development of the newly acquired lands was undertaken. Nikolaev and Sebastopol were established as strong naval bases that could directly threaten Constantinople, now two and a half sailing days distant. At the same time Russian agents continued to agitate among the Christian populations of Turkey. The Russian activities in the areas bordering on the Ottoman territories in the Balkan peninsula and Georgia caused the deepest apprehension among the great powers, Britain and Prussia in particular. Open warfare finally broke out between Russia and Turkey in August, 1787 when the sultan demanded the evacuation of the Crimea and Georgia.

Although Austria also entered on the side of Russia in this conflict, the allies were unable to achieve decisive military successes. The British government, aware of the great danger to its own interests in Russian southward expansion, sought to find

ACQUISITIONS OF CATHERINE THE GREAT

SWEDEN

• Nystadt

• St. Petersburg
• Narva

Volga River

Baltic Sea

Niemen River

• Moscow

Oka River

Vistula

Warsaw •

Bug River

Dnieper River

RUSSIA

Don River

AUSTRIAN EMPIRE

Dniester River

Prut

River

• Kiev

Danube

River

• Kuchuk Kainarji

CRIMEA

• Azov

Black Sea

OTTOMAN

EMPIRE

PARTITIONS OF POLAND

counterweights to the growth of Russian power. It first encouraged Sweden to declare war on Russia. This dispute was settled in 1790 on a *status quo ante* basis, but the Russian fleet in
the Baltic was confined during the hostilities to the northern
waters and could not be used in the Mediterranean. Austrian
participation was also brought to an end by Joseph's successor,
Leopold II. In 1791 he signed the Peace of Sistova with Turkey
and terminated the alliance with Russia. Catherine II, again without an ally, made peace with the Ottoman Empire, but with
significant additions of territory. The Treaty of Jassy in 1792
recognized the Russian annexation of the Crimea and of lands
between the Bug and Dniester. Russia, not the Ottoman Empire,
was henceforth to be the dominating power on the Black Sea.

Meanwhile, the Polish situation had again deteriorated. During
the period after the first partition to 1793 when the state was
under the political control of Russia, a strong reform movement
had developed which was directed against Russian authority. The
final partitions occurred under the shadow of the great event of
the close of the century—the French revolution. The second
partition of Poland in 1793 was again initiated by Prussia, who
feared that Russia would seize the entire territory without compensating her neighbors. In this division Prussia took Danzig and
Thorn; Russia received Lithuania and western Ukrainian lands.
This action, in which Austria did not participate, touched off a

final revolt. Prussia and Russia sent troops into the country, quelled the rebellion, and set the stage for the final destruction of the Polish state. In 1795 Austria joined Russia and Prussia in the third partition. The disappearance of Poland from the map of Europe in no way settled the Polish problem for Russia. The consequences of the policy of partition and the acquisition of a large hostile Polish population became, thereafter, one of the determining factors in Russian foreign policy.

THE FRENCH REVOLUTION AND NAPOLEON

Although the outbreak of the revolution in France in 1789 awakened enthusiasm in some elements of Russian society, Catherine was disturbed by the situation. At war at the time with both Sweden and Turkey, she wished no more complications on the international scene. In the following years, however, the events in western Europe served as a cover and a distraction for the division of Poland among the three eastern powers. Despite the fact that the execution of Louis XVI in 1792 was made the occasion of court mourning, Russia herself did not join the allies in the first coalition.

Catherine's successor, her son Paul, who came to the throne in 1796, showed early in his reign signs of great emotional instability. Like his father, Peter III, he was determined to reverse the policy of a hated predecessor. He particularly attacked the major achievement of his mother's reign—the imperial policies she had pursued. He announced that Russia would henceforth not follow a path of foreign conquest and expansion, and he denounced the partitions of Poland as a crime. Despite his aversion to the previous reign, he had to face the realities of the diplomatic situation. The victorious French armies not only threatened to upset the European balance of power, but, since they carried with them the ideas of the revolution, they also constituted a danger to the autocratic regimes.

Paul's attitude toward France and the revolution was determined finally by a relatively minor issue—the fate of the island of Malta, which was under the control of the Catholic religious order of the Knights of St. John. Under severe financial pressure because of the sequestration of its lands in France by the revolutionary government, the order sought funds in Russia and even welcomed the protectorship of the Orthodox tsar. Paul himself appears to have conceived the idea of forming an international organization, which, like the old crusading orders, would fight the menace of revolution. He was thus particularly aroused when Napoleon, while on his way to Egypt in June, 1798, occupied Malta.

Because of the French action and the real danger to Russian interests of the French victories, Russia joined with England, Austria, and Turkey in the Second Coalition. In 1799 a Russo-Turkish expedition took the Ionian Islands. The war on the continent, in contrast to that on the sea, did not proceed well, principally because of the quarrels between the allied powers. Finally, angered by apparent British and Austrian failures to fulfill their obligations to him, Paul withdrew from the Second Coalition in October, 1799.

Napoleon's seizure of power after his return from Egypt and his establishment of what was in fact a military dictatorship made possible a shift in Russo-French relations. The situation had also changed in Malta. In September, 1800 the British occupied the island to the great annoyance of Paul, who had been elected Grand Master of the Catholic order. Enraged by the British action, the tsar attempted in reprisal to form an alliance of Sweden, Prussia, and Denmark to block British interference with neutral shipping. Napoleon used the opportunity to assure Paul that he was willing to cede Malta (which was no longer his) to Russia, and he released with honors the Russian prisoners that he held. Paul was now even willing to co-operate with France in the foolhardy plan of an attack on India. The tsar's assassination in 1801 brought an end to this undertaking, and the Russian troops that had already been despatched were recalled. The death of Paul was greeted with joy in England, but Napoleon correctly saw it as a major defeat.

*   *   *   *   *

The accession of Alexander I, the son of Paul, at the beginning of the new century in effect brought to a close a century of Russian expansion in which war and war alliances had been the rule. Although Russia was to acquire Finland in 1809 and Bessarabia in 1812, the age of Russian territorial conquest in the west had in effect come to an end. Russian policy thereafter in the next century was largely devoted to the preservation of boundaries already established. The eighteenth century had thus witnessed the firm establishment of Russia as one of the European great powers. It had also brought about the weakening or destruction of the three powers bordering upon Russia—Sweden, Poland, and the Ottoman Empire. Russia now had ports on two seas, the Baltic and the Black, and she had built up a navy. The rise of Prussia to great power status, seen at first as a threat to Russian security, on the contrary provided a reliable ally for the next hundred years. The basic Russian alliance system, the union of the three northern courts of Vienna, Berlin, and St. Petersburg, was firmly founded at this time and further strengthened by the partitions of Poland. The policy of interference in the affairs of the Ottoman Empire and the use of the appeal to the subject Christians of the empire were also inaugurated in the eighteenth century, and the principles of the Treaty of Kuchuk Kainarji were to determine the future course of Russo-Turkish relations. Russian foreign policy after 1815 can thus only be fully understood against the background of the conquests of the previous century and the lines of development laid down at that time.

II

Alexander I

Alexander I came to the throne in 1801 without adequate training or preparation for the decisive role that he was now called upon to fill in European and Russian affairs. His childhood had been made difficult by the estrangement between his grandmother, Catherine II, and his father. He had been forced to divide his time between two courts organized on differing principles and hostile to each other. He had also been given full knowledge of the conspiracy that had ended in the assassination of Paul. His education, which had been under Catherine's direction, was limited and superficial. He did, however, become acquainted with the ideas of the Enlightenment through the influence of his Swiss tutor, César de La Harpe. Although thereafter general principles and lofty ideas always had a compelling fascination for him, he lacked the ability or even the firm conviction necessary to translate any of his ideals into a successful course of action. At the beginning of his reign it seemed that he would inaugurate a period of reform in Russia. He first allied himself with men such as Prince Adam Czartoryski, Count Paul Stroganov, and Nicholas Novosiltsev who wished to remodel the Russian government along more progressive lines. These early liberal inclinations of his thought soon changed, particularly after the invasion of 1812, to be replaced by a growing mystical and highly conservative turn of mind. Thus, despite the hopes that were first placed on him, Alexander's reign witnessed no improvement in the internal order of Russia.

In contrast to his relative lack of achievement at home, Alexander I throughout his career played a brilliant role on the international scene. He was able to repel an invasion launched by the foremost military power of the time, to take the lead in the organization of the peace, and thereafter to maintain the position of his country as the strongest single power on the continent. In foreign relations his propensity to base practical decisions on moral principles and general concepts was always apparent, but these considerations usually contributed in the end to the strengthening of the power of Russia abroad. Alexander's foreign policy, although often highly ideological in direction and presentation, thus also served Russian national interests.

ALEXANDER I AND NAPOLEON

At the beginning of his reign Alexander I drew back from Paul's policy of co-operation with Napoleon and sought to maintain a position of neutrality. He explained his attitude with one of those resplendent declarations that were to characterize his reign and so clearly show his mode of thought: "If I ever raise arms," he declared in 1801, "it will be exclusively in defense against aggression, for the protection of my peoples or of the victims of ambitions that endanger the peace of Europe . . . I shall never participate in the internal dissensions of foreign states." [1]

The Russian desire for a respite was shared by the other powers. In March, 1802 France and Britain signed the Peace of Amiens. This truce held scarcely a year, and in May, 1803 the conflict was resumed. In 1805 Russia joined with Britain in the Third Coalition, to which Austria later adhered. Once again the allied armies proved unable to withstand Napoleon's forces. Austria went down to defeat at the battle of Austerlitz. In July, 1806 Prussia belatedly entered the conflict only to lose the disastrous battles of Jena and Auerstädt. At the battle of Friedland in June, 1807 the Russian forces were so decimated that the commander, General Bennigsen, advised that Russia could not continue in the war. The French victories, the impotence of the Russian allies, and the entrance of the Ottoman Empire on the side of France influenced Alexander's decision at this time not only to make peace, but to join with France as an ally. Napoleon, who now also desired an end to the continental fighting so that he could concentrate on the reduction of Britain, wisely allowed Alexander a means of radically changing his policies without a loss of prestige.

Meeting with Alexander on a raft in the river Niemen, Napoleon sketched out a grandiose plan of the division of Europe: France was to rule in the west, Russia in the east. The Treaty of Tilsit, signed on July 7, 1807, provided for the joint solution of the outstanding European problems and brought Russia into the alignment against Britain by associating her in the so-called Continental System with the stringent French measures directed against the great seapower's shipping and trade. France, in return, agreed to attempt to mediate between Turkey and Russia. If this failed, the two powers were to arrange for the partition of European Turkey. The Polish question was settled by the creation by Napoleon of the Duchy of Warsaw from the Prussian territories of Poland. Although it appears that Alexander I was well satisfied

1. Michael T. Florinsky, *Russia* (New York: Macmillan, 1960), II, p. 651.

with these arrangements, the treaty was not in the Russian interest. It was not a true division of Europe, since not only was French military power greater, but the French-controlled territories far outweighed in strength and importance those held by Russia. It also created on the Russian borders a satellite Polish state that could easily be turned into a weapon directed against Russia. The Russian entrance into the commercial war against Britain also interrupted a very beneficial economic relationship and was most heartily disliked at home. In fact, the entire idea of an alliance with France was extremely unpopular with the Russian aristocracy, particularly since it coincided with the period of the attempted reforms of Michael Speransky, who was a firm supporter of the French alignment. Land reform, co-operation with the French Revolution as embodied in the person of Napoleon, and the military and diplomatic support of France, the former national enemy, were all policies that could find little sympathy among influential circles in St. Petersburg.

The union of Tilsit, moreover, never functioned smoothly, principally because neither partner was sincere in his intentions; the treaty had been designed on both sides to win time. Napoleon, in order to offer Russia some immediate concrete advantage from the pact, encouraged her to go to war with Sweden in February, 1808. A year later Finland and the Aland Islands were added to the Russian Empire. The war with the Ottoman Empire, however, continued. In 1808 when the two emperors met at Erfurt, the tension between them was already apparent.

From 1808 to 1812 an uneasy truce was nevertheless maintained. Napoleon went to war again with Austria and added Galicia to the Duchy of Warsaw. In 1810 in an effort to close the holes in the blockade against Britain, he annexed Oldenburg, Bremen, Hamburg, and Lübeck. Since the tsar's favorite sister, Catherine, was married to the heir-apparent of the Duchy of Oldenburg, this move caused a severe reaction in the Russian court, but Napoleon did not even bother to answer the Russian note of protest. The continued presence of French troops in Prussia also caused apprehension. By 1811 both sides had begun to prepare for open conflict. Napoleon had been unable to subdue Britain by commercial warfare and the Continental System, nor had he quelled the revolt that had broken out against French rule in Spain. The temptation was now great to strike against the last unconquered continental state in order that thereafter he would be free to concentrate on the reduction of Britain.

The Russians had ample warning of the French intentions, although they were not eager for a test of strength at this time. To prepare for the coming conflict they made an agreement with Sweden in April, 1812 in which they promised to support Swedish claims to Norway to compensate for the loss of Finland. In the next month the Treaty of Bucharest was signed with Turkey, and the province of Bessarabia was taken from Moldavia. On his side Napoleon forced Austria and Prussia to make treaties with him, but both of these unwilling allies subsequently secretly assured Alexander of the practical worthlessness of these pacts. Both Russia and France had therefore set the stage for the conflict, but neither had gained the real support of another power. Spain and Britain ultimately joined Russia, but only after the outbreak of hostilities, and they could offer no concrete assistance during the invasion. France's allies hoped for Napoleon's defeat.

On June 24, 1812 Napoleon crossed the river Niemen at the head of an enormous army of 600,000, composed of soldiers of many nationalities; scarcely half were French. Opposed to him were three Russian armies whose combined strength totaled around 200,000 men. This second great invasion of Russia was met by tactics similar to those adopted by Peter to meet the attack of Charles XII, but on a larger scale. Under heavy criticism from large sections of the Russian aristocracy, who wished to fight the French troops on the periphery of their nation, the Russian commander, General Michael Barclay de Tolly, adopted a system of calculated retreat. Once again the scorched earth policy resulted in the destruction of all stores of food and munitions and in the burning of villages and forests. The effect on the French communications lines was immediate and catastrophic. Without sufficient fodder the horses perished and the military supplies and provisions could not be transported in sufficient quantities to care adequately for the rapidly advancing French armies. The ravished countryside offered no relief.

Although these methods of meeting an invasion were wise under the circumstances, since the Russian armies were not strong enough to defeat the French in open battle, the Russians themselves reacted bitterly against the surrender of so much territory. The failure of Barclay to engage the French in combat finally forced Alexander I to replace him with the popular hero, Michael Kutusov. Under heavy pressure, the new commander against his better judgment made a stand at the village of Borodino. There, on September 7, the Russian forces were able to inflict equal losses on their opponents although the battle was a technical French victory, which in fact opened the doors of Moscow to them. The march into the ancient Russian capital, however, proved to be anything but a triumph. Shortly before the French arrived the Russian government ordered the evacuation of the city, including the removal of firefighting equipment. The great fire which broke out and subsequently consumed the city after Napoleon's occupation thus left the French with a deserted, gutted city without supplies or adequate shelter for the winter. Despite his failure to engage the Russian armies in a decisive battle, Napoleon expected Alexander I to sue for peace. In this vain hope he delayed five weeks in Moscow. Finally, in October the French forces, now severely reduced by war losses, disease and desertion, started the long march back to Poland. The disaster of the French retreat, in bitter winter weather for which they were not prepared, harassed by guerilla forces and by units of the Russian army paralleling their march, has long been recounted as one of the great catastrophes of warfare. Of the 600,000 soldiers who commenced the campaign, barely 30,000 recrossed the Niemen on December 14.

The destruction of the French armies forced the Russian government to make a major decision. Throughout the retreat Kutusov had tried to spare his own tired forces, who had also suffered from the conditions of the campaign, and to avoid an open battle. He wished to see the foreign armies expelled from Russian soil with the least possible loss to his own troops. However, once the French armies left Russia, the question arose as to whether they should be pursued through foreign territory. Despite strong opposition at home, Alexander I chose to continue, and in January the Russian army crossed the Niemen. Joining with Austria and Prussia, Russia was able to defeat the hastily assembled French forces. The Battle of the Nations at Leipzig in October, 1813 marked the freeing of Europe from the long period of French domination. On March 31, 1814 Alexander I, accompanied by Frederick William III of Prussia, rode into Paris at the head of the victorious allied armies.

The entrance of Alexander I into the French capital marked the culmination of a line of development that had commenced during the reign of Peter the Great. In March, 1814 Russia emerged from the period of the revolutionary wars as the strongest European power. Thus Russia, who had entered into the politics of Europe only at the beginning of the eighteenth century, now had risen to a position of military predominance.

THE CONGRESS OF VIENNA

Because of the preponderant weight of Russian military power in 1814, the views of Alexander I toward the peace were of first significance. His attitude toward the future treaty was determined by three principal considerations: first, the influence of his education and his early companions, particularly of his first foreign minister, Prince Adam Czartoryski, second, the increasing influence that religion began to exert upon his outlook on international problems, and, third, the interests of Russia as a power. Although the effect of Alexander's education, particularly of the role of La Harpe, in the formation of his later ideas, is much debated, certainly the tsar acquired during this period a tendency to look upon political questions as moral problems. His endeavor at this time to construct an international system upon principles of right remained a constant goal of his policy throughout his reign, although his judgment on what constituted the fundamental bases of such an order altered with time. Prince Adam Czartoryski in his memoirs wrote: "I would have wished Alexander to become a sort of arbitor of peace for the civilized world, to be the protector of the weak and the oppressed, and that his reign should inaugurate a new era of justice and right in European politics." [2] This aim, to be the "arbitor of peace for the civilized world" exactly corresponded with the tsar's convictions of his own destiny, a conception that was reinforced after 1812 by his religious conversion.

His inclination to broad views and general settlements was shown as early as 1804 in instructions which he drew up for Novosiltsev, who was sent to negotiate with the British government. Here the principles that states should receive institutions of their own choice and fitting their internal development, that disputes between nations should be submitted to international arbitration, and that boundaries should be drawn to coincide with the geographic, economic, and national organization of the area in question were elaborated. The tsar's belief, which he held until at least 1820, that each people should have the government best suited to it and that all should be joined together in some sort of general union to protect the security of each member, was, of course, open to widely varying practical interpretations. The principles could, and were, applicable to differing situations and could be used to justify highly liberal or strongly reactionary courses of action.

To Alexander's conception of the existence of a basic European solidarity and the need for a morally justifiable peace settlement was added a growing religious fervor, whose direction was profoundly influenced by his experiences during the French invasion. He later related: "The burning of Moscow enlightened my soul, and the judgment of God on the fields of ice filled my heart with a faith which I had never so deeply before experienced. . . .

2. *Memoirs of Prince Adam Czartoryski*, edited by Adam Gielgud, (London: Remington & Co., 1888), II, p. 8.

I was filled with the deep and mature conviction to devote myself and my government only to Him and to the furtherance of His honor. Since that time I have been another man; to the salvation of Europe from destruction I thank my salvation and liberty." [3] His feelings were also expressed in his attitude toward the defeated enemy. To his troops he declared: "God does not love inhumanity and cruelty for he is compassionate. Forget all of the evil that the enemy has done to us." [4] Alexander's emphasis on the redeeming and forgiving aspects of Christianity were also clear in his treatment of France and in the conduct of the Russian armies during the period of their occupation of French territory.

The intensity of the faith of the tsar, which resulted in manifestations of a mystical and often hysterical nature, was chiefly affected by elements outside of and often inimical to the established Orthodox Church and its authorities. Alexander's experiences came in time to result in the conviction that he, and often he alone, was acting under divine inspiration and that he was God's chosen instrument. In 1821 he wrote: ". . . I feel that I am the depository of a sacred holy mission."

Fortunately for Russia, there was no basic contradiction between Alexander's ideals and Russian national interests in Europe. In a very practical sense Russia had gained a great deal through the Napoleonic Wars. First, the reduction of the strongest power had greatly enhanced her own, and, second, additional territory was brought in to the Russian Empire. The annexation of Finland in 1809 and Bessarabia in 1812 must certainly be added to the balance sheet of the Congress of Vienna. Russian power in 1814 was clearly shown in the fact that Alexander, virtually alone, made the first settlements with France and determined the form of government that country should have after the defeat of Napoleon.

After his arrival in Paris in March, 1814 with Frederick Wil-

3. Karl Stählin, *Geschichte Russlands* (Graz: Akademische Druck, 1961), III, pp. 238, 239.
4. Valentin Gitermann, *Geschichte Russlands* (Frankfurt, n.d.), II, p. 369.

liam III, Alexander I henceforth conducted the negotiations in the name of the allies. Although he personally did not favor the return of the Bourbons and would have accepted a long list of alternatives, including Napoleon's son, the King of Rome, he finally decided upon a restoration, largely because of the influence of the brilliant French diplomat, Talleyrand. The Treaty of Fontainebleau of April, 1814 provided for Napoleon's abdication and his withdrawal to Elba. Thereafter the newly established provisional government of France proceeded to draw up a constitution, the Charter, and Louis XVIII was formally declared king of France. The first Peace of Paris was largely formulated under the tsar's direction. Prussia wished a far harsher treaty and British support for the first terms was only lukewarm. The provisions, reflecting Alexander's feelings toward the defeated country, were most generous in view of the devastation that had been inflicted by French armies since 1791. There were no annexations of French territory and no indemnities. The French boundaries became those of 1792, which meant that some of the former acquisitions were kept. The moderation of the terms also served to make the return of Bourbon rule more palatable to the French people.

With the signing of this agreement, Russian ability to influence and direct the course of the European settlement reached the limit of its extent. In the next months before the opening of the Congress of Vienna in September, 1814, the other allies, Britain and Austria, in particular, came to realize the danger to their own position in Russian predominance in Europe. Because of this division in the allied camp, Talleyrand was able to play the powers against each other to the ultimate benefit of France. The emergence of Russia to continental hegemony in place of defeated France was for Britain and Austria the replacement of one evil with another. Moreover, the statesmen were more than sceptical about Alexander's motives and his lofty declarations; they regarded him as eccentric, if not outright insane. Although they listened to his fine words, they also kept their eyes on the map of Europe. Alexander I now proposed that the peace should

include the establishment of a Kingdom of Poland to be constituted out of the former Napoleonic Duchy of Warsaw. The
state was to be autonomous in administration and organization,
but the crown of Poland would be worn by the tsar of Russia.
Prussia in compensation for her lost Polish lands was to be given
Saxony, who had remained too long a faithful French ally. To
the Austrian and British representatives, this proposal amounted
to nothing less than the absorption of all of Poland into Russia
and would signify a deep disarrangement of the balance of power,
particularly in view of the fact that Prussia was largely under
Russian influence. Metternich, whose views dominated Austrian
policy until 1848, also was concerned about the increase of territory which the Saxon annexation would have on the position of
Prussia in relation to the other German states.

Because of the conflict on the Polish and Saxon questions, the
congress thus became an instrument to prevent further Russian
encroachment in Europe, rather than a conference solely devoted
to securing the redrawing of the European boundaries and providing for the containment of revolutionary France. Before the
Russo-Prussian front, the three western powers, Britain, Austria,
and France, on January 3, 1815 signed what was in effect a war
alliance. Hanover, Bavaria, Württemberg, and Hesse later adhered. Conflict was, however, avoided when Alexander I accepted a compromise in which Prussia received back some of her
Polish land, two-thirds of Saxony, and territory on the Rhine.
Alexander I contented himself with the greater part of the Duchy
of Warsaw.

No sooner had this major agreement been reached than the
powers received the news that Napoleon had left Elba and had
again landed in France. In this last phase of the campaign Russian
troops played little part. This time the British and Prussian armies
marched first into Paris and dictated the second and stronger
Peace of Paris. France was now limited to her boundaries of
1790, an indemnity was levied, and an army of occupation was
to remain in France until the debt was paid. Napoleon was ban-
ished to the remote island of St. Helena.

The Vienna settlement ranks with the treaties of Westphalia of 1648 and Versailles of 1919 in general European history. It created political and power relationships that remained stable until the middle of the century and provided a framework for international affairs that for a century enabled Europe to avoid a major, catastrophic war. The diplomats of the victorious powers, in making the peace, were concerned first with limiting and controlling France. The indemnity and the occupation would prevent further moves in the immediate future. For a more permanent control the allies surrounded France with a cordon of barrier states who were to check renewed French expansion. To help protect this strategic area, the Kingdom of the Netherlands was formed by combining the Austrian Netherlands with the Republic of Holland. In Italy the Kingdom of Piedmont-Sardinia was assigned a similar role. The extension of the Prussian territories on the Rhine was to enable that state to serve better as a guard against France. Prussia was also strengthened through the addition of Swedish Pomerania, Sweden being indemnified with Norway.

With the containment of France geographically secured, the victorious powers then divided among themselves the remaining territories in question. The Habsburg Monarchy acquired again dominance in Italy with the annexation of Lombardy and Venetia. The smaller kingdoms went back to their old rulers, who were closely tied to Vienna. The Pope regained his power in the Papal States, and the highly reactionary Bourbon ruler, Ferdinand I, received the crown of the Kingdom of the Two Sicilies. In addition to preponderance in the Italian peninsula, Austria received Dalmatia, the Tyrol, and Salzburg. Her position in the Germanies was reasserted through the organization of the Germanic Confederation, of which she was president. Although no attempt was made to undo the reforms of Napoleon, who had reduced the number of separate German political entities from over 300 to 38, little more was done to promote the closer political unification of the land. The Germanic Confederation was thus only a loose organization. Its diet, which met at Frankfurt,

EUROPE IN 1815

UNITED KINGDOM OF
GREAT BRITAIN
AND IRELAND

▲ Sites of International
Congresses 1814-22

was attended by the instructed delegates of the rulers of the member states. The question of German unity and the rivalry of Austria and Prussia in this matter remained to be settled.

With the defeat of France, Britain had achieved her major aim —the preservation of the balance of power. It has already been mentioned how she recognized that Russia might replace France as a danger to the European equilibrium and how she had endeavored to prevent it. With the conclusion of the peace Britain remained in a most favorable position. She was the major colonial and commercial power; she stood at the beginning of that great epoch of her history marked by the industrial revolution. In the treaties she concentrated on the acquisition of strategic points that would be of value to her trade and her lines of communication with her colonies, as for example, Malta, Capetown, and the Ionian Islands, over which she assumed a protectorate. No attempt was made to acquire large pieces of territory overseas.

The peace treaties strongly emphasized, as we have seen, the principle of legitimacy. Wherever possible the former rulers were returned to their thrones, and the changes brought about by the Napoleonic occupations were annulled. In Spain and Portugal, as well as in the small states of Germany and Italy, the structure of the old regime was again introduced. This condition reflected the reaction felt in all states against the type of political experimentation embodied in the French Revolution and the universal desire for a period of stability. The international arrangements set up after the peace and the subsequent meetings of the powers therefore dealt not only with territorial questions, but also with the problem of the preservation of the political *status quo*. Although this development was to the chief benefit of Austria, it had the initial support of all of the powers.

Of the two major agreements made after Vienna, the Holy Alliance and the Quadruple Alliance, it was the first that owed its origin to the efforts of Alexander I. The Holy Alliance, which was the concrete expression of the tsar's ideas of the correct principles to be applied to international politics, was accepted with reluctance by the other powers despite the fact that it was little more than a solemn statement that the signatories would "both in the administration of their respective states and in their political relations with each other" base their actions on "the precepts of religion, namely, the rules of Justice, Christian Charity and Peace." Although all of the European powers except England, Turkey, and the Vatican adhered to this pact, none of the contracting parties, with, of course, the exception of Alexander I, took it seriously. Metternich entitled it a "loud-sounding nothing"; the British minister Castlereagh called it a combination of "mysticism and nonsense."

Although the Holy Alliance was generally regarded with some derision, the congress renewed on November 20, 1815 the Quadruple Alliance of 1814, which had been concluded among the allies against Napoleon. In this pact the four great powers, Russia, Austria, Prussia, and Britain now agreed "to renew their meetings at fixed periods . . . for the purpose of consulting upon their common interests, and for the consideration of measures which at each of these periods shall be considered most salutary for the repose and prosperity of the nations and for the maintenance of the peace of Europe." This stipulation became the basis for the congress system that functioned between 1815 and 1823 and resulted in the holding of four great international gatherings for the solution of specific problems. Although the agreement was originally established to prevent a recurrence of French aggression on the continent, the adherence of France to the Quadruple, now the Quintuple, Alliance in 1818 changed its direction. The specific system established in 1815 lapsed with the defection of Britain in the 1820's, but the principle that the great powers should meet in congress to solve by arbitration and mediation their common conflicts and disagreements remained accepted in European international relations throughout the century.

The completion of the Vienna settlement left Russia in a most advantageous diplomatic position and at a height of political power that she did not achieve again until 1945. She was recognized as the strongest military power on the continent; the acquisition of control in Poland placed her armies within striking distance of Vienna and Berlin. Her chief opponent, France, had been at least temporarily eliminated as a threat. The tripartite division of central Europe into Prussia, the Austrian Empire, and the "third Germany" of the small states gave her a great measure of protection on her sensitive western border. She could thereafter play the three political elements against each other. Her relations with Austria and Prussia were also to her great advantage. Prussia, until the unification of Germany in 1870, remained bound by strategic necessity and by dynastic ties to Russia. Austria, because of her insecure position in Italy, her rivalry with Prussia in Germany, and the ever present problem of France, could not afford to alienate Russia over questions in central Europe. Russia's neighbors, therefore, because of their need for Russian support, were valuable allies rather than rivals. Although Austria and Russia did not co-operate in the eastern question, which will be discussed in detail later, Prussia did remain a close collaborator through most of the nineteenth century.

With the attainment of a position of maximum advantage in 1815, the Russian government was thereafter satisfied with its western boundaries. From the Congress of Vienna until 1917 the primary problem for Russia was that of defending the enormous territory that had been conquered in the previous centuries. Because of the backward conditions prevailing in Russia in comparison to those in the lands of her European neighbors, the attention of her statesmen should now have turned to internal affairs. The Congress of Vienna settlement offered in the succeeding years a period of peace in which Russia was at no time faced with dangerous outside pressure and in which she therefore had ample opportunities for reform. [The great military and political defeat that she was to suffer in 1856 was a result of her failure to utilize this period in modernizing and tightening her entire internal structure. The disaster of the Crimean War was thus primarily the result of a failure of Russian domestic policies and not of international relations.

Despite the scepticism of the powers, Alexander I personally was no doubt sincere in his desire to establish a truly autonomous Poland under Russian protection. His feelings, however, were not shared by significant groups in either Russia or Poland. Although the tsar wished Poles and Russians to live together as brothers under his paternal rule, the Poles continued to prefer complete independence, and the Russians disliked the special position allowed the new government. The Poles thus carried on their struggle for full freedom; the Russians looked back to the days immediately following the partition of Poland.

According to the terms of the Vienna Treaty Poland was to be established as a constitutional kingdom under the Russian tsar. A committee composed of Polish and Russian representatives prepared a constitution, which was liberal in character for its time. A diet of two chambers was established, with the upper house appointed by the crown and the lower elected by the nobility and the middle class. Although this body was supposed to meet every two years, only four sessions were actually held between 1815 and 1830. The diet could not legislate; it could only request that the tsar accept its recommendations. The autonomous kingdom was also allowed its own army, and the administration of the country was Polish in personnel and in language. Contrary to expectation General Joseph Zaionczek, and not Alexander's former close associate Czartoryski, became the tsar's viceroy. The real control in Warsaw, however, came to rest in the hands of Grand Duke Constantine, the tsar's brother, who was given command of the army.

The special constitutional arrangements enjoyed by Poland were not unusual in the Russian Empire. Finland, the Baltic provinces, and Bessarabia all retained their unique local organizations even after their incorporation with Russia. Although this disparity in systems was generally not favorably received in Russia, Alexander I after the Congress of Vienna was sympathetic with and supported the free institutions of Poland. In a speech in March, 1818 he raised the hopes of those in Russia who wished reform when he praised the Polish constitutional system and declared that he would extend the benefits of "free institutions" to other sections of his domains.

THE CONGRESS SYSTEM

In the years immediately following the peace, Russian relations with France were particularly good despite the tsar's personal dislike of Louis XVIII and his anger with Talleyrand over the treaty of January, 1815. This favorable condition was largely a result of the activities of the Russian ambassador in Paris, Count Pozzo di Borgo, and the French foreign minister, the Duke of Richelieu, who replaced Talleyrand. Richelieu had in fact played previously a larger role in Russian administration than in the affairs of his own country. His career in Russia had commenced in 1790 and had culminated after 1800 in his appointment as military governor of Odessa and governor-general of Novorossiia. Under his able guidance the Black Sea lands had flourished and the port of Odessa had risen in size and wealth. As foreign minister for Louis XVIII he kept in close touch with the Russian government and followed policies that won its approval. Like Alexander I he opposed the extreme groups among the royalists and former émigrés who wished to restore intact the pre-revolutionary conditions. In foreign affairs he sought first to obtain the removal of the allied army of occupation from French soil and a final settlement of the war debts.

In accordance with the provisions of the Quadruple Alliance, a congress was called to meet at Aix-la-Chapelle in September, 1818. Although the other powers wished to limit the discussion to the settlement of the French problem, Alexander sought to introduce questions pertaining to Europe in general. The tsar at this time was assisted by two statesmen, who jointly held the position of foreign minister, John Capodistrias and K. R. Nesselrode. Of the two, Capodistrias was the more brilliant and the more controversial. Born in Corfu, he retained his attachment to the Greek cause and was later forced to leave office as a result of the

Greek revolution. Nesselrode, who remained to serve under Nicholas I, was of a Protestant, German Rhineland family, and his father had also been in the Russian administration. His sober, industrious and modest character made him an excellent second to two impulsive sovereigns, both of whom were determined to conduct their own foreign affairs. Conservative and moderate in outlook, he exerted a restraining influence, but he did not direct the formulation or the conduct of the main lines of Russian policy.

The principal business of the Congress of Aix-la-Chapelle was quickly settled. The occupation armies were withdrawn from France and her financial obligations were settled. Thereafter France joined the four other powers on equal terms. The major controversy of the conference occurred when Alexander I, in an attempt to extend and strengthen the Holy Alliance, proposed the signature of another pact in which the powers would guarantee one another's territorial possessions and political systems as they existed at the time. This agreement would have established a tight organization of Europe and would have permitted a virtually unlimited right of intervention by the powers in each other's internal affairs. Alexander also wished to set up an international army with the Russian forces as the center. This proposal, so idealistic in appearance, would have served Russian interests in that it would have secured more strongly the status quo in Europe, which was to the benefit of Russia.

Austria and Britain, the two states that principally opposed the plan, again represented as at Vienna by Metternich and Castlereagh, did not object to the conservative aspects of the program, but they did shrink from the vision of Russian armies marching all over Europe to suppress revolutions. The Congress of Aix-la-Chapelle brought out clearly the fundamental differences in outlook on foreign affairs held by Britain and Russia. Alexander remained firm in his desire to form some kind of European order that would guarantee the continued existence of the political and territorial conditions of 1815. The British government, in contrast, would not go further than the terms of the Quadruple

Alliance, which they maintained was nothing more than an instrument to prevent the recurrence of French aggression and not the basis of a European super-government. The British attitude was best expressed in the State Paper of May 5, 1820, which was drafted by Castlereagh and issued by Canning in 1823. In contrast to Alexander's principle of intervention and co-operation, this statement of policy declared that the European alliance ". . . never was, however, intended as an union for the government of the world or for the superintendence of the internal affairs of other states." [5]

Russian relations with Austria also cooled after the Congress of Vienna. In the peace settlement the Austrian monarchy had achieved a position of dominance in the Italian peninsula and had won a measure of superiority over Prussia in the organization of the Germanic Confederation. Russian interests in central Europe from all points of view lay in the maintenance of the system established in 1815 and in the preservation of the balance among Prussia, Austria, and the states of the second order. Tied by dynastic links with the royal houses of the small monarchies, the Russian court was anxious to protect the independence of these governments from Austrian encroachments. It soon became apparent that Austria would attempt to use the apparent threat of revolutionary conspiracies in the area as a means of widening and deepening its influence.

The national and liberal fervor that had been awakened in central Europe, particularly during the wars of liberation against Napoleon, continued into the next years, chiefly among the students and intellectuals. Their activities centered in the organization of societies for the propagation of their ideals, and the movement culminated in a meeting held at the Wartburg in 1817. Political changes, occasioned by liberal agitation, also occurred in the smaller German states. In March, 1816 the Duke of Saxe-Weimar granted a constitution; his actions were duplicated in the following year in Württemberg and Baden. All three of these courts had

5. R. W. Seton-Watson, *Britain in Europe, 1789-1914* (Cambridge: Cambridge University Press, 1955), p. 73.

close relations with Russia, and Alexander had been consulted about the new measures. Metternich regarded the tsar's actions here and in Italy with deep suspicion. In his correspondence with Nesselrode and Capodistrias and in the letters that Emperor Francis sent to Alexander I, the dangers of revolution were strongly emphasized.

As could be expected, the Austrian government took the lead in the organization of joint measures in Germany to deal with the revolutionary agitation. In co-operation with Prussia, Austria was able to obtain the sanction of the other German states for the Karlsbad Decree of 1819. The small governments also agreed to censor their publications, to control their universities, and to aid each other in the suppression of the new political movements. A central committee was established at Mainz to investigate revolutionary activities. Having instituted these measures with the co-operation of the German states, Metternich next turned to Britain and Russia for their sanction. Although Castlereagh personally supported strong action against revolutionary movements, he could not officially approve the provisions that called for interference in the internal affairs of other states. He therefore replied with the vague phrase: "We are always glad to see evil germs destroyed without the power to give our approval openly."

Alexander I, in contrast, did not hesitate to express his opposition to the Austrian actions. He had been shaken by the assassination in March, 1819 of the dramatist August von Kotzebue, who at the time was an agent of the tsar, particularly when it was reported that the murderer, Karl Sand, was acting on the instructions of a secret society. However, he had no desire to see Austria establish a firmer control over central Europe on the excuse of suppressing revolutionary dangers. Although he had himself proposed at Aix-la-Chapelle that a general alliance be established to guarantee the political *status quo* with rights of intervention, he was not prepared to grant this privilege to Austria in regard to German affairs. Moreover, Alexander I still held the belief that liberal institutions were acceptable if granted by a monarch and not extorted by revolutionary agitation. "Liberty," he stated, "is and has to be circumscribed in proper limits . . . and those limits are the principles of order." [6] He preferred that each German state adopt the measures necessary to ensure its own internal tranquillity.

Alexander's convictions were expressed in the Russian circular despatch of January 27, 1820 in which it was stated that the German states should be left free in their relations with each other, and that no league to defend absolutism should be set up. In this note the Russian government went so far as to say that it would welcome the formation of a unitary state to replace the Germanic Confederation. The Russian backing of the small states against Austria was also shown in the support that Alexander I gave his brother-in-law, the King of Württemberg, in his desire to maintain the constitution which he had granted. In the fall of 1819 the tsar massed troops in Poland as a threat to Vienna. These Russian actions were blamed by Metternich on the influence of Capodistrias. Hereafter the Austrian minister became the bitter opponent of the Russian statesman.

In the period between the Congress of Vienna and 1820 Alexander I was thus in no sense a blind reactionary in foreign politics. He accepted liberal reform in other lands when it was introduced by the legitimate ruler of the state; he opposed it when it was brought in by revolution or was based on the doctrine of the sovereignty of the people. He also sought to achieve general acceptance of the principle that the European powers acting in concert should protect reigning monarchs threatened by rebellion. He had, however, acted to prevent Austria from gaining a free hand in Germany through the use of this doctrine. Although he did not allow Austria to interfere freely in German affairs, he did after 1820 support the Austrian policy of intervention in Italy, which assured the monarchy's supremacy in that peninsula until 1860. Russian support of Austrian policies reflected the tsar's

6. F. F. Martens, *Recueil des traités et conventions conclus par la Russie avec les puissances étrangères* (St. Petersburg: A. Böhnke, 1874-1909), IV, p. 269-270.

increasing aversion to political reform and liberal ideas, which he now equated with Jacobinism and the revolution. The highly conservative emphasis that characterized Russian policies hereafter naturally led to increasing co-operation with Vienna. Austria also needed Russian assistance because of the virtual withdrawal of Britain from continental entanglements of any kind in the 1820's. The revolutions of 1820 were the occasion, therefore, of the reformation of the conservative coalition of Austria, Prussia, and Russia. Alexander I himself at this time fell more under the influence of Metternich and showed little of his old originality and spirit in the conduct of Russian policy. Vienna became again the European diplomatic center.

Although revolutions also broke out in Spain and Portugal in 1820, Austria was most concerned with the Italian revolts, since they involved her hegemony in that country. The Congress of Troppau, summoned in October, 1820, was convened chiefly to discuss the question of Austrian intervention in the Kingdom of the Two Sicilies to put down the revolutionary government. Because of their attitude toward intervention in this instance, Britain and France sent only "observers," and they did not sign the final declaration of the conference. The three conservative powers, however, co-operated well. Alexander at this time commented to Metternich: "You do not understand why I am no longer the same, I am going to tell you. Seven years have passed between 1813 and 1820, and these seven years appear to me a century. I would at no price do in 1820 what I did in 1813. You have not changed but I have. You have nothing to regret; I cannot say that of myself." [7]

The Preliminary Protocol of the Congress of Troppau, signed by the three powers in November, stressed the dangers of revolution and reaffirmed the principle of intervention. Austria was instructed to re-establish order in Italy in the name of the signatory powers. King Ferdinand I of the Kingdom of the Two Sicilies was invited to attend a second congress, which was to be held at Laibach. In this agreement Austria thus accepted and supported

7. Clemens von Metternich-Winneburg, *Mémoires laissés par le Prince de Metternich* (Paris: E. Plon, 1881), III, p. 374.

the doctrine of intervention which she had opposed at Aix-la-Chapelle and used it to protect her own interests. Britain and France did not agree to the Austrian action, not because they supported the revolutionary movements, but because they disliked the principle and feared its application under other circumstances.

Alexander's conservatism in foreign affairs increased after the outbreak of a mutiny in the Semenovsky Regiment in St. Petersburg. Although this revolt was no more than a protest against the conditions under which the troops served, the tsar preferred to regard it as part of the great revolutionary conspiracy which he saw at work everywhere in Europe. At the Congress of Laibach, which opened in January, 1821, Metternich had no difficulty in convincing Alexander I who now firmly believed in the real existence of an international revolutionary committee "which gives the signal for the revolutions in countries which have been carefully prepared by intrigues and agitations."[8] Emperor Francis and Alexander I were now close friends, and the Austro-Russian co-operation rested on the firm ground of political compatibility.

The issue that was eventually to break the combination of the conservative powers arose at this time, although its effects were apparent only much later. In March, 1821, when the tsar was at Laibach, he received word of the outbreak in Moldavia of a revolution aimed at securing the liberation of the Greeks from Ottoman rule. Since the Greek revolution played such a great role in the European diplomacy of the 1820's, it will be treated in detail in a separate section. Suffice it to say that the revolt forced the tsar to face the contradiction in principle between his position as the protector of eastern Orthodoxy and his support of conservative regimes and legitimate monarchs. Under strong pressure from Metternich, he at this time denounced the revolution and dismissed his Greek foreign minister, Capodistrias, a strong supporter of the movement. Austria thus also gained her wishes in this first round of the reopened eastern question.

In March, 1821 a rebellion also broke out in Piedmont. The

8. A. A. Lobanov-Rostovsky, *Russia and Europe, 1789-1825* (Durham, N.C.: Duke University Press, 1947), p. 387.

Austrian troops, with Russian blessing, were thus able to deal with two Italian revolts at once. Northern Italy was subdued, Ferdinand I regained his throne, and Austrian pre-eminence in Italy was restored. With the Italian question settled, the powers now turned their attention to Spain. Here the chief governments with interests at stake were France and Britain rather than Austria.

Despite their geographical separation, Russia and Spain had maintained close relations after the end of the Napoleonic Wars. During the period of the French occupation of Spanish territory, the Spanish colonies had taken the occasion to revolt; and, with peace once restored, the Spanish government naturally sought for aid to secure their restoration. The Russian government, favoring the effort, even sent some old ships to assist in the endeavor. When Ferdinand VII was made prisoner in a revolutionary movement in 1820, Alexander naturally supported intervention by the powers to aid him. France, the tsar believed, was the logical power to carry out such an action. At the Congress of Verona in 1822 the four continental states agreed upon this policy, and in April, 1823 a French army placed Ferdinand VII back on his throne. The king immediately requested assistance from his allies in the winning back of his Central and South American colonies. Here, however, the British attitude would prove decisive since she controlled the seas. No new armada could be launched against America if she opposed it. The British position had from the outset been, as we have seen, that of strong disapproval of the doctrine of intervention. Moreover, she had developed a rich trade with the rebellious colonies, which would be interrupted if they were reconquered by Spain. She therefore had every interest in blocking the action of the continental powers.

The British position was also that most favorable to the interests of the United States. In 1823 President Monroe issued a statement to the effect that the United States would regard as an unfriendly act the interference of any European power in the affairs of an American republic. The Monroe Doctrine was directed not only against the European coalition but also against British moves in the Caribbean and Russian expansion along the Pacific coast of

North America. Without adequate seapower and without British and American support, Spain could not hope to regain her colonies.

The doctrine of intervention, supported enthusiastically by Alexander I, thus resulted in the restoration of the former governments in Spain, Portugal, Piedmont, and the Kingdom of the Two Sicilies. Revolutionary movements succeeded at this time only in South America. The co-operation of Austria, France, Russia, and Prussia had thus brought about a restoration of the general conditions of the Vienna settlement. One question, nevertheless, remained unsettled—that of the fate of the Greek revolutionary movement. This issue, which reopened the entire eastern question, which had been in abeyance since the Treaty of Bucharest of 1812, was to test the collaboration that had been established between Russia and Austria. Although bound by common ties in European affairs, the two powers faced a fundamental separation of interests in the Near East.

The Eastern Question

Throughout the nineteenth century the chief center of European diplomatic activity was the Near East; and the Turkish Straits, more than any other single geographical point, held the attention of the powers. The evident fatal weakness of the Ottoman Empire by the end of the eighteenth century made it apparent that the disposition of its ill-managed territories would soon be brought into question. Throughout the eighteenth century the internal conditions in the provinces had become increasingly chaotic; the central government was unable to control the activities of its governors in the outlying lands. The Janissaries, an elite infantry corps that was the principal military support of the state, had become a national danger through their lawlessness and rebellious temper. Almost useless against a foreign foe, they plundered the countryside and menaced the government itself. In 1795 the attempt of Sultan Selim to improve his military es-

THE OTTOMAN EMPIRE IN 1815

tablishment shattered on their opposition. By the end of the eighteenth century it was clear to foreigners and even to some Turks that either the entire structure of the empire would have to be reformed or it would surely fall apart. In the bad conditions under which they lived, Christian and Moslem suffered alike.

Unfortunately for the interests of the Porte, the Ottoman Empire was in a very real sense the crossroads of the world. The great religions, Christian, Jewish, and Moslem alike, had their holy centers here. Moreover, all the powers had vital interests and historical traditions that made the fate of the territories of the Porte of grave concern to them. In the nineteenth century the chief antagonists were Britain and Russia. After Britain's loss of the North American colonies, India played the predominant role in the British imperial system. The eastern Mediterranean as a route to India and as a commercial highway to the Far East was threatened chiefly by Russia, who also appeared to menace the wealthy colony through the back door of Afghanistan and Persia. Britain was thus always particularly sensitive about the buildup of Russian sea power in the Black Sea and the status of the Turkish Straits. She wished no regime set up in this area that would allow Russian warships to move freely into the Mediterranean to endanger her shipping and would at the same time prevent British fleets from entering the Black Sea. Her greatest fear was that the entire Ottoman Empire, because of its military weakness and the claims that St. Petersburg had on the Orthodox Christians, would simply fall into the hands of Russia. Because of this extreme anxiety, British opinion tended to hold that Russian policy was in all circumstances directed toward this goal and it saw aggressive intentions in Russian actions even when these did not exist.

Certainly, Russian interests and aims in the Near East were in the nineteenth century never so extensive as attributed to her by her British opponents. As we shall see, the Russian government throughout this period was extremely aware of the problems connected with its diplomatic position. Although quite willing to make small gains at Ottoman expense, it recognized that the conquest of the entire empire, were it possible, would not be an element of strength for the Russian state. The administration and defense of the existing boundaries taxed the resources of Russia enough without the addition of further territories. Moreover, the Russian statesmen always recognized the extreme danger of the formation of a hostile coalition directed against them, which could be brought into existence by the eastern question. Since the international situation in the nineteenth century did not allow them to achieve the ideal solution from their point of view, i.e., the opening of the waterway to their fleets but its closure to the ships of other powers, they strove, in general, for the establishment of a regime at the Straits that would prevent all warships from entering and leaving the Black Sea. Since they did not have predominant seapower, they could only lose under any system that allowed British, or British combined with French, fleets to enter the Black Sea at will. In the question of the fate of Turkey, they favored in general its maintenance; if this were not possible, they preferred its partition, but in agreement with Britain and Austria.

Austria and France, as well as Britain and Russia, also had important interests in the area, although French influence declined relatively. However, France conquered Algeria in 1830, and she also played a major role in the modernization and development of Egypt under Mehemet Ali. In general, she co-operated with Britain and was in opposition to Russia, but this diplomatic pattern underwent frequent modifications in the course of the century. Austria, although an ally in central European affairs, found herself generally in disagreement with Russia in the question of the Ottoman Empire. First and foremost, the Habsburg Empire from purely military and strategic considerations could not afford to allow a major extension of Russian power on her southern flank. In addition, with her own large population of Slavic peoples, she had no wish to see the inauguration of a great emancipation movement in the neighboring empire because of the influence it might have on her own subjects. She was thus bound to oppose any significant extension of Russian control or any attempts to raise in revolt the Balkan Christians under the banner of national liberation. The Austrian position was unusually complicated because of her need for Russian support to maintain her influence in Italy and Germany. She did not wish to be forced to bargain for aid in central Europe by concessions in the Balkans. The support of the *status quo* and the emphasis on legitimacy was therefore usually the Austrian program.

The Russian government in its dealings with the Porte was thus faced with two realities: first, that the Ottoman Empire was on the verge of collapse and, second, that somehow the European balance of power must be maintained should it fall. She also had to meet a diplomatic situation in which the other major powers considered that the principal danger in the situation was that Russia would simply grab the entire Ottoman inheritance. The problem of what to do with Turkey was never adequately settled before World War I. Three major alternatives were offered for the consideration of the powers, and all were used at one time or another. A fourth possibility, the conquest and control of the entire territory by one power, presumably Russia, was not a serious consideration in this period. It is difficult to imagine a situation in which the attempt by Russia to annex Turkey would not have brought about an immediate coalition of France, Britain, and Austria. Russia was never in a condition to meet such a military threat, and her statesmen were well aware of this fact.

The first and simplest solution for all concerned was the maintenance of the empire and its strengthening through internal reform. Britain, in particular, through most of the century clung to the hope that the entire structure might be so modernized that life would be made endurable for the Christians. The fear that any other alternative plan would mean the control of the area by Russia strengthened the British conviction that such a plan was feasible, although it is difficult to conceive a program that would have made the Christians happy subjects of the sultan.

The second alternative, the partition of the empire among the great powers in a manner that the balance would be preserved, was also discussed throughout the century. Although many different schemes of partition were offered, all of them followed certain general lines: Russia would take the Principalities and perhaps the Bulgarian lands; Austria would obtain territory in the western Balkans, possibly including Serbia; Britain would receive Egypt and Crete, and France lands in Asia Minor. These ideas, although fine on paper, were very hard to put into practical effect, because, in fact, the lines of interest of the powers so crossed that a settlement satisfactory to all was impossible to achieve. For example, the Russians were not enthusiastic about an Austrian occupation of Serbia, while the Austrians did not want Russia in control of the lower Danube. The single issue of who should hold the Turkish Straits always proved impossible to settle. The entire question of partition in the end also ran against the fact that any scheme that could be devised inevitably granted Russia a disproportionate increase of power because of her geographic position and her ties with the peoples of the Balkans.

The third possibility, the establishment of independent states among the subject populations, was greeted with suspicion until the latter part of the nineteenth century by the western states, particularly Britain, because no one believed that such nations would not indeed be Russian puppets. The Russians themselves were not enthusiastic, because of the ideological implications of the national liberation movements. The achievement of independence by the Greeks in the 1820's and of autonomy by the Serbs was a result of the actions of the peoples themselves and did not come about because the powers were attempting to free the subject Christians. It was only after the Crimean War, when the idea of national unification also caused a redrawing of the map of central Europe, that the establishment of independent states was accepted as the best solution. At that time it also became apparent that independent states, far from being Russian satellites, could also be used to form a bulwark against Russian southward expansion.

Because of the innate powerlessness of the Ottoman government, Constantinople became in the nineteenth century the scene of constant duel between the representatives of the powers, particularly between Russia and Britain, although the Russian-Austrian, the British-French, and the Russian-French antagonisms also played a role. Of great interest was the attempt made by both the Russian and British governments to dominate the decisions of the Porte through intrigue, intimidation, or bribery of officials. In general, when Russian influence was paramount at the Porte, the Russian government stood for the maintenance of the empire. When, on the contrary, another power held primary control, Russia supported the whole or partial partitioning of the territory.

The Ottoman Empire was not only an area where great power interests clashed, but also where the major European religions and political ideologies were involved in the international conflicts. Of greatest importance to Russian policy before 1856 was undoubtedly the religious question. Russia at this time used freely the appeal her Orthodox faith held for the Balkan peoples, who were indeed oppressed by Moslem overlords. This policy brought her into close association with the Greeks, Rumanians, Bulgarians, Serbians, and Montenegrins, all of whom were Orthodox. The religious issue had the advantage for Russia that it was part of the conservative tradition and one of the foundations of autocracy. The appeal to the faith of the people, moreover, did not bring into play the unfavorable elements associated with the idea of freedom, the second great consideration.

Undoubtedly for its time the Ottoman Empire was the most oppressive despotic power having European possessions. Although their situation was not as bleak as it is often pictured, the Christians certainly enjoyed none of the political privileges and rights dear to the heart of the liberal west. At the time of the French revolution and Napoleon the ideas of the European revolutionary movements came into the Balkans and thereafter provided the political ideology for Balkan revolt. Thus the Balkan uprisings became strongly influenced by French ideals and French thought at the same time that the rulers of Russia came to regard France as the center of political movements of deadly danger to their own form of government. Russia, in addition, had nothing to offer of her own to combat French influence. Tsarism did not offer a political pattern applicable to Balkan conditions. It was inevitable that once free, the Balkan peoples would set up some form of government adopted from western models. Thus if the Russian government supported the freedom of the Orthodox from Moslem subjection, the danger existed that the new states would form centers of subversion against Russia itself.

The third issue, racial and national, that of Slavic brotherhood with its emphasis on the conflict between Slav and German in the larger sense, was not invoked until after the Crimean War.

As long as the Holy Alliance maintained itself, Russia could not support a policy involving outright hostility with her German allies. Although perhaps the most effective bond between Russia and the Balkan peoples, this alternative proved possible only when the entire central European area became potentially a threat to the Russian state. The policy also had the disadvantage that although it could be used to influence the Bulgars, Serbs, and Montenegrins it excluded the Greeks, Albanians, and Rumanians. As a doctrine it was better designed to secure the downfall of the Habsburg Empire, rather than the control of Ottoman, or former Ottoman, lands in Europe.

Until 1856, because of these contradictions in the courses of action open to it, the Russian government favored usually a policy of the maintenance of the empire intact but the domination of the government at Constantinople. In its relations with the Balkan peoples, the common Orthodox religion was stressed. The recognition of Russia as the protector of the Christians, in accordance with the policy established in the Treaty of Kuchuk Kainarji, thus became a major goal of Russian diplomacy, because it could be used as a means of controlling the Porte. The continued existence of the Ottoman Empire but as a weak buffer state and, if possible, as a Russian satellite was the aim of Russian policy at Constantinople before 1856. This condition was in accord with Russian general policies in Europe as the defender of the political and territorial *status quo* and, if it could have been maintained, was certainly the alternative most advantageous to Russian practical interests as a great power.

Despite this desire and the dislike of revolutionary activity shown by both Alexander I and Nicholas I, the Russian government in the fifteen years following the Congress of Vienna aided in the establishment of independent or autonomous regimes in Serbia, Greece, and the Danubian Principalities and thus, in fact, launched the Balkan liberation movements. Nationalism in the Balkans as well as in the rest of Europe was strongly influenced by the events of the French revolution and the wars of Napoleon.

At the beginning of the century the entire peninsula with the exception of one small area was under the control of Constantinople and under varying degrees of subservience. Only in the mountain kingdom of Montenegro had a Balkan people been able to maintain their freedom from Ottoman rule although the empire did claim a dominance that it was never able to enforce.

Despite the fact that Montenegro will play no important part in the following narrative, because its size precluded it from a major role in international affairs, mention must be made of the particular and close relationship of this state to Russia. As the single Slavic, Orthodox people who had successfully resisted Moslem rule and who throughout their history had waged a constant struggle for their freedom, the Montenegrins naturally appealed to the Russians in the romantic and imaginative sense. In addition, the strategic position of Montenegro made it a valuable point from which Russia could conduct policy against other powers, as was shown in the events of 1875-1878 and in the Balkan Wars of 1912-1913. This extremely primitive land with a population of less than half a million maintained close, cordial ties with Russia and with the Russian court throughout the century under discussion. The relationship was well illustrated by Alexander III's remark in 1888 that Montenegro's ruler was his "only sincere friend"; later Prince Nikola made the proud declaration: "We and the Russians are 100,000,000 strong."

THE REVOLT OF SERBIA

Although intense diplomatic activity characterized the eastern scene during the Napoleonic period, the Russian attitude toward events in the Ottoman Empire remained determined by her relations with France. At this time Russia did, however, succeed in considerably strengthening her position in the Principalities. In 1802 she protested over conditions in the area on the basis of her rights under the Treaty of Kuchuk Kainarji and succeeded in having her candidates appointed as hospodars. In 1806 in a renewed quarrel over the area, Russia went to war with Turkey. The hostilities were interrupted by the Treaty of Tilsit, which brought about an armistice and two years of negotiations. In a secret clause in this latter agreement, Napoleon and Alexander I agreed upon the partition of Turkey, but they were never able to settle the ultimate disposition of the Straits. In 1809 the war was resumed until 1812, when Russia, faced by a possible invasion by France, was forced in the Treaty of Bucharest to give back to Turkey lands that her armies had occupied. The Porte thus won again control in the Principalities and Serbia and over certain Russian conquests in Asia. Russia retained Bessarabia and the Danube delta. This treaty thus marks the beginning of the Bessarabian problem, which was to poison the future relations of Russia and Rumania. The Treaty of Bucharest, however, freed the Russian armies to march northward to meet the Napoleonic invasion.

The period of the wars of Napoleon also witnessed the first successful uprising of a Christian people against the Porte. The Serbian revolution of 1804 began not as a full-scale revolution against Turkish rule, but as a mutiny against the local administration and the atrocities of the Janissaries. Later the movement turned into a real rebellion with the aim of achieving complete independence. At the beginning of the century Serbia occupied a definite position in Russian policies in the Balkans but was subordinate to the Principalities and Greece. Moreover, there was no possibility that the Russian government would compromise its wider European interests to aid a Balkan revolt. Thus, when in September, 1804 a request for aid was received from Serbia, it met with little success. Alexander I, who at the time was more concerned with the extension of French influence in Dalmatia than with events on the Danube, did not wish to see the entire issue of the position of the Christians in the empire opened again. He, therefore, advised caution, but he did agree to send arms and officers and promised diplomatic support at Constantinople.

At first the Serbian insurgents were able to win real victories.

In 1806 Belgrade was captured by the rebels, who next gained control of northern Serbia. However, the entire movement soon fell victim to the changing diplomatic conditions in Europe. In 1806 Selim joined with Napoleon; and, in an attempt to end the fighting, the Sultan offered autonomy to the Serbs. The revolutionary leader, Karageorge, preferred instead to join Russia. In July, 1807 an alliance was concluded, and a real war for independence was launched. The agreement with Russia, signed three days after the Treaty of Tilsit, was never honored. Instead of supporting the Serbs, the Russian government concluded an armistice with the Ottoman Empire. Free from the threat of Russian arms, the Turks could concentrate on the reduction of Serbia. Although in the Treaty of Bucharest Russia gained from Turkey the assurance that the Serbian rebels would receive full amnesty and that the country would be autonomous, the Porte failed to carry out these terms. With Russia engaged with France, Turkish troops were concentrated in Serbia, and Karageorge was compelled to flee. By 1813 the Ottoman forces had reoccupied Belgrade and were in effective control of the country.

The second stage of the Serbian revolution was carried out under the leadership of Miloš Obrenović, who at first adopted a policy of co-operation with the Turks. The retaliatory measures taken by the Ottoman officials and the Janissaries upon reoccupying the country were so violent that a second rebellion broke out in 1815. Faced with the possibility of renewed Russian intervention after the defeat of Napoleon, the Porte in December, 1815 recognized Miloš as Prince of the Pashalik of Belgrade and allowed the Serbs a large degree of autonomy. They were granted the right to retain their weapons and to have their own national assembly, but the usual taxes and tribute would be levied and Turkish troops would remain in occupation. Thus with indirect Russian help, Serbia won a measure of freedom from Ottoman control. The next stage in the winning of Serbian independence was closely connected with the Greek revolution of the 1820's.

THE GREEK REVOLUTION

Although the great powers were not drawn directly into the events leading to the achievement of Serbian autonomy, the Greek revolution was, in contrast, an event of general European importance and one that dominated the diplomatic history of its decade. Of the Christian inhabitants of the Ottoman Empire, the Greeks enjoyed a distinct and privileged position and, as such, were best qualified to lead a revolt against the dominating power. In the eighteenth century they had achieved a certain amount of control in the administrative and commercial system of the empire. Greeks from the Phanar district of Constantinople were regularly employed as secretaries and interpreters by Ottoman officials. Three important posts, that of grand dragoman (chief interpreter) of the Porte and the two hospodarships of the Danubian Principalities were traditionally held by Greeks. Because of the responsible offices which they occupied, Greek nationals came to have close relationships with Russia, particularly after the Russian conquest of the northern coast of the Black Sea. Many of them, as, for example, Capodistrias and K. K. Rodofinikin, rose to high positions in the Russian state service.

The Greek domination of the Orthodox ecclesiastic organization of the empire and their commercial supremacy in the Black Sea and the eastern Mediterranean also resulted in frequent meetings with their Russian counterparts. The great Orthodox ecclesiastical centers, such as the monasteries of Mt. Athos and the Holy Places of Palestine, were largely administered by Greek clerics. Greek merchants throughout the eighteenth century, but particularly during the wars of the French revolution, were able to extend their commercial ventures over the entire area. The carrying trade of the Ottoman-controlled seas was in Greek hands. Over the years Greek and Russian worked well together, and the Greeks regarded Russia as their protector against Ottoman tyranny.

Because of Greek commercial interests in the Black Sea and their relations with Russia, it was natural that the port city of Odessa should become a center of conspiracy against the Ottoman Empire. There in 1814 the society Philike Hetairia (the Society of Friends) was founded with the aim of achieving Greek freedom. In view of the Russian past policy in the Balkans and the patronage offered Balkan Christianity, the organizers of the Hetairia expected to secure Russian aid. They were able to obtain financial support for their ventures from the wealthy Greek Black Sea merchants, and Greeks in Russian or Ottoman service in the Balkans were drawn into their plans. Revolts were organized both in Greece proper and in the Principalities, which were in the hands of Greek administrators. The headship of the revolution was first offered to Capodistrias, who, although refusing the titular leadership, did what he could to bring Russia behind the Greek cause. Thereafter Alexander Ypsilanti, a major-general in the Russian army and an aide-de-camp of the emperor, led the movement. On March 6, 1821 he invaded Moldavia, and he promptly sent an appeal to the tsar for assistance. Simultaneously, a Rumanian national revolt under the leadership of Tudor Vladimirescu broke out. Although both Greek and Rumanian shared a common interest in achieving freedom from Ottoman rule, the two groups soon came into conflict and Vladimirescu was executed on Greek authority.

Though the Greek rebellion received some support, principally from the hospodar Michael Sturdza, the uprising in the Principalities soon met with complete disaster. First, Alexander I was at the time at the Congress of Laibach, where, as we have seen, he had succumbed to the influence of Metternich's arguments. The Austrian chancellor, fearing the opening of the eastern question, convinced him that this revolt was just another manifestation of the revolutionary spirit in Europe. Capodistrias, who remained the champion of Russian intervention, was dismissed. Russian troops were therefore not sent across the Prut in aid of the Greeks as they had hoped. Second, the hatred of the Rumanian for the Greek-dominated administration of the Principalities soon became apparent. The Rumanians had no desire to change from Turkish to Greek rule; they sought an end also to Phanariote control. Without strong Russian aid, the Greek rebellion in the Principalities could only have succeeded if it had won the adherence of all of the Christian subject peoples, Rumanian, Serbian, and Bulgarian alike, and had joined them in a common uprising. Despite efforts by the Greek leaders, this endeavor proved impossible.

The suppression of the revolt in the Principalities, however, in no way marked the end of the Greek revolution. A rebellion that had broken out in the Morea proved more difficult to crush. Greek geography, with its wealth of islands, peninsulas, and high mountains, was well adapted to guerilla warfare and continued resistance. Throughout the Greek revolution the Turks never solved the problem of how to defeat decisively rebel groups who could always retreat to places inaccessible to the regular Ottoman troops. The Greeks, although divided among themselves, were thus able to prolong their resistance and create a condition in the Balkans that eventually forced the great powers to intervene.

The issue of the Greek revolution was complicated for the European governments by the hold that the idea of Greece had on the imagination of the educated public of Europe. In the west the close identification of classical Greece with the Greece of 1820 and the general association of that land with the idea of human liberty resulted in the great movement of Philhellenism. In Russia, sympathy for the Greek cause was based on the common Orthodox and Byzantine heritage of both peoples, a far more valid association. As a result of this wave of sympathy and ardent support, every power was faced with public pressure to act in the Greek interest. The Greek forces were swelled with men who came from all over Europe to fight for Greek freedom.

Despite the fact that Alexander I refused to send troops to the Principalities, he too was moved by opposing influences. Although he feared the spread of revolutionary movements, he could not allow a massacre of Balkan Christians. The defense of Orthodoxy was part of his conservative system; Russian prestige was deeply involved. The Treaty of Kuchuk Kainarji appeared to impose upon Russia the obligation as well as the right to protect threatened Balkan Christians. Russian economic interests were tied to the fate of the Greek merchant community; the sympathies of the Russian public were openly with their co-religionists. The action of the Russian government in the crisis was thus bound to depend upon the reaction of the Porte and the speed with which the rebellion could be crushed.

The first reaction of the Turks to the revolution was a direct challenge to the Russian position in regard to the protection of Balkan Christians. On Easter night Patriarch Gregory along with some of his bishops was seized by a group of Janissaries and hanged in front of his own church. This atrocity was followed by a general massacre of the Greeks of Constantinople. The violence of the Turkish reprisals and the choice of the target, the head of the Orthodox church, forced Russian action. In a strong note the Russian government warned the Porte not to use the occasion of the suppression of a political rebellion to open a religious war against its Christian subjects. Although the Turkish actions brought about a real Russo-Turkish crisis, culminating in the withdrawal of the Russian ambassador in June, Alexander I did not resort to war. Under the influence of Metternich, who saw the danger to Austria in a Russo-Turkish conflict, the tsar preferred to regard the revolution as the revolt of a people against their legitimate ruler rather than as a quarrel between Christians and Moslems. Moreover, the new situation in the Near East brought up for Russia, as for all of the powers, the question of the fate of the Ottoman Empire.

Thereafter the Greek question, which was not finally settled until 1832, became enmeshed in the far greater issue. Each power in the ensuing negotiations considered the revolt from the aspect of the effect that the weakening of the Porte would have on the balance of power and on its own position. Seen in this light, none of the great powers favored Greek independence. Britain and Austria continued to fear that Russia would use the situation to go to war with Turkey; Prussia with little to gain from a Near Eastern war wished to prevent a crisis. Russia, as we have seen, had sought to avoid a conflict. Moreover, the Greek constitution of 1822 was firmly based on western political principles; a free Greece would clearly be a liberal Greece. Neither Russian interests nor tsarist ideology would thus be benefited by Greek success.

The Greeks gained no aid from the Russian government, but they did obtain assistance from official and unofficial sources in Britain. In 1822 George Canning succeeded Castlereagh as foreign secretary. In no sense a partisan of Greece, he was nevertheless faced by the pressure of British opinion, particularly after the massacre of Chios when Turkish troops killed or sold into slavery all but 2,000 of a population of around 45,000 on the island. In 1823 the British government recognized the Greek rebels as belligerents; in 1824 they received the first of a series of British loans, which, in effect, made the City of London the financier of the revolution. British interests, public opinion, and fear of what Russia might do finally forced the government to seek an agreement with Russia for joint action.

Meanwhile the sultan had been unable to make headway against the Greek rebellion. Finally, in 1825 in desperation he called upon the Pasha of Egypt, Mehemet Ali, for assistance. He promised his vassal the gift of the island of Crete for his son Ibrahim. Egyptian troops first took Crete and then landed in the Morea. Their early successes and the devastation they caused brought about a strong reaction among those sympathetic to the Greeks. British interests were also endangered by the increase of Egyptian power in the area. At this crucial point Alexander I suddenly died, leaving to his successor the solution of the Greek problem. Before his death, however, the possibility of British-Russian co-operation had already been discussed. Nicholas I thus continued a policy that had been inaugurated under his predecessor, but, as shall be shown, he carried it to its conclusion with a new strength and directness.

*   *   *   *   *

Although in internal affairs Russia advanced but little during the reign of Alexander I, in international affairs she had, as we have seen, won a position of continental superiority. As for all of the allied states, the period of the Napoleonic wars had been for her a time of trial and danger. Revolutionary France threatened Europe both as a military aggressor and as the carrier of an idea that could have subverted the regimes in power in the other states. At the Congress of Vienna Alexander I, like the other statesmen, made peace with the intention of ensuring that the upheaval of 1791-1814 would never be repeated. Far from being an uncritical reactionary, he wished not to enforce the acceptance of autocratic regimes everywhere, but to see that all received political forms corresponding to their historical development and general background. Having little feeling for political evolution, he then wished to solidify the system through an international organization that would, in effect, guarantee the *status quo*.

Despite the fact that the tsar's ideas were often presented in a form that made others doubt his emotional stability, they were in fact an example of wise statesmanship. The years after 1815 are known as the "era of Metternich," but Russia as much as Austria benefited from the system then established. The protection of the territorial settlement of Vienna and the defense of the principle of legitimacy gave the Russian government a lever for interference in any continental crisis. The ultimate dependence of both Austria and Prussia, in both a strategic and political sense, assured Russia that, where continental affairs alone were in question, she would have dependable allies. Austrian adherence was made more necessary by the British withdrawal from continental entanglements, particularly after 1820. The great danger to Russian policy lay in the eastern question where "traditional" and "legitimate" interests might in fact involve the support of revolutionary movements against the Ottoman Empire. There also any Russian advances met with Austrian and British opposition and carried the threat of the formation of a continental coalition. Thus, although Alexander I bequeathed to his successor an enviable inheritance in foreign affairs, the basic contradiction, which Nicholas could never resolve, was already apparent. Alexander died during one eastern crisis; Nicholas on his assumption of power was thus immediately faced with the general problem that was in the end to bring Russia a bitter defeat in the 1850's.

III

Nicholas I

Although in many ways profoundly different from his brother, Nicholas I, during his reign, made no fundamental alterations in Russian foreign policy. However, his character and temperament made it inevitable that his methods of dealing with situations would alter. In contrast to Alexander I, with his complex emotional structure, the new tsar was direct, blunt and stubborn. With none of Alexander's inclination to high idealism or religious mysticism, Nicholas I clung to a few principles with strong tenacity. His ideal was that of the perfect military order, where everything had its place and all functioned on a chain of command. Like Alexander I, Nicholas I also felt convinced that he held his power directly from God and that his decisions had thus divine sanction. He, therefore, preferred collaborators who would serve him as secretaries and not criticize or oppose his plans; Nesselrode was an ideal subordinate. Nicholas' political ideas had much in common with those of Alexander in his last years. Hereditary monarchy remained for him the only legitimate form of government; regimes based on revolutionary action or on doctrines of popular sovereignty could, in his eyes, never have real validity. The circumstances of his assumption of the throne reinforced his natural inclinations. During the reign of Alexander I the presumed heir to the throne was not Nicholas, but his elder brother Constantine. Since his marriage was morganatic and his children could not succeed him, Constantine preferred not to become tsar. Although Alexander I did indeed name Nicholas, this decision was kept secret from those directly concerned. As a result, when Alexander I died, Nicholas recognized Constantine, but at the same time the latter proclaimed Nicholas tsar. For a period of approximately three weeks political life in Russia was in a turmoil. This confusion gave the opportunity for a political disturbance, organized primarily in the guards regiments. Although this event, the Decembrist revolt, was in no sense a great national uprising, Nicholas I felt that he had crushed a real revolution and also that he had done this with the aid of God. His subsequent attitude toward European revolutionary movements was deeply influenced by this early experience, which he profoundly misinterpreted.

In addition to the questions connected with the internal rebellion, Nicholas I also inherited the unresolved Greek revolt and the problem of Russo-Turkish relations based on past treaties. In this field he acted with more vigor and decision than Alexander I. In fact, it is to be noted that throughout his reign Nicholas I showed more flexibility in eastern affairs than in his dealings with the continent itself. However, as has been emphasized, the interests of unreformed Russia demanded the maintenance of the *status quo* in central Europe. Nicholas' policies directed toward the suppression of liberal and national movements in that area, while motivated chiefly by ideological concerns, were to his country's advantage as long as the internal conditions in Russia remained in a state of stagnation and repression. The Near East, in contrast, offered a freer field of activity.

THE RUSSO-TURKISH WAR OF 1828

The principal international questions with which Nicholas I had to deal in the first years of his reign were those concerned with the Greek revolution and the events in the Balkans connected with it. Continuing the policy inaugurated by Alexander I, Nicholas I laid particular emphasis on the past agreements that Russia had made with the Ottoman Empire. These pacts, although not referring to Greece directly, covered, as we have seen, certain general Russian claims to the protection of the Balkan Christians and also specific rights in regard to the Principalities and Serbia. In the next years in his negotiations with the powers on the Greek question, Nicholas I made a clear separation in his policy in the east. Russian interests, he believed, were directly involved in questions of dispute between St. Petersburg and Constantinople, as, for example, the problem of the Principalities, Serbia, and Russian commercial rights in Turkish territories. In contrast, the Greek revolution was not treated as the primary issue. In fact, Nicholas shared Alexander's tendency to treat the Greeks as rebels against the authority of a legitimate ruler, although this feeling appears not to have influenced Russian decisions after 1825. In matters affecting the direct relations of Russia and Turkey, Nicholas I always negotiated with the Porte unilaterally and without reference to other governments. In the Greek affair, on the other hand, he accepted a wide measure of co-operation, particularly with Britain, and he acted in concert with his allies.

Agreement with Britain was made possible by the simultaneous desire of that government to settle the Greek question by mediation and joint action with Russia. The British prime minister, Canning, hoped that by working with Russia he could moderate and direct her actions and thus prevent a Russo-Turkish war. Moreover, neither Russia nor Britain had an interest in the increase of Egyptian power, which would result should Mehemet Ali achieve a real triumph in Greece. In March, 1826, therefore, the Duke of Wellington was sent to St. Petersburg to greet the new monarch. There in April the Protocol of St. Petersburg was signed—a document in which Russia and Britain agreed upon a policy of mutual co-operation in the Greek revolution. Britain, with Russian support, was to attempt to act as mediator with the aim of securing the establishment of an autonomous Greek state under the sovereignty of the sultan. Should the British efforts fail, the two powers were to act in concert to set up an independent Greece.

Russia was thus obligated to act together with her British partner in the Greek question, but no such limitations hindered her activities in the other matters in dispute with the Porte. In April, 1826, in a virtual ultimatum, Nicholas called upon the Ottoman Empire to restore the conditions of 1821 in the Principalities and to carry out the provisions of the Treaty of Bucharest in regard to Serbia. After the rebellion of Ypsilanti, Turkish troops had occupied the Principalities and had failed to leave; the situation in Serbia was equally unsatisfactory. Caught in a moment of domestic weakness occasioned by his abolition of the Janissary corps, Sultan Mahmud was without the means to defend himself. In the Convention of Akkerman, signed on October 7, 1826, Russia gained not only the recognition of her demands for Serbia and the Principalities, but also disputed territory in the Caucasus, the right of navigation in Turkish waters, and permission for commercial vessels to pass through the Straits.

With the chief Russian objectives secured in this pact, the Russian government was less anxious to hasten the implementation of the Protocol of St. Petersburg. On July 6, 1827 France joined Britain and Russia in the Treaty of London, which, like the previous agreement, called for the establishment of an autonomous tributary Greece. The powers, in addition, agreed to try within a month to induce both the rebels and the Porte to conclude an armistice. This agreement, which was not signed by Austria or

Prussia, marked a break of the Holy Alliance. Metternich throughout the crisis stood strongly against action in favor of the Greek revolution. He failed, nevertheless, to exert the same restraining influence on Nicholas I as he had on Alexander I.

Meanwhile, in an attempt to force an armistice on the Ottoman Empire through a blockade of the Morea, the combined French, British, and Russian fleets trapped the Turkish navy in the Bay of Navarino on October 20. In the surrounding confusion, fighting broke out, and as a result the Turkish fleet was destroyed. This unexpected and dramatic event changed the entire course of the Near Eastern crisis. The Russian government immediately expressed its enthusiastic approval of the event; the British government, in contrast, was deeply disquieted. The policy of co-operation with Russia had been designed to restrain the menacing northern neighbor and not to bring about the destruction of the Ottoman Empire. After the death of Canning, the Duke of Wellington in 1828 became responsible for British policy. Reversing the stand of his predecessor, the general now allowed Russia and the Porte to settle their quarrels alone. That conflict was inevitable was shown by the reaction of Constantinople to Navarino. The Convention of Akkerman was denounced and a Holy War proclaimed.

The Russo-Turkish War, which finally commenced in April, 1828, proved anything but an easy victory for the Russian troops. Nicholas I, who insisted upon heading the campaign personally, showed that despite his military training he was an inept commander. During the Russo-Turkish hostilities the three allied powers, France, Britain, and Russia, maintained the fiction that this conflict had little to do with the Greek revolution. They, therefore, continued to negotiate on the question. With the assent of Russia and Britain, French troops were landed in the Morea in 1828, and the Egyptian forces were compelled to leave. Despite their surface co-operation, relations between France, Britain, and Russia were characterized by mutual distrust and suspicion. In April, 1827 Capodistrias was chosen as the first president of Greece. His election marked the victory of the Russian party and gave Russia the hope that the new state would be strongly under her influence. Inside Greece, French and British agents co-operated to block such an occurrence.

Despite the difficulties they encountered, Russian troops were finally able to march down the Balkan peninsula to Adrianople, where they arrived in August. The seizure of the city and the fact that Russian armies were now within striking distance of Constantinople offered Russia the possibility of attempting the conquest of the city and the destruction of the empire. This grave question was discussed at this time by a special committee appointed by the tsar. It was decided here that the maintenance of the empire was more to the Russian advantage than any possible alternative. Although the work of the committee did not influence the terms of the Treaty of Adrianople, which was signed on September 14, 1829 before the decision had been reached, the agreement reflected as a whole the same general policy. The empire was to be preserved, but it was to be kept in subjection to Russia. This principle was clearly expressed in a secret circular of May, 1830 in which it was stated that the terms of the treaty should make it clear to the Turkish government that: "if it is still able to live, it will be only the life that the emperor is pleased to allow it . . ." [1] Despite these strong words, Russia was in fact in no position to effect the outright partition of the empire. Such an action could only have been carried out at this time against the strong opposition of Britain, France, and Austria and would certainly have led to the formation of a coalition against Russia. The performance of the Russian forces in the Balkan campaign had shown that Russia was not prepared to fight Europe.

Despite the fact that the Treaty of Adrianople was regarded as a moderate peace, Russia had indeed gained much. The provisions of the Convention of Akkerman were reaffirmed, and Russia

1. Barbara Jelavich, *Russia and Greece during the Regency of King Othon: Russian Documents on the First Years of Greek Independence* (Thessaloniki: Institute of Balkan Studies, 1962), p. 138.

TREATY OF ADRIANOPLE

now acquired a protectorship in the Principalities and special commercial privileges in the empire. The control she gained over the Sulina channel of the Danube, the one navigable arm, gave her dominion over the mouth of the river. Serbia received the autonomy promised in the previous agreement, and Turkey was compelled to pay an indemnity. Article X provided that Greece should become an autonomous, tributary state in accordance with a protocol that had been signed between the powers in March, 1829. The Russian victory over the Turks thus resulted not only in the securing of further advantages to Russian commerce and certain territorial gains, but also in further freedom from Ottoman control for the Serbs, Greeks, and Rumanians.

Although the Treaty of Adrianople provided only for the establishment of an autonomous kingdom, Greece received in the London Protocol of February, 1830 full independence but with restricted frontiers. After the refusal of Leopold of Saxe-Coburg to accept the throne, the crown was finally given to Otto, the second son of the Philhellene King Ludwig of Bavaria. The prince ascended the Greek throne in 1832 as King Othon. The attitude of Russia toward Greece after this date was determined by the policy she had adopted at the time of the Treaty of Adrianople—that of preserving the empire intact, but in a state of dependence. Although the drawing of the Greek frontiers, which left most of the Greeks outside of the state, was bound to become again an international question, Russia acted to maintain the integrity of the lands of the Porte. Moreover, after the assassination of Capodistrias in 1831, Russia had little chance of securing the predominance of her partisans in the Greek government. Her interests in the new kingdom thus never became as important as her links with the Principalities, Serbia, or later, Bulgaria. Her aims within Greece remained, in general, limited to the securing of a diplomatic position of balance against the rival parties of the British and French. French influence in Athens was particularly disliked because of the revolutionary tendency of French politics and because of the links that country had with Egypt. The Russian government repeatedly pressed for the establishment of a strong monarchical regime in Athens, and the granting of a constitution was opposed on the grounds that

GREECE IN 1832

Black Sea

Adriatic Sea

M A C E D O N I A

●Adrianople

Constantinople●

Thessaloniki

Sea of Marmora

EPIRUS

CORFU

THESSALY

Aegean

LEMNOS

Sea

MYTILENE

Ionian Sea

CHIOS

Athens

SAMOS

CYCLADES

DODECANESE

PELOPONNESUS
(MOREA)

Original Greek Kingdom 1832

RHODES

CRETE

it was first necessary to set up an orderly government and ac-
custom the people to the new political conditions.

On one issue, however, the Russian government in its relations
with Greece remained firm—that of religion. This question in
future years was to determine the Russian attitude toward King
Othon. Although Russia had been forced to accept a Catholic
king, because of the lack of a satisfactory alternative, she remained constantly concerned about the status of the Orthodox

church in the state. When in 1834 the Greek church was separated from the Patriarchate of Constantinople, the position of Othon, a Catholic, as head of the national institution was obviously not satisfactory. Thereafter Russia continued to press Othon to secure the promise that at least his heirs would adopt the Orthodox faith.

The Greek question, as a major disturbing element in international relations, now receded into the background until its revival in the 1890's. The other major powers also had no wish to see a strengthening of the Greek nation. The growth of Greek merchant seapower was as little favored by Britain as by Russia. The establishment of a strong Greece or of a revived Byzantine Empire was to the advantage of no major government. When in subsequent years King Othon was to attempt to win popularity among his people by a policy of expansion abroad, he was met with the united opposition of the Mediterranean powers.

Despite the Russian government's lost influence in Greece after the death of Capodistrias, its position, in contrast, in the Principalities was assured through the Convention of Akkerman, which was reaffirmed in the Treaty of Adrianople. The Russian protectorate established at this time lasted until the Crimean War. In accordance with the agreements existing between Turkey and Russia, the hospodars in both Wallachia and Moldavia were to be elected for terms of seven years and they could be deposed only with the assent of Russia. In addition, the wishes of the Russian government were to be taken into consideration by the administrations. A new statute was to be drawn up for each principality, which would regulate the form of its government. In the Treaty of Adrianople, Russia also received the right to leave her troops in the Principalities until the Porte had paid a heavy indemnity.

Under the able and enlightened direction of P. D. Kiselev, the Russian governor-general, the Russian representatives in subsequent years did attempt to introduce a good system of administration into the Rumanian lands. With the co-operation of the boyars, the great landowners of Moldavia and Wallachia, the so-called Organic Statutes were drawn up for each principality. These documents established separate but parallel institutions in each section. Both states were to be governed by a hospodar, now chosen for life, and an assembly composed of the highest boyars. In the period of the protectorate, Russia supported the political position of the large landowner, who, in turn, was able to extend his control over the Rumanian peasant. Domination of the political life of Moldavia and Wallachia was exercised through the Russian consuls in Jassy and Bucharest, who interfered constantly in Rumanian internal affairs. Despite the good intentions of many in the Russian service, the years of the protectorate won for Russia the dislike and distrust of those who, in the future, were to direct the country. Strongly supporting conservative forms of government, Russia could not hope to win the sympathy of the group that was rising to power and was also liberal and strongly influenced by France. The Rumanian national liberation movement, as a consequence, became directed as much against Russian protection as against Ottoman domination.

PERSIA AND THE CAUCASUS

The attainment of the major Russian objectives in the Balkans in the 1820's was paralleled by similar successes in the Caucasus and against Persia. The tripartite struggle over Georgia between Russia, Persia, and the Ottoman Empire had its origins in the eighteenth century, but this area of diplomatic conflict had always remained distinctly secondary in Russian policy to the developments in Europe and the Balkan Christian territories. Here, as elsewhere in the east, the Russian activities were determined by general European considerations, particularly by the relations with France and Britain.

Russian penetration in the Caucasian region commenced in the reign of Catherine; under Paul, eastern Georgia was annexed to Russia. Although the ruler of the state had requested Russian protectorship against Persia and the Ottoman Empire with the condition that he remain as sovereign, Paul decided instead upon outright annexation. Despite the fact that this measure went against the wishes of the peoples concerned, Alexander I confirmed the decision, which made the later administration of the land more difficult. Russian expansion into and beyond the Caucasus principally affected Persia, but also the Ottoman Empire, particularly in view of the strategic value of the territory. During the Napoleonic wars the Russian government continued its efforts toward the gradual penetration and control of the Caucasian states. A policy of seeking to obtain the co-operation of the ruling families was adopted, and Russia sought to win them by offering them high ranks and positions in the Russian state.

The strengthening of the Russian hold here alarmed Britain because it brought up the question of the control of Persia, which was part of the system of buffer states that British policy favored as a protection for India. The entire diplomatic situation at the beginning of the century was somewhat complicated by the fact that the French government too attempted to exploit Persia as a weapon against its European enemies, Britain and Russia. Under foreign impulsion, Persia twice before 1830 attempted to block Russian expansion toward her borders. First, in 1805 under French influence a war was inaugurated, but the Persian armies soon met with defeat. In 1807, after the Treaty of Tilsit, France joined with Russia, and thereafter Britain became the dominating power at the Persian court. In 1812 Persia met further reverses, and in 1813 she was forced, in the Treaty of Gulistan, to recognize the Russian rule over the disputed Caucasian states. After this defeat, Britain still remained predominant in Teheran and maintained her position with promises of subsidies and military assistance.

A second attempt to halt Russia was made in 1826, but again the Persian armies failed to win victories. In the Treaty of Turkmanchai in 1828 Russian possession of Erivan and Nakhichevan was recognized. These annexations brought into the Russian Empire large Armenian populations whose acquisition was to have a great influence on the Russian attitude toward the Armenian question in the 1890's. The Treaty of Adrianople, as has been mentioned, also had given to Russia Caucasian lands. Despite these military and diplomatic victories, Russia still faced a difficult and protracted struggle to enforce her control, particularly over the Caucasian mountaineers, who strongly resisted Russian domination. In 1830 the rebels found a real leader in the person of Shamil, who was not finally defeated until 1859. The Caucasian campaigns, which extended into the 1860's, had a great influence on Russian culture, and they strongly appealed to the Russian imagination despite their relative insignificance in international diplomacy. The poets Lermontov and Pushkin participated in the fighting; the music of Rimsky-Korsakov, Balakirev, and Borodin reflected the exotic quality the Caucasus held in Russian eyes.

The area was eventually subdued, but Russian relations with Persia remained unsettled; and throughout the century their course was determined by the wider Russo-British rivalry. In Teheran, as in Constantinople, Russian and British diplomats vied in their attempt to control the government of the eastern state. In the 1830's the center of conflict shifted from the Transcaucasian lands to Afghanistan, and here Persia acted in the interests of St. Petersburg. In 1837, under Russian influence, Persia commenced a war against Afghanistan in an attempt to seize Herat, a point Britain regarded as vital to her control of India. As a result of this struggle and its ensuing complications, Britain in 1839 brought about the First Afghan War, which led to the establishment of her domination over the country and eventually to a war with Persia in 1856. Although in the 1830's the principal attention of the European diplomats was centered on the Straits and the Egyptian question, the involvement of Britain and Russia in Persia and Afghanistan always played a determining role in the formulation of policy by the great powers. The fate of Afghanistan again came into question in the 1870's when

Russia moved against Khiva, Bokhara, and Kokand as well as Transcaspia. The larger problem of the control of Persia, waged on both the political and economic level, continued throughout the century and up to the outbreak of the First World War.

THE EGYPTIAN QUESTION

The granting of independence to Greece and the signing of the peace with Russia did not put an end to the difficulties of the Porte. Sultan Mahmud II was still faced with the challenge of his ambitious and resourceful ally, Mehemet Ali. Although the ultimate aims of the Pasha of Egypt are a matter of conjecture, he had by 1830 built up what could have become the center of a future great Arabian empire, and he had the power necessary to challenge the sultan himself. He first added the Sudan and part of Arabia to his lands; he received Crete in payment for his aid in the Greek revolt. Unlike other Ottoman governors, he had modernized and developed his territories, and his finances were in good condition. His military forces, the best in the east, had been built up with the aid of French advisors. With these advantages behind him, Mehemet Ali in 1831 revolted and embarked upon the invasion of Syria in an attempt to join this province to his own lands. His son Ibrahim, the commander of his armies, quickly reduced the Syrian cities and fortresses and in December 1832 at the battle of Konya destroyed the main Turkish army. Constantinople now lay before the Egyptian forces, and the great powers were again faced with the danger that the Ottoman Empire might collapse or fall into the hands of a strong power.

Although Russia was directly affected by this challenge to her predominance in Constantinople, the Egyptian venture in its final outcome served to reinforce her position at the Porte. Faced with the new threat, Sultan Mahmud first appealed to Britain for aid, but that country, deep in the reform crisis of 1832 and the problems involved in the Belgian revolution, refused to accept further commitments. France, because of her relations with

Egypt and her position in Algeria, regarded Mehemet's victories with a sympathetic eye. The Ottoman Empire was thus left with the sole alternative of accepting Russian aid. With reluctance and with the explanation "a drowning man in his despair will clutch at a serpent," the sultan in 1833 agreed to the presence of Russian soldiers and sailors at the Straits. Russian protection, however, did not spare Mahmud the humiliation of yielding to Mehemet's demands. In the Convention of Kutahia, Egypt received Syria, including the disputed district of Adana.

In this moment of Turkish defeat and isolation, Nicholas I sent to Constantinople an able and tactful statesman, Prince Orlov. Under the influence of the diplomat's conciliatory and charming manner, the sultan himself proposed a Russo-Turkish agreement and consented to the terms of the Treaty of Unkiar Skelessi. This pact, signed in July, 1833, had the effect of making Russia the guarantor of the Turkish Empire and marked the height of her influence in Constantinople. The terms of this treaty of peace and alliance provided that each partner should protect the other's lands and render aid in case of aggression. An additional article, however, limited the assistance to be given by the Porte to Russia to the closing of the Straits to armed vessels of other nations in time of war. Although this clause was secret, the British government learned of it four days later. The great significance for Britain lay in the interpretation of the article. If the agreement sealed the Straits to all warships, it was not dangerous, but if the Russian fleet were allowed to pass freely in and out of the Black Sea, without a similar privilege being allowed to the ships of her opponent, then Russia had indeed gained a major victory. In the following years Nesselrode was to give repeated assurances that the Treaty of Unkiar Skelessi was no more than the reaffirmation of previous agreements and that Russia had gained no new rights. The British government, ever suspicious of Russian intentions, did not fully accept his words.

With the privileged position of St. Petersburg reaffirmed, the Russian policy, adopted in 1829, of the preservation and control of the Ottoman Empire was given new strength. The Russian ascendancy in the east was reinforced in September, 1833 by the Treaty of Münchengrätz with Austria. As we have seen, the Holy Alliance of the three conservative powers had broken on the Greek question. Throughout this crisis Austria and Prussia had remained to a large degree aside; Russia had followed a policy of co-operation with Britain and France in the achievement of Greek independence. However, the increasing division of interest with Britain after Navarino and with France after the July revolution made the continuation of close co-operation impossible. To meet this situation, Nicholas once again was able to join his policy in Europe with that in the east. Seeking to preserve the *status quo* in both areas, he turned back to his original partners. In the Treaty of Münchengrätz both Austria and Russia agreed to oppose Mehemet Ali should he attempt to obtain further gains at the expense of the Porte and to seek jointly the maintenance of the Ottoman Empire. Should the empire, despite their wishes, collapse, they were to co-operate to arrange a new system and to maintain the balance of power. Prussia later adhered to the general policies of this agreement.

After the conclusion of the Treaty of Unkiar Skelessi, affairs in the east entered upon a period of relative calm. A Russo-Turkish convention signed in January, 1834 provided for the evacuation of the Russian armies from the Principalities and a cancellation of a portion of the Turkish debt arising from the Treaty of Adrianople. Russia thus emerged from the period of the prolonged eastern crisis, which had begun in 1821, in a considerably strengthened position. Control had in effect been established over the empire through the Treaty of Unkiar Skelessi. Although the Russian government did not claim that it had received new rights in regard to the Straits, it did believe that the pact obligated the Ottoman Empire to consult first with Russia in all crises, and to accept Russian assistance before that of any other power, a situation that meant, in the words of Lord Palmerston, that "the Russian Ambassador becomes the chief Cabinet Minister of the Sultan." With Russian armies stationed on the Prut and the Russian fleet only a few days sailing distance from Constantinople,

Russia believed that it had the military strength necessary to maintain these terms. Moreover, Nicholas, with the re-establishment of the bonds with Austria and Prussia, had brought his central European allies behind the eastern settlement, which was much to the Russian advantage.

The relatively strong increase of Russian power and influence naturally aroused the concern and hostility of Britain, who was most directly affected by the events. Although it was largely due to British negligence that the Porte had been led to accept Russian assistance, Britain resented the diplomatic defeat she had suffered at Constantinople. Thereafter the tone of British policy became more aggressive and dynamic, particularly under the direction of the Liberal foreign secretary, Lord Palmerston. An ardent exponent of imperial power and glory, he became the chief influence in the shaping of British foreign relations. His opinion of Russia was expressed in a letter to his brother, written in 1835, whose words also give a clue to his way of thinking:

The fact is that Russia is a great humbug, and that if England were fairly to go to work on her, we should throw her back half a century in one campaign. But Nicholas the proud and insolent knows this, and will always check his pride and moderate his insolence when he finds England is firmly determined and fully prepared to resist him.[2]

The British distrust of Russian intentions combined with the threat to British interests implicit in the Treaty of Unkiar Skelessi gave rise to a great deal of anti-Russian feeling among the British statesmen and the public. These feelings also characterized the attitudes of both British ambassadors to Constantinople before the Crimean War, Lord Ponsonby, who held office from 1831 to 1841, and his successor, Stratford Canning, who remained there from 1842 to 1858. The most effective publicist of Russophobia, David Urquhart, was first secretary at the embassy from 1836. The importance of the conflict between the British and Rus-

2. Seton-Watson, *Britain in Europe* (Cambridge: Cambridge University Press), p. 184.

sian ambassadors in Constantinople in the following years cannot be overestimated. After 1833 the sultan always found in the British embassy firm support and encouragement for resistance to Russia.

In the 1830's the principal concern for Britain in her relations with the other powers in the eastern question was the protection of her rich possession, India. At this time events in Afghanistan and Persia, as well as at the Straits, led the British statesmen to fear that the Russian government intended a giant pincer movement to force Britain out of these areas and perhaps eventually to rob her of her costly prize. Relations with France and the rise of Egyptian power were also seen in this context. France, having increased in strength in the western Mediterranean after the conquest of Algeria, was thus seen as a potential enemy. Britain had won the duel with France for colonial supremacy in the eighteenth century, but the danger of a revival of the conflict was always present.

The increased power of Mehemet Ali was viewed with apprehension for the same reasons. With the introduction of the steamship and the growth in trade with the Orient, the British laid more weight on the possibilities of developing further the trade routes through the Red Sea and Suez as an alternative to the long stretch around South Africa. The erection of a modern powerful state, controlling this area, was viewed with great disfavor. A great Arabian empire was an equal danger to that presented by Russia. Moreover, the diplomatic possibilities in the situation were also menacing. France openly favored Egypt's power and growth. There was always the chance that Russia might join with France and Egypt, and Britain would be faced by a coalition that she could not defeat.

To meet these potential threats to their empire, the British statesmen launched an active policy in the Ottoman Empire. They now sought to bolster the power of that state so that it could remain as an effective buffer against the threats of its neighbors. Ottoman control of the routes to India was judged the most advantageous of the alternate possibilities for the protection of British interests. The British representatives, therefore, now pressed for the introduction of a program of reform within the empire that would strengthen the state as a military power and also conciliate the subject peoples so that they would not seek an independent existence. In 1835 British officers were sent to aid in the reform of the Turkish army. Due to quarrels that arose in this connection, the Turkish government finally dismissed these advisors and appointed instead Prussian officers, among them Helmut von Moltke. Britain also constantly advised a policy of resistance to Egyptian demands. In 1838 the very favorable commercial Treaty of Balta Liman was signed. Despite the fact that its provisions were not faithfully fulfilled by the Porte, it did signify a diplomatic victory and showed the increase in influence that Britain had won at Constantinople.

Although Mahmud gladly listened to advice on resistance to Egypt, he wished to proceed one step further and initiate a policy of revenge. He had never accepted the Peace of Kutahia as final, and he waited only for the proper moment to go to war with his rebellious vassal. Despite his strong pleas he was not able to win British support. The British government wished to reform and strengthen the empire but not bring about a war. It was justly feared that a severe crisis would lead Russia to implement the Treaty of Unkiar Skelessi by rushing to the aid of the Porte, by occupying the Straits, and by remaining there indefinitely.

The British aims were thus clear. They would uphold the Ottoman Empire as the best guarantor of British interests in the area. They also wished if possible to secure the abrogation of the Treaty of Unkiar Skelessi and its replacement by a general European agreement. The Russian plans, in contrast, were not so clearly formulated or vigorously pursued. Like Britain, the Russian government wished to support the Ottoman Empire and maintain the *status quo* in the Near East. The tsar desired also to exploit the opportunity presented by the French and British differences of opinion over Egypt to improve his own diplomatic position. Austrian and Prussian support was assured through the Treaty of Münchengrätz. If now Britain could be brought into this system, France would be isolated in Europe. The eastern question, which usually served to drive Russia's potential adversaries together, could now be used to divide them.

It is interesting to note that despite his dislike of liberal and constitutional governments, Nicholas I showed a great preference for working with Britain. It was France, with its revolutionary past and its sponsorship of subversion abroad that bore the chief weight of his disapproval. Throughout his reign, from the Greek crisis to the Crimean War, the tsar sought to solve the successive eastern crises, if possible, by agreement with Britain. The Russian policy in the Egyptian crisis of 1839 to 1841 was thus that of co-operation with Britain to the exclusion of France. The fact that both Russia and Britain favored the upholding of the sultan's power made such an agreement possible.

At the end of April, 1839 Mahmud precipitated the renewed crisis when his armies attacked Egypt. This rash act resulted in the resounding defeat of the Ottoman forces and the desertion of the entire fleet. At this grave juncture Mahmud died, to be succeeded in June by the sixteen-year-old Abdul Mejid. The great nightmare of the diplomats, the collapse of the Ottoman Empire, again appeared to be at hand. The powers were particularly apprehensive that Russia would now go to the aid of Turkey under the terms of the Treaty of Unkiar Skelessi. Austria, who, despite the Münchengrätz agreement, had no desire to see Russia act, proposed collective action. Nicholas I at first balked at the idea of a conference that would subordinate Russian interests to the desires of the majority of the powers. Nevertheless, in July, 1839 the Russian ambassador in Constantinople also signed a joint note addressed to the Porte that requested the Ottoman government not to take independent action, but to consult with the powers.

The decisive step toward co-operation with Britain was taken in September when P. I. Brunnov was sent to London to propose Russo-British co-operation. Russia at this time offered not to seek the renewal of the Treaty of Unkiar Skelessi, which was to lapse in 1841, and agreed that no attempt would be made to defend Constantinople by the occupation of the Straits without the agreement of the other governments. The closure of the Straits was also to be made part of the public law of Europe. Russia's intention was that France be excluded from any agreement that might be made.

Although Palmerston was not able to accept these terms at once, negotiations continued. France and Britain were now in disagreement on general policy in Europe. Finally, spurred partly by the fear that France might negotiate a Turkish-Egyptian peace, Palmerston joined with Russia, Prussia, and Austria in July, 1840 to negotiate the "Convention for the Pacification of the Levant" with the Porte. This agreement set the terms for a settlement of the Egyptian question. The exclusion of France from the negotiations marked a break between the French and British governments and a reversal of former British policy. When Mehemet Ali refused to accept the terms dictated by the powers, on September 14 the sultan deposed him. During the crisis the French government pressed Egypt to yield, particularly when it became obvious that the Egyptian forces could not withstand the allied attacks. British, Austrian, and Turkish naval squadrons defeated the Egyptian fleet, and a successful rebellion broke out in Syria against Egyptian rule. Although there were rumors of war and a French attack on the Rhine, there was little that France could do in its position of diplomatic isolation and in view of the Egyptian defeats. In November, 1840 Mehemet was forced to yield. In the peace the Porte received back what it had lost at Kutahya, but Mehemet Ali retained his independent position in Egypt with the recognition of his hereditary right to rule the country.

France rejoined the European concert in July, 1841 and signed the Convention of the Straits with Britain, Russia, Austria, and Prussia. Russia now allowed the Treaty of Unkiar Skelessi to lapse, and the Porte passed under the joint patronage of the powers. It was also agreed that the Straits would be closed in time of peace to the warships of all countries and that this settlement could only be changed by a European conference. This agreement, a victory of British diplomacy, placed the Straits for the first time under international control. The Russian gains of 1833 had been annulled, and the Ottoman Empire remained as a great buffer state protecting the routes to the Orient.

In the next years the Russian government attempted to continue and to extend its policy of co-operation with Britain with the aim of isolating France. The Russian statesmen did not see the abandonment of Unkiar Skelessi as a diplomatic retreat; they, too, were for the preservation of the *status quo* in the Near East, and the new treaty served this purpose well. Peace was thus preserved in the Egyptian, as in the Greek, crisis because the principal opponents, Russia and Britain, found a ground of common agreement in the upholding of Turkish power. The great issue, that Russia should not fall heir to the empire, remained in existence. Neither Austria, Britain, nor France could allow Russian control over the area; it was an issue on which all would fight. Russia, well aware of this condition, continued throughout the 1840's to base her policies on the principles adopted at the time of the Treaty of Adrianople.

THE REVOLUTIONS OF 1830

Despite the surrender of the privileged position won in the Treaty of Unkiar Skelessi, Russia had made considerable gains in the years after the accession of Nicholas I. Similar diplomatic successes were also characteristic of her policy in Europe proper in the same period. Here Russian interests called for the maintenance of the political and territorial conditions of 1815, which were so much to her advantage. The Vienna settlement was challenged twice between 1830 and 1850 by national and revolutionary forces. In the first crisis, in 1830, Russia was able to repress the movements directly dangerous to her, and in the second, in 1848-1849, she was able to reassert her position as final arbiter in the political balance in central Europe. Although the ideological emphasis in Nicholas' foreign policy becomes more pronounced in the affairs of continental Europe in comparison to those of the east, it must be remembered that Russian interests were bound more closely to the maintenance of the *status quo* in Europe proper than in the Ottoman Empire.

The revolutions of 1830 commenced in France with the overthrow of Charles X and the accession to the throne of Louis Philippe of the house of Orleans. Despite the fact that Nicholas I himself had warned against the repressive measures that Charles X took in the last days of his reign, the tsar was not willing to admit the right of the French people to change kings. With the Decembrist revolt still fresh in his mind, he was disturbed by any sign of the renewal of revolutionary activity. His anger was not directed so much against Louis Philippe as a person; he had met him in 1815 at Neuilly and had found both the man and his family highly sympathetic. It was the challenge to the principle of legitimacy and the danger of the influence of the movement on Russia that he feared. He was also concerned that the revolution would initiate a new wave of French imperial expansion and possibly a revision of the treaties of Vienna.

At the time that the July revolution occurred in Paris, Metternich and Nesselrode were by chance both in Bohemia. They were thus able to meet and come to an agreement on how the new events were to be met. In the so-called *chiffon* of Karlsbad, they declared that their two governments would not intervene in French internal affairs unless France inaugurated an active policy abroad. This agreement marked the recommencement of practical co-operation between the two conservative powers against the forces of revolution, a policy that had been interrupted by the eastern crisis. Both statesmen were chiefly concerned lest France again take up the Napoleonic tradition and initiate a new age of imperial expansion.

Nicholas I, in contrast to the more conciliatory attitude of his minister, immediately attempted to adopt positive measures against the revolutionary movement. He instructed the military governor of Kronstadt not to admit to Russian ports any French ships flying the tricolor, which now replaced the white flag of the Bourbons as the official French emblem. He also applied similar petty and vexatious measures to hinder the activities of French citizens in their relations with Russians. Determined on strong action, he then dispatched General Dibich to Berlin to try to persuade Frederick William III to mobilize his forces on the Rhine. With territories bordering on France and Belgium, the Prussian government had no desire to see its lands become a battlefield and, therefore, declined to follow a provocative policy. Nicholas met a similar check in his attempts to block the recognition by the powers of Louis Philippe's title. Four months after Austria, Britain, and Prussia entered into relations with the new regime, Russia finally followed. Despite the formal acceptance, Nicholas I always regarded Louis Philippe as a usurper and not as the legal king of France. Kingship could come only by inheritance; the position could never be changed or legalized by a revolution.

Despite the apprehensions of many statesmen, Louis Philippe soon proved himself an entirely safe ruler. A moderate in politics and chiefly interested in maintaining his own power, he embarked upon no adventures and he did what he could to conciliate the tsar. Although pressed strongly by popular opinion on the Polish and Belgian questions, he was able to maintain the peace and refrain from crusades in the interest of Belgian or Polish freedom. Nevertheless, he was not able to establish a satisfactory relationship with Russia. As we have seen, in the eastern question the Russian government had followed a policy that had as its aim co-operation with Britain and the isolation of France.

The revolutions of 1830 had thus brought a new king to the throne of France. The next major upset to the Vienna pattern occurred in the Netherlands, where the Belgian population rose against their king and demanded separation from Holland. The union of the two peoples, which had been supported by Britain in an attempt to raise a barrier against France, had not been a success. King William openly favored the Dutch section of his kingdom, despite the fact that it represented only a third of the nation. Dutch officials dominated the administration, and the tax system was organized to the detriment of the Belgians. On September 26, 1830 the revolutionary parties were able to set up a provisional government in Brussels. King William, faced with the revolt, at once appealed for assistance to the four powers that had constituted the Quadruple Alliance. Nicholas I, who received the request on October 15, was naturally ready to intervene immediately to protect the rights of a legitimate monarch faced with a rebellion of his people. Once again he turned for support to Berlin and Vienna. Prussia, however, declined to act without the co-operation of Britain; Austria, despite her conservative principles, also showed no eagerness to intervene. In this question Nicholas I based his call to strong action not on the immediate issue of the union of the two peoples but on the general principle of change through revolution. "I am not fighting Belgium here," he declared, "it is the general revolution . . . which threatens us if we are seen to tremble before it." [3] Russia alone, however, could do little. The final outcome of the revolt rested more in the hands of the statesmen of Paris and London.

The British capital thus became the center of the negotiations on the Belgian question. Britain, more directly concerned in the matter than Russia, was chiefly afraid that if the Belgian territories were separated from Holland, they would either be annexed by France or formed into a state that would become a French satellite. It was clear that a strong party in France favored annexation and that there were influential pro-French groups in Belgium. The Wellington government, which was in office at the time of the revolt, did not favor the establishment of an independent state. The Liberal administration of Grey, which took power in 1830, was in contrast willing to approve this settlement.

The London Conference of the powers, which opened on November 4, succeeded first in arranging an armistice between the Belgian and Dutch forces and then proceeded with a discus-

3. J. A. Betley, *Belgium and Poland in International Relations, 1830-1831* (The Hague: Mouton, 1960), p. 43.

sion of the terms. Nicholas I was willing to accept a new administrative relationship between the two states, but he insisted that William must remain the king in both sections. He favored the separation of the territories with perhaps the heir to the Dutch throne, the prince of Orange, established as viceroy in Brussels. He also believed that the decisions of the conference should be backed by force, and he prepared his own troops in Poland for this purpose.

In these circumstances, the attitude of the French government was of first importance. France now had the choice of co-operating with the powers or of attempting to exploit the situation to gain more territory. Louis Philippe, despite pressure at home, chose to follow a moderate path and to co-operate with Britain. He therefore supported the establishment of an independent Belgium under a separate ruler. This proposal was strongly in opposition to the Russian insistence that William's position be protected, but Russia was not able to act because of the outbreak of the Polish revolution in November. Austria alone was not strong enough to stand up for the rights of legitimacy and she too was involved with the events closer to home. With the major opponent of an independent Belgium neutralized, the powers on December 20 finally agreed upon the establishment of an independent Belgium; in the following month it was decided that the new state should be declared neutral and that this condition should be guaranteed by all of the states. The choice of a ruler proved less difficult when Louis Philippe did not press the candidacy of one of his sons. Prince Leopold of Saxe-Coburg, the final choice of the powers, entered Brussels in July, 1831. Determined to protect his rights, William despatched an army into Belgium in August. In reply to this display of force, France sent troops and a British fleet enforced a blockade. Although William was thus compelled to withdraw, he did not officially accede to the settlement until 1839. The Russian attitude toward the new state also remained distinctly unfavorable. The Russian signature was affixed to the treaties establishing Belgian independence and neutrality, but the tsar did not thereby signify his approval of the act. A minister was not sent to Brussels until 1852.

The revolution in Poland in November, 1830 faced Nicholas I with an event far more serious than the change of monarchs in Paris or the separation of Belgium from Holland. Both of these questions had involved matters of principle and the maintenance of the Vienna settlement, but Poland reflected upon the tsar's prestige as a monarch and upon the integrity of his empire. After the Congress of Vienna, Grand Duke Constantine, as viceroy, became the effective ruler of the kingdom. Influenced by his Polish wife and his advisors, he was sympathetic to Poland and to its institutions. At the time of the Decembrist revolt he protected the rights of the Poles accused in the conspiracy to be tried according to Polish procedures. Nevertheless in the eyes of the Poles, he remained a Russian administrator and as such was not popular. Nicholas I, although it could not be expected that he would ever be well-suited to the role of a constitutional monarch, allowed himself to be crowned king in May, 1829 and he took the oath to support the constitution. This position of subservience to Russia and the Russian tsar, no matter how enlightened the domination might have been, could never have been acceptable to the politically active and nationalistic Polish gentry. Moreover, the majority regarded the true boundaries of their state as those of Poland before the partitions. They, therefore, saw with increasing dissatisfaction the Russian measures taken to assimilate the Western Provinces into Russia proper. The mobilization of troops on Polish territory and the possible use of Polish soldiers against the Belgian revolution also caused consternation. The revolutions in Paris and Brussels had already contributed to an increase in Polish restlessness. The rebellion, which broke out in November, thus expressed the desire of the Polish leadership to be freed from Russian rule and to re-establish the conditions of the early eighteenth century.

The rebels were at first considerably aided by the weak attitude of Constantine. Faced with the revolt, he chose to withdraw the loyal troops from Warsaw and to wait. The revolutionary forces thus gained time to organize, and they were able to place remarkably many men in the field. In the end the forces were numerically not too far apart. The Polish insurgents, 100,000 strong, faced Russian armies numbering about 120,000. The Polish troops, however, were considerably hampered by a lack of equipment. Moreover, the revolution, which began without adequate preparation, was further troubled by a division of leadership. Since the political right and left could not agree on the question of land reform, the revolution never gained the support of the mass of the peasantry.

At the beginning of the rebellion the Polish leaders immediately sought assistance from abroad. Since the Polish Kingdom had been created as part of the Vienna settlement, they hoped that the powers would be compelled to intervene. In reply to their requests, they received expressions of sympathy but no practical aid. The revolution had indeed been badly timed. The British government, chiefly concerned with the Belgian question, did not wish to endanger its relations with Russia although many liberals felt great sympathy for the cause of Polish freedom. Louis Philippe, despite the French tradition of the support of Poland against Russia, could also do nothing. The Polish revolt served instead greatly to assist the French government in the Belgian problem. Without foreign intervention the Polish revolution had little hope of success.

Once again in firm control of the country, the Russian government abolished the Polish Constitution of 1815 and replaced it with the Organic Statute of February, 1832. Had this new arrangement been faithfully executed, the Poles would still have enjoyed a favorable political position within the Russian state. Although the Kingdom was now declared an "indivisible" part of the Russian Empire, the guarantees of civil liberties, a free press, the inviolability of person and property, and freedom of religion were retained. Rights of local government and the use of the Polish language were similarly kept. These provisions were, however, ignored or violated by the succeeding Russian administrators. The country now fell under the rule of General I. F. Paskevich, who had commanded the troops that crushed the Polish revolt. Unsympathetic to Poland's particular position, he worked against the maintenance of autonomous Polish institutions and special privileges. The policy of repression, which he instituted, resulted in the growth of the underground political organizations that again in 1863 were to challenge the Russian rule.

After the defeat of their forces in Poland, large numbers of the Polish leaders fled abroad. Thereafter the Polish emigration was to exert influence on international diplomacy far out of proportion to its real strength. The center of Polish activities became Paris; the Hotel Lambert was the gathering point of the conservative elements of the Polish leadership. Here Czartoryski, the former comrade of Alexander I and the recognized Polish leader, organized what was in effect a state in exile and conducted a foreign policy worthy of an established government. The left groups, although in opposition to Czartoryski, also continued a policy of active opposition to Russia. Many co-operated with the radical movement Young Europe, organized by Mazzini. Henceforth in every great European revolutionary action, Polish participants could be found. The direction of all Polish activity, whether liberal or conservative, was in every circumstance highly anti-Russian. The Polish exiles were very successful, particularly among liberal circles, in building a picture of tsarist Russia as the embodiment of all that was reprehensible and reactionary in politics. The Polish emigration as a group added immensely to the numbers of those whose activities Nicholas I principally feared—the revolutionary who worked underground through secret societies to destroy the autocratic political system of Europe, that of Russia in particular.

The revolutions of 1830 thus succeeded in Paris and in Brussels, but failed in Warsaw. Similar movements in the Germanies and Italy were also suppressed, largely through the agency of Austria. Although France at first protested, Louis Philippe was not able to prevent the Austrian government from re-establishing the old order in Italy, which had also been threatened in this year of revolution. Austria acted with similar vigor in the German states. She used the occasion of the Hambach National Festival of May, 1832, an event organized by journalists and attended by around 25,000, to act against the growth of liberal and national movements. She was able to push through the federal diet the Six Acts, which limited the right of assembly and subjected the press and the universities to strong controls. The right of intervention in the affairs of states threatened by revolution was also reaffirmed. Austria thus brought central Europe and Italy back to the conditions of 1815.

Though the revolution in Paris and the division of the Netherlands had been opposed by Nicholas I, Russia as a power was not adversely affected by either event. The accession of Louis Philippe had not resulted in the revival of French imperialism across the Rhine or the sponsorship of liberal and national revolutions. The revolt in Poland had been quelled, but at a high cost to Russia. Austria had suppressed the resurgence of the spirit of revolution in her neighboring lands. Moreover, the revolutions had served to point out again to the conservative monarchies, particularly to Austria and Russia, that they should co-operate in European affairs. Divided in interest in the eastern question, they needed to follow a policy of mutual support in order to protect their political systems and their empires. The settlement of 1815 was to the maximum advantage of both powers; neither could benefit from the spread of national or liberal sentiment. With the adoption by Russia of a policy of preserving the *status quo* in the Ottoman Empire, the great issue separating Vienna and St. Petersburg was removed. Russian and Austrian interests both in the east and in Europe could thus be covered in one general agreement.

The Treaty of Münchengrätz, signed in September, 1833 has already been discussed in connection with the Egyptian crisis. It marked the formal renewal of the policies of the Holy Alliance, which had shattered on the Greek issue. In October, 1833 Prussia joined her neighbors in the Berlin Convention, whose articles were an open reaffirmation of the spirit of the old agreement. Here again the three monarchs supported the right of any ruler threatened by revolution to appeal for outside aid. They also agreed that should one of the three signatories, when engaged in the suppression of such a revolt, be threatened by an outside power, then the two other partners would come to her assistance. These agreements became the basis of Russian continental policy until the Crimean War.

With the conclusion of the agreements of Münchengrätz and Berlin, the Russian government had again established in Europe a political system that was not only in line with Nicholas' ideological convictions, but that also served to protect Russian state power. Prussia stood guard on the Rhine; Austria took over police duty in Italy and Germany. Russia guaranteed the preservation of the *status quo* in the East. Together the three powers were guarantors of the Vienna settlement and of each other's territorial possessions and conservative forms of government. Faced by this combination, which was united on lines of interest and ideology, Palmerston attempted to erect a counter-alliance of France, Britain, Portugal, and Spain. The agreement was, however, never the counterpart of the conservative alliance since Britain and France were not joined by the same ties of common interests and needs that united the conservative empires.

After 1833 the three courts continued a policy of mutual cooperation despite numerous petty disagreements between statesmen and rulers. As a result, central European affairs assumed an appearance of outward calm until the great revolutionary year of 1848. The single important disturbance was the Austrian annexation of Cracow in 1846, an act carried through with the approval of the other partition powers. At this time, but particularly during the reign of Frederick William III, Russo-Prussian relations were particularly close. Nicholas I, married to the Prussian king's daughter Charlotte, valued his family ties with the Prussian court and remained always a great admirer of the Prussian military tradition. In this relationship it was clearly Russia who predominated. Although Prussia could withstand Russian demands on minor issues, she stood always in the shadow of St. Petersburg, particularly as long as she remained in a position of rivalry with Vienna over German affairs. This situation was slightly altered in 1840 when Frederick William IV came to the throne. Unlike his father, the new ruler not only failed to develop close personal ties with the tsar, but he became increasingly drawn toward liberal ideas. Under the influence of his liberal advisors, he considered a change in Prussian institutions and a policy of closer co-operation with Britain. Such a change of political orientation naturally involved great dangers to Russia. If Britain should find a friend and ally in Berlin, Russian policy in the east would be paralyzed and her vital western front would be endangered. This close relationship of ideology and national interest in central Europe was clearly shown in the revolutions of 1848.

The Revolutions of 1848

Although the revolution of 1830 had resulted in the Polish rebellion, which had directly challenged Russian power, the movement in 1848 presented an issue of potentially greater danger to the Russian government—that of the unification of central Europe, possibly under liberal and national forms of government. As has been mentioned, the settlement of 1815 in central Europe had been to the Russian interest. The area, split in three political directions, allowed the Russian government a wide field in which to manoeuvre. The maintenance of the Austro-Prussian rivalry in German affairs and the protection of the independence of the states of the second rank was the best policy open to Russia. Moreover, the ideological unity of central Europe protected Russia from political influences from the left that might affect either her own population or that of Poland. The alliance of the three conservative courts, whose aim was the maintenance of the *status quo*, also assured the Russian government of the support of two of the four other major powers. This extremely favorable situation was threatened by the wave of revolution that began in

January, 1848 in Italy and that had spread by March across Europe to the borders of Russia itself.

The revolutionary tide caused little surprise to Nicholas, since during his entire reign he saw the spirit of revolt behind every unpleasant event. Like Metternich, he expected that some time a great political catastrophe would hit them all. Nevertheless, the fall of the July Monarchy in February, 1848 was a shock to the Russian court. Grand Duke Constantine reported in his diary: "It was as if we had all been struck by lightning." [4] Nicholas was delighted at the fall of the man he regarded as a usurper and saw in this act of retribution the hand of God and a justification of his own stand. As in 1830 he thought of direct and immediate military action, and he called upon his ally Prussia to co-operate with him. The feelings of the conservative courts remained similar to their apprehension in 1830—that revolutionary France might again initiate aggressive moves toward the Rhine or might patronize revolutionary movements in Italy or Germany. Nicholas I thus sought to organize a coalition to meet these threats. He wished Prussia and Russia to handle France; Austria was to deal with Italy.

Nicholas' desire for immediate action met with little response in Berlin. Instead, Frederick William IV suggested a meeting, the purpose of which would be the strengthening of the Germanic Confederation. Further action on the part of Prussia was made impossible when in March the revolution spread into the Germanies and into Berlin. On March 18 Frederick William IV was forced to concede to the revolutionary demands; already on March 13 Metternich had fallen from power in Vienna. Thus in March, 1848 all of central Europe stood under the control of the revolution. Nicholas I had to meet not the problem of a movement in distant Paris or Turin but on his very doorstep. His great conservative allies had also fallen victim to the dangers he had foreseen. The Holy Alliance had been defeated by the forces of rebellion; Russia stood alone in Europe.

4. A. S. Nifontov, *Russland im Jahre 1848* (Berlin: Rütten & Leoning, 1954), p. 228.

The events of March thus destroyed the Vienna settlement in central Europe and faced Russia with the general condition that would be of the greatest danger—the possibility that the center of the continent might unite under general theories that might ultimately lead to the destruction of the tsarist autocracy and defeat of the Russian state. Although the map of 1815 was most favorable from the Russian in point of view, the Russian government had not at all times looked with disfavor on a degree of consolidation in the area. Still, it had no desire to see one power dominate. From 1848 to 1851 three alternate solutions to the problem of German unification were offered; each was in turn defeated. Despite the Russian interest in their suppression, these movements failed primarily because of the inner rivalries within central Europe itself, that is, because of the split between conservative, liberal, and socialist political factions and the conflict for power between Prussia, Austria, and the smaller monarchies, rather than through foreign intervention.

The first solution, that of a liberal, national Germany, which was offered by the Frankfurt assembly in 1848, was that least desired and most feared by Russia. This Germany would be ideologically inimical to the Russian autocracy. Pro-Polish, it would tend in time naturally to ally with Britain or France. The strong bulwark of Russia against Europe, the Prussian army, would fall into the hands of the enemy. A second solution, offered by Austria in 1850, that of the incorporation of the entire Austrian Empire into the Germanic Confederation, to form an empire of 70 millions, was preferable to the Frankfurt proposal largely because the federal form and conservative basis of this union would make it more compatible with tsarist Russia. The third possibility, the unification of Germany, or at least of the states north of the Main river, under the leadership of Prussia, was for Russia the preferable solution, provided that the Prussian government remained conservative in form and oriented its foreign policy eastward. An autocratic Prussia, united with Austria and Russia under the Holy Alliance, was thus the preferable alternative should it prove impossible to maintain the settlement of 1815.

In 1850 Russia opposed Prussian moves more because of Frederick William's liberal inclinations and his actions in the Schleswig-Holstein affair, rather than because of any direct opposition to the principles involved.

Before the threat offered by the March revolution in the Germanies, there was little that the Russian government could do. Although the tsar had been most bellicose in January and February, when the revolts occurred in Italy and France, the advice of his counsellors, who pointed out the financial and military conditions of the country, calmed his crusading zeal. An isolated Russia could indeed do nothing. In March Nicholas I gave vent to his feelings in a strongly worded manifesto, which ended with the declaration: "God is with us. Understand ye people and submit; for God is with us." Although this statement was understood abroad as a call for war against the revolution, such was not its intention. Nesselrode was forced to issue an explanatory circular in which he stated categorically that Russia would not intervene in the affairs of other nations as long as they did not interfere in Russia.

Although the policy of nonintervention in central European affairs was in contrast to his previous actions, Nicholas I was hampered by the unsatisfactory state of his own country and his military unpreparedness. The dangers of the general situation also became immediately apparent, particularly in regard to Poland. On March 17 the foreign minister of the new government in Prussia, Arnim, called for the restoration of an independent Poland. On March 28 Czartoryski appeared in Berlin. Prussian liberals at the same time called for a union of free Poland, liberal Prussia, France, and Britain. The possibility of a crusade of liberal Europe under Prussian leadership against autocratic Russia was also discussed. Russia thus faced the danger that she might find Europe united against her and that she might have to deal with revolutionary uprisings in Poland and in her own territory. At this time she could also call on no other power for assistance; Austria, with similar interests, was herself unable to handle her domestic rebellion.

The gradual withdrawal of this threat was due not to Russian actions but to the internal conflicting forces of the German revolution. Prussian enthusiasm for Polish freedom ended when the conflicts in Posen led the Prussian government to abolish the Polish administration that had been established on the basis of liberal, national principles. Even more significant was the split within the revolutionary forces on ideological grounds. Unlike the revolutions of 1830, the movement in 1848 contained a strong socialistic and radical element, which soon came into conflict with the moderate liberals. Moreover, the preserve of the old conservative tradition, the army, remained intact in most of the states. With the passage of time, therefore, the revolutionary groups became divided against each other, whereas the counter-revolution gained in strength and unity of purpose. The Russian government could thus afford to maintain its position of enforced waiting until it could intervene effectively on the side of its choice. The victory of Russia, for in the end she was called upon to act as judge and final arbiter of the central European settlement, thus came not so much from the wisdom and strength of the Russian statesmen, as from the division and lack of a common purpose within the revolutionary forces.

Active Russian intervention in the revolutionary situation was first exercised in the area of most immediate concern—the Danubian Principalities, which were under Russian protectorship. In June an insurrectionary movement, directed against Russian predominance, swept through both Moldavia and Wallachia. Despite the fact that the revolutionary governments had reached some understanding with the Porte, Russian troops marched into the country and put down the revolt. This action in a land within the Russian political orbit called forth protests from both France and Britain, but caused no further diplomatic repercussions. The second action, the intervention in the affairs of Schleswig-Holstein, by contrast involved negotiations with the other powers and affected greatly the course of the German revolution.

The Schleswig-Holstein question, a quite complicated issue, became the first international question arising from the revolutions of 1848 in the Germanies. The two duchies, of which Holstein was German and Schleswig predominantly so, belonged to the Danish crown. Holstein was a member of the Germanic Confederation; Schleswig was not. Both duchies wished to remain politically united. Unfortunately, the entire question of their status was opened at this most inopportune time by the problem of the succession in Denmark and the actions of Danish nationalists who wished to form a centralized state. A revolt broke out in the duchies, who then appealed for assistance to the Frankfurt assembly as the successor to the German diet. At the end of April, Prussian troops, acting in the name of the assembly and joined by soldiers from other German states, invaded the duchies. In this situation the King of Denmark, Frederick VII, appealed to the powers. Quite naturally, the tsar was sympathetic to the Danish king. Here was clearly a case of a rebellion against a legitimate monarch and a violation of the treaties of 1815. The entire international balance in the Baltic area was also affected when the victorious Prussian troops pressed into Jutland and thereby brought into question the continued independent existence of Denmark. The governments of both Sweden and Britain were vitally concerned with the status of the area, which dominated the entrance to the Baltic Sea. Prussia thus found herself faced with a coalition of powers who were determined to maintain the *status quo*. In the humiliating armistice of Malmö of August, 1848, the victorious Prussian troops were forced to turn back. This pact in no way settled the problem of the duchies. Instead the entire issue remained a point of conflict between Berlin and St. Petersburg and contributed to the eventual option of Russia for Austria in the German question by 1850.

The acceptance of the armistice by Prussia, which was done without consultation with the Frankfurt Assembly, did nothing to ease the internal German situation. This question had meanwhile become an issue in German politics, far out of proportion to its real importance. The revolt of the duchies had become deeply enmeshed with the German national question and had become a symbol to the German liberal. For the great powers

the issue was the balance in the Baltic and the maintenance of
treaties; for the German nationalist foreign hostility signified the
determination of the others to prevent German unification.

By the fall of 1848 the anti-revolutionary forces were able to
regain power everywhere. After the destruction of the socialist
strength by the French army, France, too, received a political
system more acceptable to Nicholas I. In the Habsburg lands the
power of the Austrian army slowly began to assert itself. Nicholas rejoiced greatly at the news of the defeat of the Sardinian
armies at Custozza and the subsequent securing of Italy under
Austrian control. In June, General Windischgrätz had taken
Prague; in October he recaptured Vienna from revolutionary
control. In December the incompetent Emperor Ferdinand was
replaced by his young nephew, Franz Joseph. Thereafter the
Austrian policies were influenced predominantly by the counsels
of an extremely able statesman, Prince Felix Schwarzenberg, who
also proved most adroit in his dealings with the tsar. With the
accession of the new monarch, in whom Nicholas I proclaimed a
fatherly interest, Russo-Austrian relations gradually tightened at
the expense of the ties between Russia and Prussia.

Throughout the revolutionary crisis, Nicholas I remained dissatisfied with the actions of Frederick William IV. The vacil-
lating, unstable, and liberally inclined character of the Prussian
king was hardly found sympathetic by the tsar, who erred on the
side of impetuosity, strong action, and intensity of feeling. Certainly, Nicholas I could never obtain in Berlin the same unswerv-
ing support of conservative ideals that he received in Vienna. This
difference, of course, reflected the divergent interests of the two
German courts. Like autocratic Russia, the Habsburg Monarchy
as such could only lose by the introduction of liberal, national
ideas into central Europe. Because of its preponderant Hungarian
and Slavic populations, Austria could never use the weapon of
nationalism in the interest of state power. Prussia, nationally
homogeneous, could, in contrast, find its power enhanced should
it assume a position of leadership in a liberal, national movement.
In 1849 and 1850 the Prussian government was not yet strong

enough, nor was the international situation favorable, to exploit this advantage in order to defeat its Austrian rival. In these two years the victory went to the combined forces of Austria and Russia; in 1866-1870 this situation was to be reversed in the Prussian favor.

The Austrian armies were able to restore imperial control in Italy and Austria, however, Hungary remained in rebel hands. The Hungarian revolution had commenced in March, 1848, and by October Vienna and Budapest were at war. The danger of the Hungarian revolt was intensified in Russian eyes by the participation of large Polish forces and by the activities of General Joseph Bem, who had been one of the leaders of the Polish rebellion of 1830. The establishment of an independent Hungary was thus correctly regarded as the forerunner of renewed revolutionary activity in Poland. Therefore, in April, 1849 Nicholas I, in answer to an Austrian appeal, agreed to send troops into Hungary. His intention was to defeat the "enemies of order and tranquility in the whole world" as well as to aid the monarchy.

In June, 1849 the main Russian forces entered Transylvania. Together the Russian and Austrian armies numbered around 270,000 in comparison to the Hungarian forces of about 170,000. With their advantage in size, the allied armies were able to defeat the revolutionary forces by the end of August. Refugees from the Hungarian revolt thereafter fled in great numbers into Turkish territory, where the protection offered them by the Porte resulted in a diplomatic crisis in Constantinople. The joint campaign, instead of producing a feeling of comradeship, resulted in much bitter feeling between the two armies. Each held the military qualities of the other in low esteem; the Russians felt they had been cheated by the Austrian commissary. The vindictive punishments meted out to the captured Hungarian leaders, many of whom were delivered by the Russians to the Austrians, was bitterly resented. The estrangement between the military leaders, however, did not affect the political support that Russia continued to offer Austria in central European affairs.

The re-establishment of control over her empire now enabled

Austria to turn again to the German scene. Meanwhile Frederick William IV had again aroused Russian distrust by his actions in the Schleswig-Holstein affair, which had reopened in April, 1849. He was also further compromised in the tsar's opinion both by his failure to make a clean break with the revolution and by his failure to return his kingdom to the political conditions prevailing before the March revolt. In April, 1849 he had, however, refused the crown of the united Germany offered to him by the Frankfurt Assembly.

Although the liberal movement of 1848 collapsed with this refusal, ideas and plans for German unification did not. Frederick William IV proceeded to attempt to unite at least the northern German states under Prussian leadership; he first approached the kings of Hanover and Saxony. The Erfurt Union (as the Prussian plan was now called), which aimed at the ultimate unification of central and northern Germany, aroused at once the antagonism of Austria and the states of the second rank, such as Bavaria, Württemberg, and Baden. Under the able leadership of Schwarzenberg, the Austrian government now attempted to resurrect the old federal diet at Frankfurt and to gain the support of the south German states. With the German powers thus ranged against each other in 1850, Russia was able to intervene decisively and to arbitrate the German settlement.

The issue that brought the Austro-Prussian clash into the open involved the Electorate of Hesse-Cassel, where the elector and his assembly had quarreled. The elector appealed to the Austrian-dominated Frankfurt diet for assistance, and Prussia claimed an equal right to interfere since her military road to her Rhenish provinces ran through the state. In this crisis the position of Russia was determined by considerations already mentioned: the revival of the Baltic problem, the tsar's dislike of Frederick William's politics, and the Russian belief that Austria was militarily the weaker of the two German powers. Faced with Austrian and Russian opposition, Prussia was forced into a humiliating surrender. At Olmütz in November, 1850 Edwin von Manteuffel, the Prussian representative, and Schwarzenberg agreed upon the restoration of the pre-March conditions in Germany. The political organization of central Europe most advantageous to Russian interests was thus re-established. Later, at Dresden, the Russian government also secured the defeat of Schwarzenberg's proposal that the entire Habsburg empire be brought into the Germanic Confederation, thus bringing to an end the Austrian dream of the "empire of seventy millions." Russia had thus seen defeated the major schemes for the unification of central Europe. The settlement of the revolutions of 1848 was therefore a victory for conservatism, the Habsburg Empire, the small German monarchies, and Russia.

The restoration of 1850 was in the interest of Russian policy, yet it cannot be demonstrated that this was the goal of Russian diplomacy throughout the revolutionary years. Nicholas appears to have been influenced by immediate events and to have made his decisions on a day-to-day basis. The defense of conservatism and the Russian position in Poland remained, however, constant preoccupations. The division of forces within Germany saved Russia from the necessity of taking strong action or of resorting to outright military intervention. Moreover, at no time was Russia faced with the necessity of vetoing German unity outright, although political unification was a danger to her. It was instead enough to support the re-establishment of Habsburg power through assistance in Hungary; Vienna then undertook the task of thwarting the expansion of Prussia. In 1848 and 1849 Russian interests demanded the preservation of the Austrian Empire for the same reasons that the continued existence of the Danubian state was a political necessity for the German empire in 1914. Russia needed an ally of a similar ideological pattern. With the re-establishment of the division of central Europe and the securance of Austrian domination in Italy, the conditions of 1815 were again in effect. The Holy Alliance was apparently again an effective diplomatic combination. Outwardly Russia appeared to have achieved a position of new power and prestige.

Undoubtedly much of the influence which Russia was able to exert in international affairs, particularly in central Europe, was due to a gross overestimation of Russian military strength. In the period after the Napoleonic Wars Russian troops fought only the Turkish border tribes in the Middle East and revolutionary forces in Poland and Hungary. Although here she enjoyed an advantage at all times in manpower and matériel, her victories had not been impressive. Her opponents, however, remained hypnotized by the mass of the Russian territory and the size of the Russian army. As long as these arms were not tested on a major battlefield against modern enemies, Russia could still win diplomatic victories on the basis of her presumed strength. The weakness of her internal system and its effect upon her military potential was not to be demonstrated until the Crimean War.

However, in 1850 Russia did indeed still appear to be the most powerful continental state. In the preceding years she had suppressed the rebellion in Poland, come to the aid of Austria, and, finally, had dictated the re-establishment of the old order in central Europe. The combination of the three northern courts remained the strongest diplomatic alignment; France and Britain, separated by constant petty quarrels, formed no adequate counterweight. When Schwarzenberg died in 1852 and was succeeded by Buol, Russia lost a sympathetic statesman, but the significance of the change was not at once apparent. Prussia, although similarly torn between an eastern and western orientation, continued to base her policy on co-operation with St. Petersburg. Moreover, Nicholas I never lost hope that he could reach an accommodation with Britain over the eastern question. We have seen how he had even sought to bring her into the Holy Alliance. France, Nicholas' chief opponent in his own opinion, after 1848 went through a series of political changes. The election of Louis Napoleon as president for life and his assumption of the position of emperor in 1852 were clear violations of the treaties of 1814 and 1815. Nevertheless, the European powers did nothing, and Russia and France engaged in a petty interchange concerning the way in which Napoleon should be addressed. The revolutionary influence of Napoleon's ideas on Europe were to appear only after the Crimean War. Thus in the early 1850's Russia appeared to have won a most favorable diplomatic position and to have the power to protect her own interests both in Europe and in the east.

THE CRIMEAN WAR

After the signature of the Straits Convention of 1841 a period of relative inactivity followed in the Near East. In 1843 King Othon of Greece, as the result of a military coup, was forced to accept a constitution, but this event caused no serious international complications. The first major diplomatic incident that arose was a result of the defeat of the Hungarian revolutionary forces by the Austrian and Russian armies. At this time approximately 3,600 Hungarian, and 800 Polish refugees crossed into Turkish territory. Austria and Russia immediately demanded their return, a move that was in accord with their treaties with the Porte on extradition. Unwilling to agree, the Ottoman government appealed to France and Britain, both of whom prepared their fleets for possible action in aid of the empire. In the course of the negotiations the British fleet on November 1, 1849, using the excuse of bad weather, moved into the Dardanelles in violation of the Convention of 1841. Palmerston, realizing the implications of the act for the future, at once apologized. Both Russia and Britain thereafter agreed that both the Dardanelles and the Bosphorus must remain closed to their fleets. The question of the refugees was settled with the withdrawal of the Russian demands and the granting of amnesty by Austria to some 3,000 of them. Others, such as Kossuth, emigrated or became Moslems and entered the Ottoman service. The crisis was thus amicably settled with no further repercussions.

A second incident, the "Don Pacifico affair," occurred in January, 1850, when in support of the claims of a Portuguese Jew whose house had been burned by a Greek mob, a British squadron applied a blockade to Greece. The act followed a long

series of minor disagreements between the governments of Lord
Palmerston and King Othon. At this time the French and Russian
governments joined together to protest the highhanded British
methods. The episode, which caused a break between London
and Paris, thus was in the Russian interest in that it brought about
a division between her potential rivals in the east.

Although no major crisis involving the fate of the empire
took place in the 1840's, the problem of the future of the Turkish
state always remained in question. Nicholas I, in view of his
successful co-operation with Britain in the past, tried repeatedly
to continue this policy and, if possible, to bring Britain into a
closer and more definite arrangement with Russia. He did not
seek the dismemberment of the Ottoman Empire, but he had
no faith in its durability. He thus wished to make a firm agreement with Britain that would obligate that power to consult with
him first should the eastern question again open. He also wanted
to negotiate a partition treaty to be applied should the Turkish
state collapse. His approaches met with little success, largely
because of the British aversion to accepting prior commitments
or treaties of a general nature. The tsar also seems never to have
understood the constitutional limitation on the actions of a British
cabinet, which could not without parliamentary consent make
agreements that would bind its successor. As a result, Nicholas I
appears to have believed that he received in his conversations
with British statesmen in 1844 and 1853 more firm commitments
than he actually had.

In 1844 the tsar, accompanied by Nesselrode, visited Britain,
where he discussed the eastern situation in detail with Lord
Aberdeen. As a result of these conversations Nesselrode drew up
a memorandum, which he communicated to the British foreign
secretary, that stated that both powers would co-operate to
preserve the *status quo*. Should this prove impossible, they would
come to an agreement on what should be done next. Although
this was not the firm pact that Nicholas I had hoped for, the
tsar now believed that he had obtained prior arrangements with

Britain as well as with Austria and Prussia to deal with an eastern crisis.

In 1853 Nicholas I again attempted to approach the British government in order to obtain a more detailed agreement. Once again Aberdeen, whom the Russians much preferred to the belligerent Lord Palmerston, was in office as prime minister with Lord Russell as foreign secretary. In January and February Nicholas I held a series of conversations with Sir Hamilton Seymour, the British ambassador in St. Petersburg. Again the tsar warned of the impending collapse of the Ottoman Empire and the necessity for a prior arrangement. He then offered a wide plan of partition based upon familiar lines: Wallachia, Moldavia, and Serbia would be under Russian protection; Crete and Egypt might go to England. It was assumed that Austria would support the Russian position. Seymour also reported that the tsar stated: "Constantinople must not belong to any Great Power, nor must there be a new Byzantine Empire: still less could he allow Turkey to be partitioned into small Republics, as asylums for the Kossuths, Mazzinis and other revolutionaries of Europe."[5]

To these open overtures the British government was entirely unresponsive. They had no interest in, nor did they expect the imminent collapse of the empire. They saw in Nicholas' attitude only the desire to hasten the demise of the Porte and to extend Russian power. London continued to believe that Turkey could be reformed.

The Russian attempt to strengthen the ties with Britain coincided with the rise of a dispute between France and Russia over Catholic and Orthodox rights in the Holy Places in Palestine. Despite the fact that Nicholas I looked upon France as the most dangerous of the powers, the interests of the two states clashed on few points. There had certainly as yet been no occasion for an open quarrel after the settlement of the Egyptian question. The clash between the Christian churches was, however,

5. Seton-Watson, *op. cit.*, p. 306.

an issue of deep significance for both governments. The protection of Orthodoxy had always been one of the bases of Nicholas' policy. Napoleon III needed the support of the Catholic church for his internal policies and to maintain himself in power. The prestige of both rulers was thus deeply involved.

The conflict commenced as a result of the gradual loss of rights suffered by the Orthodox before a militant Catholic offensive. In the first half of the nineteenth century, because of the anti-clerical influence of the French revolution, the Catholic position had been weakened in favor of the Orthodox. After 1840, with the growth of the Ultramontaine party in France, the situation was reversed. Large numbers of French pilgrims appeared and the Catholics pressed their claims vigorously. Soon open fighting broke out between the two religious groups. Both the French and Russian governments then put pressure on the Porte, each in the interests of its own church. The French based their claims primarily on the capitulations of 1740; Russia on the Treaty of Kuchuk Kainarji. The Russians threatened with their army on the border of the Principalities; the French with their Mediterranean fleet.

Before these rival pressures the Porte, as was its custom, wavered. When the French threats appeared the more convincing, the sultan in December, 1852 made a judgment in favor of France. The Catholic monks received the key to a door of the church of Bethlehem and the right to replace at the birthplace of Christ a star that had been removed by the Orthodox in 1847. Nicholas I answered this blow to his prestige by mobilizing two army corps and sending Prince A. S. Menshikov as a special envoy to the Porte to discuss the entire question. In this dispute Nicholas I felt diplomatically secure because of his Prussian and Austrian allies and because of what he regarded as his understanding with Britain.

In February, 1853 Prince Menshikov arrived in Constantinople; the object of his mission was to block the French in the question of the Holy Places and to re-establish Russian prestige. His objectives were thus in many ways similar to those of Prince Orlov in

1833. However, unlike his tactful predecessor, Menshikov was an arrogant and overbearing diplomat. Instead of achieving his goal of reasserting Russian influence in the Turkish capital, he brought Britain and France together to face what they now regarded as an attempt of Russia to control the empire. Menshikov first forced the replacement of the Turkish foreign minister Fuad with Reshid, who was regarded as being more favorable to Russia. He then presented the Russian terms. Although ostensibly in Constantinople to settle the religious dispute, he now demanded what amounted to the recognition of a Russian protectorate over the 12 million Orthodox subjects of the sultan, and a treaty similar to that of Unkiar Skelessi. The basically religious question of the Holy Places had thus now been turned into a dispute over the survival and domination of the entire empire. The eastern question had thus been opened again, but in a manner unfavorable to Russian interests.

At Constantinople Menshikov faced the opposition of a very formidable adversary in the person of the British ambassador Stratfort Canning, now Lord Stratford de Redcliffe, a recognized Russophobe. His instructions advised him to counsel moderation and reform to the Porte, but he was also given the right to call the fleet from Malta in an emergency. The presence of a strong man of anti-Russian inclinations considerably strengthened the hands of those in the Ottoman government who favored resistance to Russia. Stratford now wisely advised the Porte to separate the issues of the Holy Places and the protectorship of the Christians. In May a compromise solution on the religious question was reached, and the debate over the Holy Places played no further part in the relations of the powers. Firm resistance was, however, offered on the other Russian demands.

Since his proposals had not been accepted in their entirety, Menshikov left Constantinople on May 21. Ten days later Nesselrode issued a declaration, stating that if the entire Russian proposal were not accepted, the Russian armies would occupy the Principalities. Simultaneously, the British and French fleets were ordered to Besika Bay, from whence they could easily enter the

Straits. The major opponents now stood face to face. British and French seapower lay off the Straits; Russian land power was concentrated in the Balkans. Russia was opposed by the diplomatic combination she had hoped to avoid; the policies of separating France and Britain in the eastern question and of co-operating with Britain had both been abandoned. Nor was the issue of the conflict clear. Nicholas I, in sending Menshikov to Constantinople, had not sought to destroy the empire but, at the most, to re-establish the conditions of the 1840's and what he regarded as the rights assured to Russia in previous treaties. The questions involved were in no sense great enough to warrant a war against the western powers.

In this moment of stress Russia turned to her allies. Basing her hopes on the agreements of Münchengrätz and Berlin and on the assistance rendered in 1849, the Russian government believed that it could count on Vienna. However, once again the division of interests between the two states in eastern affairs became apparent. Austria had no interest in increasing Russian power in the Balkans. Moreover, she feared that support of Russia would lead to French intervention in Italian affairs. Her control in that peninsula remained at all times precarious. In an impossible diplomatic situation the Austrian government, under the leadership of Buol, saw its interests tied with those of the west, but it was well aware of the dangers of antagonizing Russia. Throughout the Crimean War the Austrian policy of hesitation and half-measures won Austria the disdain of both sides.

Sentiment in Prussia was also divided; the humiliations of Olmütz and the Schleswig-Holstein affair were not forgotten. As usual, those with liberal inclinations favored co-operation with the west, whereas the conservatives stood behind the Russian alignment. As a result, Prussia adopted a policy of strict neutrality, which won her the lasting gratitude of St. Petersburg. During the Crimean War the Russian government did not have to fear that Prussia would join the allies and thus face Russia with the threat of a direct overland invasion. In contrast, Austrian neutrality always contained such a possibility. Prussia reaped the rewards of her restrained neutrality after 1856.

Not only was Russia without the active support of a strong ally, but she was also in no condition to enter upon a major war. The catastrophic state of Russian finances was reflected in the army, which, because of the cost involved, had not been equipped with modern weapons. The Russian network of railroads had not been developed to the south and Russian communications between the north and center of the country and the Black Sea were very bad. The bureaucracy, which was characterized by graft, corruption, and inefficiency, had not the ability to prepare the nation for a national crisis. The Crimean War was to demonstrate how thoroughly Nicholas I had failed to develop the internal organization of his country in order to enable it to keep pace with its international position and its external claims and commitments.

The summer of 1853 was filled with great diplomatic activity. Since Vienna held the key to the future, attention was concentrated on this city. For Russia, in particular, the Austrian attitude was bound to be decisive. Austria and Prussia together protected the Russian western frontier; the Austrian armies stationed in Transylvania could nullify Russian action in the Balkans. Russian armies could not march toward Constantinople if the danger existed that they might be cut off by Austrian action in the Principalities. Yet without a Balkan invasion the Russian government had no possibility of defeating the Turks or ending the war with a victory. Since Russian naval power could not hope to challenge France or Britain, Russia could menace Constantinople only by land.

In its approach to Vienna, however, the Russian government met only with rebuffs. Not only was the debt of gratitude for 1849 ignored, but Russia had also more recently supported Austria in a quarrel with the Porte over Montenegro. Before Russia had occupied the Principalities, she had invited Austria to act with her and to take Bosnia and Serbia. Vienna had refused to co-operate and had advised against the move. Austria certainly had every reason to prevent the crisis from developing further. In an attempt to save the situation, Buol and the ambassadors of the powers in the Austrian capital drafted the "Vienna Note" of July 28, 1853, which in effect reaffirmed the Russian rights under Kuchuk Kainarji and Adrianople. Russia accepted the proposal at once, but Turkey, by suggesting amendments that were unacceptable, in fact rejected it. The Porte, convinced that Britain and France would give their support, now was eager for a Holy War and a showdown with St. Petersburg. The effect of the apparent willingness of Russia to accept mediation was undermined when it became known that the Russian interpretation of the Vienna note was such that she would have more rights of interference in behalf of the Christians than was originally intended. Nicholas himself did not know exactly what had been gained at Kuchuk Kainarji. Although the tsar later withdrew this "violent interpretation" at a meeting with Franz Joseph at Olmütz, confidence in his sincerety of purpose was weakened.

Meanwhile, despite the continued diplomatic negotiations, the situation grew more critical. At the end of September, without consulting the cabinet, Aberdeen and Clarendon ordered the fleet to Constantinople. Confident of British backing, the Ottoman government on October 4 issued an ultimatum to Russia to evacuate the Principalities; on October 23 Turkish troops crossed into Russian territory. With the British fleet at the Straits and Russia and Turkey thus at war, public enthusiasm for participation in the conflict increased in both France and Britain. It took only a perfectly legitimate act of war on the part of the Russian fleet to make the final decision almost unavoidable. With the deliberate aim of provoking a Russian attack, the Ottoman government sent a squadron into the Black Sea. On November 30 at Sinope the Russian fleet met and annihilated the Turkish force. About 4,000 men were lost. Despite the full legitimacy of the Russian action, the western press dubbed it the "massacre of Sinope" and branded it a Russian outrage. Stratford de Redcliffe was delighted with the battle: "for that means war. The Emperor of Russia chose to make it a personal quarrel with me: and now I am avenged." [6]

The war still took long in starting. In January, 1854 the allied fleets entered the Black Sea; in the next month diplomatic relations were broken. At the end of February the allies sent Nicholas I an ultimatum giving him two months to evacuate the Principalities. The tsar did not bother to answer this communication, but on March 20 he despatched Russian troops across the Danube. Thus by slow stages the battle was finally engaged. The issue on the allied side was straightforward: the prevention of Russian preponderance over the Ottoman Empire. For Russia the reasons for the war were not so clear. At the time she had no immediate desire to partition the empire, although Nicholas I had repeatedly sought to provide for such an eventuality. The Russian government was also fully conscious of its own weaknesses and of the dangers of a coalition war. It had been, nevertheless, pushed into the conflict by a series of events that involved Russian prestige. The test of strength in the Near East between Britain and Russia, which had been years in preparation, was now to be fought under circumstances of maximum advantage to the British. Although it may well be argued that such a conflict was at some time inevitable, it was certainly a failure of Russian diplomacy, and of Nicholas I personally as the responsible head of the government, that the war came at a moment so unfavorable for Russian interests.

With the war now underway, the choice of a battlefield remained to be made. Since Russian seapower was inferior, it was obvious that it would be the allies who would determine where the armies would meet. Because of the attitude of Sweden, a Baltic campaign was not deemed advisable. Neutral Prussia closed that area. A Balkan venture remained a possibility, but here Austrian actions prevented that region from becoming a battlefield. In April, 1854 Prussia and Austria signed an alliance in which each guaranteed the other's territory and both agreed

6. *Ibid.*, p. 320.

to allow no further Russian expansion in the Balkans. Prussia later gained the adherence of the German diet to this agreement. Thereafter Prussian influence was directed toward the preservation of Austrian neutrality. With her position in central Europe secure, the Austrian government next turned to the Turks and made an agreement on the Principalities. To the intense indignation of the Russian government, whose armies were winning victories, the demand was then made that the Russians evacuate the Principalities. After the forced withdrawal of the Russian troops, Austria occupied Moldavia, and Austrian and Turkish troops together held Wallachia. As long as Austria remained neutral, it would be impossible for the allies and Russia to meet in combat in the Balkans.

With the Principalities in its hands, the Austrian government continued its efforts to find a basis for peace. On August 8 the allies and Austria issued the Vienna Four Points, which, because they eventually became the basic terms of the peace, are of immense significance. The declaration contained the following provisions: (1) the Russian protectorate over the Principalities and Serbia was to be replaced by a European guarantee; (2) the navigation of the Danube was to be made free; (3) the Straits Convention of 1841 was to be revised; (4) a five-power guarantee of the Christians of the Ottoman Empire was to substitute for the Russian rights in regard to the Orthodox. Since the Russian armies had not yet been defeated in battle, Nicholas rejected the proposals.

With all other possible areas eliminated, the allies were left with the Russian Black Sea coast as the only available area for combat. Thus the Crimea, with Sebastopol as the main objective, was selected as the point of invasion. Although this land was remote from their home base, Britain and France had absolute command of the Black Sea, and sea transport at that time was preferable to overland carriage. In September, 1854 a combined force of British, French, and Turkish troops landed, to be met by about 35,000 Russian defenders. Later in the campaign Sardinian troops also joined the allies. The first engagement on the Alma resulted in a defeat for the outnumbered Russians, but delay and divided council prevented the victorious troops from exploiting their gains. The Russian forces were thus given time to reassemble and to fortify Sebastopol more strongly. The seige of this city thereafter became the central point of the military operations of the war. Although the Russians were able to hold the position for eleven months, they were unable to dislodge their opponents; unsuccessful attempts were made at Balaklava in October and at Inkerman in November. Finally in September, 1855, after its long resistance, Sebastopol was finally captured by the allies. The only bright spot in the Russian military picture in the war was in the Caucasus where Russian troops took Kars in November, 1855. Nicholas I was spared the knowledge of the final defeat of his armies, in whom he had shown such intense interest and pride. On March 2, 1855 he died, leaving his country in a disastrous internal condition and faced with a war against dangerous opponents.

* * * * *

With the death of Nicholas Russia lost the unique position in Europe that she had won in 1814. Another century was to pass before Russian military power and prestige was to enjoy a similar advantage. Nicholas' entire reign has in retrospect been harshly judged, particularly because of his blind failure to institute some kind of internal reform. Although it is indeed difficult to justify his internal administration, the thirty years of his leadership in foreign policy do not present such a dark picture despite the final catastrophe. Until 1854 Russian policy in the east had been quite successful. The Russo-Turkish war had ended in a Russian victory; the Treaty of Unkiar Skelessi was an undoubted diplomatic triumph. The policy of co-operation with Britain in the Greek and Egyptian questions had led to solutions satisfactory to Russia and had prevented France and Britain from forming a united front against her. In central European affairs his success was even more marked. Certainly, his recognition that liberal and national movements could be potentially dangerous to

Russia was correct. He also kept Germany divided and Poland in political bondage. Although this condition was not to the benefit of the Poles or Germans, unreformed Russia could not be expected to welcome the formation of modern national states on her doorstep. The Crimean War, thus, did indeed mark a failure of policy, but the weakness of the system lay in the internal affairs of Russia. The new tsar, Alexander II, was to take this lesson to heart and, in concentrating on the domestic needs of his country, was to commit a blunder in foreign relations far greater than any in his father's reign in allowing the consolidation of central Europe.

IV

Alexander II

The reign of the new tsar, Alexander II, commenced under the most unauspicious of circumstances. Ascending the throne at the age of 37, he was, however, better prepared for this high position than his father had been. Keenly aware of the deficiencies of his own training for the demanding office, Nicholas I had associated his son with him and given him administrative duties. Alexander II had also functioned as regent in his father's absence. Unlike many royal heirs, Alexander II showed no signs that he did not fully share his father's basic political principles, although the weaknesses of the system had been shown in the Crimean War. Despite the fact that reforms were inaugurated under his administration and that he did initially follow a policy of alliance with France, he accepted these changes because of immediate necessity. At the end of his reign he returned to the old principles, particularly in foreign policy, and favored a rebuilding of the former conservative coalition.

Nevertheless, Alexander's reign as a whole is chiefly notable for the internal reforms in the state. The necessities of the domestic situation determined the shape of Russian foreign relations for the greater part of the period. The Crimean War had shown with great clarity how far Russia was behind the western states in military power; without a fundamental change in its basic structure it was apparent that the vast empire could not be maintained intact. The new reforms were therefore initiated much in the spirit of those of Peter the Great, although with less of the vigor and direction of purpose of that monarch. The reforms of the 1860's quite understandably concentrated on the question of serfdom since it was in this aspect that Russian society now differed markedly from that of the rest of Europe. Serf labor and a serf-based economy had also proved inefficient and uneconomical. Although there was little or no approval of the idea of serfdom itself, the problem remained of how this condition could be changed without at the same time severely damaging the position of the gentry, who in turn were the support of the autocratic system. The question was discussed and debated by various committees and the entire matter was energetically pushed by Alexander II with the argument that "it would be better to abolish serfdom from above than to wait till it will begin to liberate itself from below." The final measures of 1861 were a compromise between the interests of the gentry and the serfs. Although the conditions of emancipation differed in the various regions of Russia and among the categories of peasants, in general the former serf received land, somewhat less in extent to that which he had previously cultivated for his own use, in return for a sum of money to be paid to the government in forty-nine annual installments. The state then in turn indemnified the landlord. The village community and not the individual received actual jurisdiction over the land and held the responsibility for the redemption payments. The peasant was thus bound to his community as he had formerly been tied to his landlord. Instead of receiving real personal freedom, he remained in a special status where he was freed from the old bonds of serfdom, but he retained many of the former limitations on his free activity. His social and legal position still set him apart from the others.

The emancipation of serfs required other reforms closely linked with this fundamental social change. New regulations for local government and for legal proceedings were enacted; in the 1870's military reforms followed. Despite the fact that Alexander II supported these changes, it is to be noted that he did not surrender any of his political powers. Russia remained an autocracy and the support of conservative, legitimate governments was to become again, after a brief entente with France before 1863, a determining consideration of foreign policy. The peasant emancipation was in the end neither an economic nor a social success. The land the peasant received was too small in extent and his payments were calculated too high. Nevertheless, these acts did bring social conditions in Russia more in line with those of her western neighbors. The reforms also for the moment served to calm internal criticism. Reform from above without revolution was accomplished despite the weaknesses of the autocratic regime that were exposed in the Crimean War.

The Crimean disaster and the subsequent concentration of Russia on internal development removed her from an active, aggressive role in European affairs for almost twenty years. During this period the map of Europe was remade and the balance of forces on the continent was radically altered. The first part of the reign of Alexander II thus contrasts strongly with that of Nicholas I, who, as we have seen, intervened actively wherever Russian interests or those of the conservative order were affected. The change reflected not only the weakness of Russia as a power, but also the disinclination of the new tsar and his ministers to continue the role of the "gendarme of Europe," the defender of the conservative order and the treaties of Vienna.

The Peace of Paris

The first sad duty that Alexander II faced was the liquidation of a war he could not hope to win. In September 1855 the fortress of Sebastopol, despite a brave and able defense, fell to the western allies and the Russian troops were forced to withdraw in the Crimea. This victory, although welcomed as the first major success of the campaign, did not bring France and Britain much further. Obviously they were in no position to launch a major invasion of Russia, particularly as long as both Austria and Prussia remained neutral. Moreover, the French government had now become reluctant to press forward the expensive campaign in the Crimea. Britain, with more at stake in the defeat of Russia in the area, preferred to continue the war. The French proposal that the allies should call for a general uprising of the Russian subject nationalities in Finland, Poland, and the Caucasus was, however, strongly opposed. The separation in aims and objectives of the two major allies was here clearly apparent.

Because of the deadlock on the military level, the position of Austria remained decisive for all of the combatants. In November the allied powers with Austria agreed upon a new protocol based upon a strengthened interpretation of the Vienna Four Points. The full demilitarization and neutralization of the Black Sea was now demanded; Austria also obtained the provision that southern Bessarabia be returned to Moldavia, thus removing Russia from the Danube river shore. When the Austrian government agreed to enter the war should these terms be rejected, Russia was forced to accept. Austrian participation on the western side would have made a true invasion of Russia possible; the Russian statesmen also feared a rising of their minorities. The hostile attitude in Vienna throughout the war had aroused Russian anger, but it was this final action that was most bitterly remembered and most strongly influenced the subsequent decisions made in St. Petersburg.

Although the Russian diplomats subsequently went to the peace conference with the expectation of meeting British and Austrian hostility, they had some hopes of receiving support from France. As had been the case in Vienna in 1814, the war coalition had showed signs of cracking even before the fighting had ended. Throughout the war France had maintained indirect connections with St. Petersburg, and at the conference itself the basis for the subsequent friendship was laid. It was soon shown that Austria and Britain had more interest in checking Russia in the east than did France, who wished Russian co-operation for its own interests.

The peace conference that opened in Paris in February, 1856 was the first general European meeting of its kind since the Congress of Vienna. The powers who had participated in the war—France, Russia, Britain, Sardinia, and Austria, because of her actions at the end—sent representatives. Due to the opposition of Britain, Prussia was allowed to attend only the sessions concerning the revision of the Straits settlement, of which she was also a signatory power. Orlov and Brunnov represented Russia; Napoleon and Walewski were the French members. Clarendon and Cowley represented Britain; Cavour spoke for Piedmont, and Buol for Austria. Since the terms had been agreed upon beforehand, no great controversies threatened the success of the conference. In general, the Russian delegates sought to obtain a soft interpretation of the terms while the British attempted to impose as restricting a peace as possible upon their eastern antagonist. In the end the treaty was singularly mild when it is considered that the Russian government could not have continued with the war. The final terms reflected carefully the Vienna Four Points with their later modifications.

The section of the treaty that aroused the greatest resentment within Russia was undoubtedly that concerned with the demilitarization of the Black Sea since these stipulations reflected directly upon the Russian territorial integrity and upon her national honor. According to these, both Russia and Turkey were forbidden to maintain warships or arsenals on the shores of the Black Sea. The Straits were, of course, to continue to remain closed to warships of all nationalities, but open to the merchantmen of the powers. In the succeeding years the issue of the enforced neutralization of the Black Sea played a disproportionate role in the determination of Russian foreign policy. In fact, the breaking of these clauses became the chief single issue in Russian foreign relations until 1870.

The annexation of southern Bessarabia to Moldavia, who had lost it in 1812, removed Russian control from the mouth of the Danube in accordance with the Austrian desires. This action was certainly to the benefit of all of the powers since the Russian role of custodian of the navigable Sulina channel had been anything but praiseworthy. In the interest of her own Black Sea ports and her agriculture, she had allowed the channel to silt up and she had taken measures detrimental to the river trade. The administration of the Danube river was now placed in the hands of a commission of riverain states from whose number Russia was excluded. The question of Bessarabia, like that of the neutralization of the Black Sea, became henceforth for Russia a matter of national honor, despite the fact that the territory was not Russian in nationality and had been acquired only during the Napoleonic period.

The principal general issue leading to the Crimean War, the Russian claim to the protectorship of the Balkan Christians, was met by establishing the principle that the European powers jointly should assume responsibility in this question. The Ottoman Empire was also expressly admitted to the concert of the European powers and the governments promised to respect the independence and the territorial integrity of the Porte. It was agreed that should a conflict arise between one of the powers and Constantinople, the other governments would be consulted. These terms were an expression of the continued British hope and conviction that the Ottoman Empire could be reformed and reorganized into a political body acceptable to its citizens. On the vigorous prompting of Stratford de Redcliffe, the sultan on February 18 issued the reform decree of the Hatti-Humayun of 1856, which promised religious and legal equality for Christian and Moslem alike. In this respect this measure resembled the similar decree of the Hatti-Sheriff of November, 1839, whose promises had never been fulfilled.

The Russian government was also forced to give up its protectorate over Serbia and the Danubian Principalities. Serbian autonomy was reaffirmed, but Turkish garrisons were allowed to remain in the country. The question of the ultimate political organization of Moldavia and Wallachia brought up one of the major disputes of the conference and demonstrated the basic lack of unity between the Crimean allies. The issue was from the beginning of great interest and importance to Napoleon III, because he could by strengthening the Rumanian position serve French national interests and also forward his ideas on the national organization of Europe. Under the Russian protectorate, as we have seen, the liberal elements of the Rumanian leadership had been educated in Paris and had turned to France for inspiration and ideas. The ruling boyars in the country regarded themselves as linked to France in culture and civilization and wished to be regarded as an outpost of that nation in eastern Europe. At the congress Napoleon, therefore, supported the program of the liberal, national party and called for the union of the Principalities under a foreign prince. This plan met with the strongest opposition from Vienna, which did not wish to allow the formation of a strong state, linked with France, on the lower Danube. The effect that this action would have both on the balance of political power in the immediate area and on the Rumanian nationals under Austrian control was considered. This position was supported by the Porte, which naturally wished to avoid any further infringements or limitations on its sovereignty in the territory. Britain at first maintained a moderate position, but she also preferred not to allow a weakening of Turkish power. Faced by this division among its adversaries, the Russian government decided to support the French stand, chiefly in order to separate France from Britain. When it was found impossible to achieve an acceptable arrangement at the congress, the powers decided to refer the Rumanian question to a special commission to be appointed to study the problem. It was also agreed that assemblies would be elected in both Principalities in order to determine the opinion of the population concerned.

In other sections of the treaty Sweden obtained the demilitarization of the Aland Islands. Cavour was also allowed to speak at the conference on conditions in Italy, in particular in regard to the Kingdom of the Two Sicilies and the Papal States. In April, 1856 the British, French, and Austrian governments signed a treaty of guarantee in which they agreed to go to war should Russia break the treaty. Although this pact was in theory secret, Napoleon communicated it to the Russian government. Its conclusion had no further significance in international diplomacy.

Despite the fact that Russia lost the right to maintain armaments on the Black Sea, that she yielded southern Bessarabia, and that she was forced to abandon her general claims to act as the protecting power of the Balkan Christians, the treaty brought no great changes in the map or any clearly apparent shift in the basic balance of political power in the Near East. To many at the time the results seemed hardly to justify the losses in men and matériel; over a half million died in the war, the majority of disease and lack of care. The finances of all of the participants had been gravely affected by the burden of fighting at a great distance from the centers of the countries involved. Nevertheless, the Crimean War was perhaps the most decisive single conflict of the entire period since Peter the Great, because it created the general political conditions that ultimately brought about the national unification of central Europe and a radical change in the European balance. The results of the Crimean War were thus not to be seen in the terms of the Treaty of Paris but in the history of the next fifteen years.

The war and the conditions of the peace had also a profound effect upon the position of Russia as a great power and upon the opinion that was held of her military capacity. The ineptness of her fighting forces had shown both to the west and to the Russian statesmen the hollowness of her claims to military might. Not only had the Russian armies proved incapable of winning battles on their own soil, but the Holy Alliance, the diplomatic combination on which Russia had relied, had proved no guarantee of international security when it was tested. After 1856 St. Petersburg was no longer able to play the predominant role that it had enjoyed in European affairs since 1814. The center of European diplomacy now shifted back to Paris, and the chief protagonist on the European scene became Napoleon III.

THE FRANCO-RUSSIAN ENTENTE, 1856-1863

After the war the task of guiding Russian foreign policy fell into the hands of a new minister, A. M. Gorchakov. Nesselrode, who now left office, favored the return to the conservative alliance system despite the Austrian betrayal because he believed that Russian policy must remain "monarchical and anti-Polish." In many respects, Gorchakov was better fitted to the changed conditions than was his predecessor. Of an ancient and pure Russian lineage, he was more acceptable to the nationalists who had deeply resented the place occupied by those of German nationality in the Russian army and bureacracy. His prior career had centered on posts in Stuttgart and Vienna. Since his appointment in Württemberg also necessitated his attendance at the diet of the Germanic Confederation in Frankfurt, he had come to know Bismarck as a colleague. His chief position had undoubtedly been the post of ambassador in Vienna, which he held during the difficult days of the Crimean War. There he had come into strong conflict with Buol and he returned to St. Petersburg determined to obtain revenge for what he regarded as a flagrant betrayal of faith on the part of Austria. With this attitude he was well qualified to lead in the inauguration of an anti-Austrian orientation in foreign relations, a course of action that fitted with the convictions of most of the influential Russian statesmen of the time.

The policy that Gorchakov directed and implemented at the commencement of his period in office was referred to by his colleagues as that of *recueillement,* based on the minister's words, "*La Russie ne boude pas, mais se recueille.*" It was recognized that for a period of years Russia would of necessity be forced to devote its principal strength to internal reform and reorganization. The Crimean War had demonstrated the weakness of the state and had shown again that an invasion by a hostile coalition of the powers of Europe was always a possibility that must be reckoned with. In these circumstances, the policy of Nicholas I would have to be abandoned until Russia was again strong enough to assume wide commitments. Thus Russian armies could no longer remain poised to intervene in European affairs; nor could Russia defend conservative causes all over the map of Europe. Foreign policy would henceforth be conducted on the clear assumption that foreign adventures should be avoided and that for a period Russia could not play a great role in European affairs.

Despite these considerations it was also recognized that because of her continental position Russia could not, like Britain, maintain a policy of diplomatic isolation. In addition, Russian aims did include certain limited goals, such as the breaking of the Black Sea clauses of the Treaty of Paris and the regaining of southern Bessarabia. Russia thus needed an alliance system of some kind, even though she intended to maintain a defensive policy. The previous tie with Austria had proved valueless. Prussia had acted in Russian eyes as a true friend, but in 1856 Prussian power was not highly rated. The Russian statesmen did not believe that alliance with Berlin alone was sufficient to offset the dangers of a hostile coalition. Britain remained the chief Russian opponent in the east; moreover her avoidance of general treaties, as had been shown in the negotiations with Nicholas I, rendered her unsuitable for Russian purposes. France alone of the powers therefore appeared to be a possible ally. In considering and in accepting the idea of co-operation with the French government, Gorchakov and the tsar reversed the entire course of Russian relations as they had been carried on under Nicholas I and inaugurated a new period in Russian diplomacy.

The policy of working with France, which Russia now

adopted, signified the abandonment of two fundamental bases of policy that had been maintained since 1815—first, the defense of the territorial settlement of Vienna, and, second, the protection of legitimate monarchs against revolution. Instead Russia now entered into a period of co-operation with Napoleon III, who actively sought to remake the map of Europe on national lines and to break the Vienna settlement. The French emperor thus stood in opposition to all that Nicholas I had held sacred in international relations—the sanctity of international treaties and the necessity for the rulers of Europe to make a common stand against revolutionary movements. In agreement with France, Russia was now to enter upon a period in which she would accede to, or actively aid in, the breaking of international agreements by revolutionary methods.

The Russian willingness to co-operate with France was a result not only of her need for an ally but also of her altered relations with her neighbors after the Crimean War. The Napoleonic policy of national unification affected at first primarily the Habsburg Empire. Russia was, after 1856, perfectly willing to accept a severe weakening of Habsburg power, and she welcomed the chance to secure revenge for the Austrian attitude during the war. However, even more important, Russia had changed her general attitude toward the Vienna settlement. Since the Russian government now openly sought to break the restrictions imposed upon her by the Treaty of Paris, it could no longer be expected to be the enthusiastic upholder of the sanctity of other international guarantees, particularly of those that benefited Austria. In order to destroy the clauses detrimental to Russian interests in this new treaty, modifications in the settlements of 1815 could be accepted. Moreover, alliance with revolutionary France no longer held the dangers to Russian internal policy of the previous era. Russia itself was undergoing a period of reform and change. Gorchakov prided himself on his liberal inclinations. Thus, once the Russian government abandoned its attempt to maintain the old conditions intact, France, as the center of change and new political ideas, no longer appeared in so dangerous a light.

Although no formal alliance was signed, Russia worked with France in international affairs with varying degrees of co-operation from 1856 to 1863. The entente was carried forward through a series of meetings between diplomats and rulers and through agreements on specific questions. The Russian government throughout these years attempted to use this policy of co-operation to divide France and Britain and to secure the humiliation of Austria. Within the period of the entente five revolutionary movements occurred in Europe—in the Danubian Principalities, Italy, Serbia, Greece, and Poland. In all but the final revolt in Poland, the Russian government either supported the changes or remained neutral. It thus concurred in the overthrow of established regimes and in the policy of the unilateral breaking of international engagements. In the following pages the three events in the Balkans, the unification of the Danubian Principalities, the change of dynasties in Serbia, and the overthrow of King Othon in Greece will be discussed together. The events in Italy and Poland will be described separately, although these occurrences overlap in time those in the east.

1. The Balkans, 1856-1863

The first major diplomatic event after the end of the Crimean War was the unification of the Danubian Principalities and the formation of the Rumanian state. The Russian protectorate over the territories, established after 1829, had, as we have seen, won Russia the enmity of the liberal, national groups. The Russian intervention in the revolutions of 1848 had caused particularly bitter resentment. Yet it was the program of those who had been foremost in their opposition to Russian domination that the French government now supported. At the peace conference Napoleon III championed the position of the Rumanian liberals, who wished a united state under a foreign prince. Russia, because of her new political orientation, in the next years followed the French lead and sponsored the attainment of the Rumanian national desires, although this action was in strong contrast to her previous position in the Principalities. In the negotiations, the French and Russian governments received support also from Sardinia and Prussia. The chief opposition to Rumanian unification lay, as before, in Vienna and Constantinople. Britain, however, because of her desire to support the Ottoman Empire also worked against the Rumanian national ambitions. The chief issue was the form of government to be given the two Principalities and the degree of unity to be permitted. In July, 1857 elections were held in the Principalities in accordance with the agreement reached at Paris. In the elections, which were characterized by extreme corruption, the vote went against the unionist party. The obvious fraudulent character of the whole transaction led to a major crisis between France and Britain, which was intensified by the rivalry of the ambassadors of the two powers in Constantinople. However, in August, 1857 a compromise solution was agreed upon between Napoleon III and Queen Victoria, accompanied by their ministers, in a meeting held at Osbourne. Britain accepted the annulment of the elections; in return Napoleon agreed not to press for the unification of the Principalities. Although this arrangement satisfied the powers, it was difficult to enforce because of sentiments of the Rumanian elector. After a more honest election held in September, 1857 the assemblies in both provinces again proceeded to vote for unification and a foreign prince. Thus the powers were forced to meet again and draft another convention affirming once more the separation of the Principalities. In the winter of 1858-1859 a third election resulted in the choice of assemblies who then elected the same man, Alexander Cuza, as hospodar (governor) in both provinces. This clear violation of the will of the great powers and of the treaties was only maintained because of the general international situation and the events in Italy. Austria, with her attention occupied elsewhere, could not actively intervene. France as usual remained the friend of the Rumanian nationalist. Under the circumstances, the powers agreed to accept the double election, but only as an exception, and they insisted upon the con-

RUMANIA IN 1861

tinued separation of the two provinces in administrative matters.

Cuza was thus able to retain his governorship over the two Principalities, but he had great difficulty in internal affairs. In order to secure support for his domestic policies, he gained the consent of the Porte in the spring of 1861 for the unification of the administrative apparatus and the assemblies of the two provinces. Thus he secured the real unity of the state. Rumania had, therefore, been created with French support and because the events in central Europe precluded intervention by the powers hostile to the development. In the question of Rumanian unification, Russian policy in this period underwent a gradual change.

Although at first favorable to the French position, the Russian government, after the double election of Cuza, gradually stiffened its outlook. It was certainly no more to the Russian than to the Austrian advantage to have the establishment of a united Rumanian state, particularly if it were liberal in politics and tied to France in international affairs. The national movement on the Danube also exerted the same attraction on the Poles that it did on the Austrian Slavic and Magyar subjects.

In 1866 the final stage of the program of the Rumanian nationalists of the 1850's was accomplished with the expulsion of Alexander Cuza and the election of a foreign prince, Charles of Hohenzollern-Sigmaringen. This revolt, carried through because of internal political conditions in Rumania, was strongly opposed by Russia, who withheld recognition of the new ruler for two years. However, again the powers did not act, although the event openly violated existing international treaties. In the next years Russian-Rumanian relations remained, in general, bad. The Russian government retained its desire to regain southern Bessarabia, which it continued to regard as part of the lands legitimately belonging to the Russian crown. It was clear that the territory would be retaken at the first opportunity.

Although the unification of the Rumanian Principalities was to prove disadvantageous to Russia in the next years, events in a neighboring state, Serbia, proved more favorable to Russian interests. Here Prince Alexander Karadjordjević, who had not supported Russia to the extent desired by his people, was replaced by the pro-Russian Miloš Obrenović. After his death two years later, his son Michael Obrenović continued his father's policies of seeking to remove the remaining rights in the state of the Porte, which was still the suzerain power, and, if possible, of extending the Serbian territories. Because of the Russian entente, the French government supported the Serbian national policy. France also co-operated with Russia in coming to the aid of the Montenegrins in their uprising against the Porte in 1858. An extension of the Montenegrin boundaries was obtained because of the intervention

of the two great powers. Therefore until 1863, when the Franco–
Russian alignment finally broke, France did assist Russia in the
Balkans by favoring the national aspirations of the two Balkan
Slavic states who were at the time in close relation with Russia.

The third important political upheaval that occurred in the
Balkans involved the expulsion of King Othon of Greece in the
winter of 1862-1863. The internal politics of the kingdom had
been complicated since its founding by the rivalry of the powers
for predominant influence in the country and by the fact that
the state as established in 1830 contained within its boundaries
only a minority of the Greek people. In 1844 Othon accepted a
constitution and with it limitations of his political power. Thereafter he relied for political support on Kolettes, the head of the
French party. Both the king and his minister pursued the one
aim that was desired by all the Greeks and that would assure them
the backing of their people—the national expansion of their country. In this policy they were principally opposed by Britain, who
in Greek affairs as elsewhere upheld the rights of the Ottoman
Empire. During the Crimean War the relations between Greece
and Britain were particularly bad, largely as the result of the desire of the Greek government to use the opportunity to gain
more territory. To prevent Greek action against the Porte,
British and French fleets were sent to Pireus in 1854. King
Othon had thus by 1860 antagonized the western powers. Russia
was also not satisfied with his rule. As has been mentioned, from
1832 until the expulsion of Othon the Russian government in its
relations with Greece placed great emphasis upon the question of
religion. When Othon, who had no children of his own, failed to
designate an heir of the Orthodox faith, or one who could be
expected to be converted, he lost the support of St. Petersburg.
Thus when a revolution forced his abdication in 1862, he found
that none of the great powers regretted the event.

With the expulsion of the Greek king, France, Russia, and
Britain as the protecting powers were faced with the problem
of finding a successor. Here the British government with its fleet
in the Mediterranean was in the most advantageous position to

influence the choice. Moreover, it could and did use its possession of the Ionian Islands as a lever to insure the return of a suitable candidate. Although Britain had decided to relinquish the islands, it was made clear that this would be done only if the new king won British approval. Finally, the powers agreed upon the name of Prince William of Denmark, the second son of the future King Christian IX of Denmark. In 1863 he became King George I of Greece. The religious issue was settled by the postponement of the question for another generation. The new king was also to govern under a constitution of a very liberal character. The change of regime in Athens thus did not fulfill the Russian desire that an Orthodox king should rule Greece. In the negotiations the French government followed willingly the British suggestions and demonstrated that in questions involving Greece there was little chance of separating the two western powers.

The seven years after the Crimean War thus witnessed revolutionary changes in three Balkan states. In each case the Russian government had approved or supported armed revolts against legitimate rulers as well as actions in violation of international agreements. Autocratic Russia was clearly not the firm supporter of legality in international relations that she had been in the previous reign. The alterations in the conditions in the Balkans, however, brought no immediate repercussions in general European or Russian politics. In contrast, the revolutionary movements that took place concurrently in Europe proper had a deep significance for the future of the Russian state.

2. Italy and Poland

Napoleon III had gladly supported the unification of the Danubian Principalities, however, his chief interest lay in the national unification of two other peoples—the Poles and the Italians. Since friendship with Russia demanded the temporary abandonment of Poland, he, therefore, concentrated on Italian unification. He pursued this aim with particular vigor after an attempt was made upon his life by the Italian nationalist, Orsini, in January, 1858. In meeting with Cavour at Plombières in July, 1858 he agreed to support the unification of northern Italy under Piedmont in return for the Italian provinces of Nice and Savoy. Thereafter he turned to Russia to assure this nation's neutrality. In March, 1859 Russia signed a secret agreement promising to maintain an attitude of benevolent neutrality in a future war between France and Austria. In this tense situation the Austrian government made the mistake of delivering an ultimatum to Piedmont, thereby precipitating on her own initiative the conflict that both Napoleon III and Cavour wanted. In the resultant war between Piedmont (which was supported by France) and Austria, Russia played her role of benevolent neutrality to the full satisfaction of France and she concentrated troops on the Austrian border. She also acted to restrain the enthusiasm of the smaller German states who wished to go to the aid of Austria. Russia and Britain together put pressure on the Germanic Confederation not to act to assist their member state.

Despite the initial military victories that he won and the support he received from Russia, Napoleon III was not content with the course of events. Like Russia, he did not fully approve of the rapid progress of the revolutionary movement in the Italian peninsula. At the outbreak of the war, revolts had overthrown the governments in Tuscany, Parma, and Modena. Moreover, the attitude of Prussia was not clear, and the French government was well aware that Russia would not act against Berlin. Moreover, the Austrian strongholds in northern Italy remained unconquered, and the German states were clearly restless under their enforced neutrality. With these considerations in mind Napoleon III met with Franz Joseph at Villafranca in July and made an agreement that in effect halted the Italian national movement at the half-way point.

Although the great powers were now in agreement on the question, the forces of Italian nationalism, like those previously in Rumania, made a compromise solution impossible. Parma, Modena, Tuscany, and Romagna proceeded immediately to vote union with Piedmont, and the revolutionary movement took hold throughout Italy. The expedition of Garibaldi, who in May, 1860 landed in southern Italy and then marched up the peninsula, brought an end to the reactionary Kingdom of the Two Sicilies. The campaign of Garibaldi with its clear leftist and revolutionary implications caused great concern in Russia. The Kingdom of the Two Sicilies had always enjoyed particular Russian favor. When the armies of Piedmont occupied the Papal States, relations were broken between Turin and St. Petersburg, not to be re-established until August, 1862. The unification of Italy thus took place in face of the clear disapproval of Russia, despite the fact that her original agreement with France had made the event possible.

The entire episode of the Italian unification thus cast a deep shadow over Franco-Russian relations. The ousting of long-established dynasties in the Italian states was bound to disturb the Russian court. It was also quite obvious that the policy of friendship with France and enmity to Austria could have dangerous repercussions within the Russian controlled lands, particularly Poland. The old vision of France as the patron of revolution and the friend of free Poland again became apparent. In 1862 the firm supporter of the French alignment, Kiselev, was replaced as ambassador in Paris by Baron Budberg, a Baltic German, and a proponent of the Holy Alliance. Even before the outbreak of the Polish insurrection, the policy of alignment with France had thus been modified.

It was, however, undoubtedly the Polish insurrection that broke decisively the ties between Paris and St. Petersburg. With the accession of Alexander II, reforms had been introduced in the administration of Poland as well as in Russia. Changes in the government of their country, nevertheless, in no way met the demands of the Polish leaders who, as in 1815 and 1830, wished a complete end to Russian domination. As in the previous decades, the Polish national movement remained divided between the so-called Whites, under Czartoryski, who sought aid from France and Britain and were essentially conservative, and the

Reds, who wished to establish a democratic republic through a national uprising. The aim of both groups was the re-creation of a completely independent Poland with the pre-partition boundaries. Quite obviously these ideas could not be understood in St. Petersburg. By 1860 Poland had become in Russian eyes an inalienable part of the Russian crown possessions and the Western Provinces were regarded as clearly Russian in character. Although the liberal Russian leaders favored the granting of a wide measure of autonomy to Congress Poland, no responsible Russian statesman considered the re-establishment of prepartition Poland. Such an event could occur only after Russia had been defeated in a war against a coalition of European powers. The international aspects of the problem made the Russian government particularly sensitive to the interference of other governments in Polish affairs.

Under the viceroyship of General Michael Gorchakov, the brother of the foreign minister, a policy of further concessions was inaugurated. In 1861 and 1862 the Polish statesman Marquis Alexander Wielopolski sought to implement a program that would have established a regime in conformity with the statute of 1832, which had not been put into effect. The Polish politician, however, was extremely unpopular among his own countrymen because of his espousal of co-operation with Russia. A series of demonstrations against Russian rule were held, which showed the strong feelings of the Polish nationalists. In an attempt to suppress this agitation, Wielopolski introduced special measures, which led to the drafting into the army of the young men most prominent in the national movement. This action was the occasion of the outbreak of a revolt in January, 1863.

The Polish revolutionary movement of 1863, in contrast to that of 1830, had very little chance of success from the outset. The revolutionaries had no adequate arms or supplies, and their forces numbered only about 10,000 as against 80,000 Russian troops. Without foreign intervention, the movement was from the beginning doomed to failure. Hopes for a rising within Russia were soon dashed; the Polish peasants also failed to rally in strength to the national cause. Fighting against impossible odds, the revolutionary forces soon were defeated, and the country was subjected to a far more extreme measure of control. The Polish kingdom was incorporated into Russia and a policy of Russification was introduced. Instruction in the schools was thereafter given in Russian with the exception of the classes in religion and in the Polish language. In an effort to undercut the Polish gentry and middle class and win the support of the peasantry, the Russian government introduced a system of peasant emancipation in Poland far more beneficial than that in effect in Russia. The peasants paid no redemption dues and secured rights in excess of those allowed in Russia.

Although the Polish revolutionaries were unable to obtain concrete outside assistance, both France and Britain did offer encouragement and moral support to the movement. At the outbreak of the revolt Napoleon III had attempted to concert with Britain on common action. Throughout the rebellion the two powers had together sponsored a series of protests, which were delivered to St. Petersburg. These measures, unsupported by any actions of a practical nature, in no way aided the insurrection, but they did convince the Russian government of the impossibility of the policy of co-operation with France. The French support of national unification movements, which Russia had approved in Rumania and, initially, in Italy, had now inevitably also affected Poland. Moreover, the role of the Catholic clergy in the Polish revolt had been particularly active; the position of France as a Catholic power was an added danger.

In this crisis, in which the powers of the Crimean coalition were again united on a single issue, Russia found once more that Prussia was the only power that would stand by her. At the beginning of the revolt in February, Russia and Prussia signed the Alvensleben Convention, in which it was agreed that Russian forces could pursue Polish rebels into Prussian territory. Although this agreement was never implemented, it remained a sign of the solidarity of the two powers in the Polish question. Certainly, Prussia had even a greater interest in the maintenance of the partition of Poland than did her neighbor. Bismarck expressed an obvious fact when he stated that it would be impossible for Prussia to hold her Rhineland territories against France with a free Poland at her back. The rebellion demonstrated once again to both states the practical value of their continued friendship.

The Polish insurrection therefore served the double purpose of completely discrediting the policy of co-operation with France and of re-emphasizing the value of close political connections with Prussia. As long as that state remained under conservative political leadership, Prussia was indeed the ideal ally for autocratic Russia. She provided a barrier between the revolutionary west and the Russian lands. With no interests in the Balkans, she did not compete with Russian objectives in the area. Close family ties and old traditions bound the two courts closely together. Moreover, after 1814 Prussia had to an extent existed in the Russian shadow; at no time did she take a stand in opposition to St. Petersburg in vital matters. The single great qualifying factor in the assessment of the value of Prussia as an ally was her actual military strength. The Russian statesmen seriously doubted if Prussia alone was a strong enough ally to protect Russia from the danger of the formation of a hostile coalition and to save her from invasion. This consideration was to play the major role in the Russian attitude toward the unification of Germany in the next years.

The Franco-Russian entente, which had lasted from 1856 to 1863, thus ended. With Russian consent Napoleon III had gained the unification of Rumania and Italy. In return Russia had received little more than the satisfaction of securing the humiliation of Austria. Her interests in the east had not been pushed forward nor had she obtained a revision of the treaty of 1856. The rise of nationalism in Europe, aided and abetted by the Napoleonic policies, had ended with a rebellion in her own lands. The policy of co-operation and alliance with Paris was now abandoned, to be resumed again almost thirty years later under greatly altered circumstances.

The Russian dislike for and distrust of French policy had by this time also come to be shared by Britain. Napoleon's restless temperament and the combination of idealism and strongly practical considerations in his policy awakened British suspicion. Quite obviously the national reorganization of Europe, if carried out in the manner Napoleon intended, would have resulted in French hegemony in Europe. The British in particular feared that the emperor would attempt to annex Belgium, Luxembourg and territory on the Rhine in the way in which he had taken Nice and Savoy during the period of Italian unification. The French-British entente, which had lasted since the Crimean War despite numerous differences of policy, received a severe blow when Britain in November, 1863 rejected a French proposal for the summoning of a European conference whose purpose would be to discuss general European questions and, if necessary, to revise the treaties of 1815. British fear of possible French aggression in areas of vital interest led the British statesmen, like the Russian, to look with favor on any diplomatic combination which might provide a counterweight in Europe to France. Thus Prussia, under the brilliant leadership of Bismarck, was able to exploit a general situation, which had been prepared by the mistakes of French policy.

THE UNIFICATION OF GERMANY

With the suppression of the Polish revolt and the disintegration of the political ties of both St. Petersburg and London with Paris the stage was set for the unification of Germany under Prussian leadership, the single most fateful event of the century for Russia. Although the genius of Bismarck as a statesman is without question, it must also be recognized that the international situation was most favorable for the realization of his objectives. For both Britain and Russia the chief danger to the peace and stability of Europe now appeared to be France under the leadership of Napoleon III. In such circumstances the building up of central Europe as a counterweight to this restless, unstable power would obviously be an advantage to both countries. For Russia a strengthening of Prussia or a furthering of German unity would provide a more effective shield for Poland; for Britain this condition would offer better protection for Belgium. Neither power foresaw the consequences of its actions. Russia, as we have seen, throughout the sixties remained preoccupied with the problems of internal reform; Britain after the death of Palmerston in 1865 entered a period of withdrawal from active intervention abroad and also concentrated on the domestic problems connected with the passage of the reform bill of 1867. Bismarck, therefore, inherited a diplomatic situation in which two of the great powers were deeply involved in questions of internal political reform, while a third was isolated and regarded with suspicion and distrust.

For Bismarck the relations between Berlin and St. Petersburg remained always of first importance. Throughout his career he sought continually to follow a policy of close collaboration and to maintain the traditional dynastic ties. As ambassador in St. Petersburg from 1859 to 1862, he had come to know the country and its principal statesmen. Because of his temperament and political convictions Bismarck as a person was also entirely acceptable in Russia. Throughout his own career Bismarck had always to meet the opposition of the Prussian liberals, who were pro-British and pro-Polish in inclination. Their victory in Prussian politics would have constituted a real danger for Russia. Therefore the protection of the position of Bismarck became a consideration of Russian policy during the years of German unification. In the 1870's Russo-Prussian relations were made difficult by the antagonism that developed between Bismarck and Gorchakov, but these feelings were not apparent at the beginning. After the great Prussian victories, Gorchakov, always vain and superficial, came to resent the successes of his colleague. The slow realization of the great significance of the unification of Germany also contributed to strengthen the dislike of the Russian minister and his assistants.

The unification of Germany was accomplished through a series of three wars in which Russia in every case maintained a position of benevolent neutrality in favor of Prussia. Without this attitude on the part of St. Petersburg toward Berlin, which was, after all, in contradiction to her policy since 1815, which had been to maintain a balance in Germany, it is difficult to imagine how the Prussian efforts could have met with success. Although the Prussian military establishment was in fact far more potent than was actually believed at the time, Prussia could not have withstood a two-front war or a conflict with a coalition. Only the abandonment by Russia of the traditional policy of enforcing the division of central Europe and of active intervention in the political affairs of the small monarchies made possible the subsequent Prussian actions. It is to be noted that in the two crucial conflicts, the Seven Weeks War and the Franco-Prussian War, Russia, in tying down Austrian forces on the Galician frontier, did in fact also render military assistance.

The first war, which arose over the vexed question of the duchies of Schleswig-Holstein, originated in a revival of the same issues that had played such a major role in the revolution of 1848 in Germany. Once again the German states saw in the question a problem of German nationalism; the other powers regarded it in the light of the necessity of maintaining the balance of power in the Baltic. In addition to the national and constitutional problems involved in the relation of the duchies to the Danish monarchy, the question of the succession to the Danish throne, since King Frederick VII had no direct heirs, was again brought up. The duchies, governed by the Salic law, would accordingly go to the Duke of Augustenberg, whereas Denmark proper would be ruled by Prince Christian of Glücksburg. In May, 1852 the powers had attempted to avoid future conflict by agreeing that both the duchies and the kingdom should together be inherited by Christian. Although Russia, France, Britain, Austria, Prussia, and Sweden signed the pact, the two German powers were not enthusiastic about the decision. The entire situation became more tense with the continuing rise of Danish and

German national feeling and its involvement in the dispute. In 1863 a new Danish constitution was drafted which provided for the incorporation of Schleswig into the Danish state in violation of the previous treaties. In answer the German diet sent an ultimatum to Denmark. At this critical moment, Frederick VII died and was succeeded by Christian IX. Pressed by his Danish subjects, the new king accepted the constitution. The diet then sent troops into the duchies in December, 1863.

War was now being waged between the diet, which favored the candidacy of Prince Frederick of Augustenberg, and the Danish monarchy. The small powers of Germany supported, in general, the actions of the diet. In contrast, Prussia and Austria, who continued to stand for the Treaty of 1852 and the candidacy of Christian IX, now separated their actions from that of the other German powers. On their own initiative, and ignoring the diet, they sent their troops into Danish territory. In the resultant fighting Denmark was defeated and forced to cede the disputed duchies. In the Convention of Gastein in August, 1865, the German powers divided the provinces, with Austria receiving the right to administer Holstein while Prussia took Schleswig. The successful acquisition of the duchies by the two powers at this time marked a strong contrast to the events of 1848-1850.

The Austro-Prussian victory and the loss of the territory by Denmark was certainly not welcomed by the other powers, but the swiftness of the event had precluded intervention. Moreover, Britain hesitated to act. She had no ally with a continental army on which she could depend and only about 20,000 troops that she could use. She was also extremely suspicious of French intentions and feared that Napoleon would use the struggle over the duchies as an opportunity to take territory on the Rhine or in the Low Countries. A strengthening of the German powers was preferable to this. Russia too had no ally, but again in contrast to 1849 and 1850 she felt no desire to check Prussia. In fact, the chief concern in St. Petersburg at this time appears to have been that war would break out and that the Prussian armies would be unable to withstand the French. Prussia as a barrier against the

west would then fall. At the time that the troops entered Schleswig-Holstein, Gorchakov assured the German minister Redern
that although war might occur, Russia would not join. "She will
never march against Prussia," he declared.[1]

The disunity of the great powers also allowed Prussia, in the
second episode, to settle the long struggle for the control of the
German lands with Austria. Britain in 1866 and 1867 was chiefly
concerned with her internal reform problems. In addition, a strong
reaction to the meddling and provocative policies of the government of Lord Palmerston had set in. Britain, thus, for the moment
played a less active role in continental politics. France remained
a problem, but Bismarck assured her initial neutrality by vague
hints of later compensation. Italian support was gained through an
alliance and the promise of Venetia. The Seven Weeks War,
which originated in a dispute over the duchies, resulted in a sud-
den and disastrous defeat of the Austrian armies. Only with great
difficulty was Bismarck able to pursuade his king not to press the
victory but to remain content with the removal of Austria from
the German political scene. The Treaty of Prague of August,
1866, in accordance with Bismarck's desires, thus cost Austria no
territory and only a small indemnity. The chief significance of
the peace was that it ended the long duel for supremacy in
Germany and it marked the dissolution of the Germanic Confederation. Prussia was now free to organize Germany north of
the river Main; the four south German states, Bavaria, Baden,
Württemberg, and Hesse remained independent.

Thus, once again the Russian government had allowed Prussia
to move forward and to increase substantially her power and
political position. The Prussian activities this time, however,
aroused great concern in the Russian court, where members of
the tsar's family had close links with the German dynasties. Although Alexander II felt closely tied to Prussia because of his
mother, his wife was from Hesse-Darmstadt. Others in the court
were linked with the rulers of such states as Hanover and

1. W. E. Mosse, *The European Powers and the German Question*
(Cambridge: Cambridge University Press, 1958), p. 172.

Württemberg. The outright Prussian annexation of Hanover, Cassel, Nassau, and Frankfurt was also unpopular. When Prussia formed the North German Confederation out of the lands north of the Main, the Russian government was also concerned about the liberal character of the constitution of the new organization.

Since the political framework of central Europe, which Prussia had now overturned, had been part of the Vienna settlement and was thus the concern of all of the powers, Alexander II proposed the holding of a conference to discuss the question. In reply to the tsar's request, William sent General Otto von Manteuffel to St. Petersburg to argue the Prussian claims. In his conversation with the Prussian general, the tsar first protested strongly over the dispossession of the small German monarchs, who, he argued, held their power from God just as surely as did the rulers of Prussia and Russia. In answer to these protests, Manteuffel emphasized the conservative aspects of Prussian leadership in Germany and he argued that a strong political organization in the area was the best guard against revolution. He thus returned to the basic emphasis of the former Holy Alliance—the conservative monarchies should remain united against liberal and revolutionary dangers. He also let it be understood that Prussia would support any Russian attempt to break the Black Sea clauses of the Treaty of Paris. Although Russia now accepted the Prussian victory and the new conditions in northern Germany, the hope remained that the southern states would retain their independence and that the tripartite division of Germany would be preserved despite the enormous strengthening of Prussia.

The severe defeat suffered by the armies of the Habsburg Monarchy forced that state to reorganize its internal structure, which it did in a manner that was to have an enormous effect on its subsequent relations with Russia. The expulsion of Austria from Germany and the national unifications of Rumania and Italy, events that were accomplished against the strong opposition of Vienna, made the further maintenance of her old political organization impossible. The monarchy was now encircled by national states; in internal affairs the Slavic and Magyar inhabitants of the empire were increasingly discontented with their status. Some compromise had to be made with the forces of nationalism. The empire met this problem by coming to terms with the strongest and most active of their minorities—the ·Magyars. In 1867 the state was in effect transformed into a partnership of the dominant nationalities: the Germans and the Magyars. Under the *Ausgleich* (Compromise), the lands belonging traditionally to the Hungarian crown were divided from those of Austria, and henceforth the two sections were joined only in the person of the emperor and by common ministries of war, foreign affairs, and finance as related to the first two offices. Although this political arrangement was made necessary by the pressure of events, it was to be highly detrimental to the future relations of Russia and Austria. Magyar policy in their lands became ever more nationalistic and was directed toward the further subjugation of their own Slavic and Rumanian inhabitants; in the empire as a whole the Magyar statesmen blocked reform measures. In foreign policy the memory of the Russian intervention in 1849 ensured that policies originating in Budapest would be anti-Russian. Magyar nationalism thus came increasingly into opposition to the rising Slavic national consciousness of the years after 1870, which, in turn, was to find a patron and supporter in tsarist Russia.

The clash of Magyar, Slavic, and German national feeling was further accentuated by the diplomatic consequences of the events of the sixties. The Habsburg Monarchy had lost her hegemony in Italy, and she had been forced out of Germany. Her Polish frontier was stable, and Rumania was united. She thus had left only one direction in which she could hope to make conquests— southeast toward the Balkans. The late nineteenth century witnessed a revival of imperialism and the desire for the acquisition of territory among all the powers; the Dual Monarchy, without effective naval power and hemmed in by her neighbors, could only direct her national energies toward the territory of the Ottoman Empire. Whereas before Austria had in general supported the maintenance of that state, she became henceforth more willing to participate in its partition. The territories first under consideration were the provinces of Bosnia-Hercegovina, which were inhabited by a South Slavic population. Like Russia, Vienna again became concerned with the fate of the Balkan Christian and his relations with his overlord. With the revival of a strong Balkan policy on the part of the monarchy, the question of the possibility of agreement with Russia again came into question. If the two powers could agree on a line of partition, which Bismarck always favored, conflict could be avoided. If, however, both governments sought influence and control over the same lands and peoples, a major clash would be inevitable. It was this issue that was to become and to remain the most dangerous single question for the peace of Europe in the coming years.

By 1866 Bismarck had thus succeeded in uniting Germany north of the Main; the four southern states, however, remained out of the union. After the Peace of Prague, Prussia proceeded to make defensive and offensive alliances with these monarchies, who were also brought into the Zollverein. The final stage in the unification of Germany would, of necessity, be their incorporation into the Prussian organization of north Germany. This policy could obviously be carried out only against the strong opposition of France. After the Austro-Prussian war, Napoleon III immediately sought to claim the compensation to which he believed himself entitled by the Prussian gains. In the next years he turned his attention to lands on the Rhine, to Luxembourg, and to Belgium. Although he was able to persuade the King of Holland to agree to the cession of Luxembourg, that ruler in the end backed down because of his fear of the reaction of the other powers. After this failure Napoleon remained unsatisfied and discontented with his role in European affairs.

Despite the tremendous shift in the balance of power occasioned by the Prussian victories, it is interesting to note that the state that continued to arouse the suspicions and fears of the others remained France. Moreover, despite frequent efforts, Napoleon III was unable to take his country out of its position of diplomatic isolation. Britain held firmly to its policy of non-involvement. Negotiations were initiated with Vienna, but the Dual Monarchy's interests were now primarily in the Balkans, an area where France could offer little assistance. The renewal of ties with St. Petersburg foundered as usual on the rocks of the Polish problem and the revolution. In 1867 the tsar visited the Paris exhibition of that year. Not only was he coolly received by the French crowds, but he was also shot at twice by a Pole. It appeared quite clear that a conservative Prussia-Germany was a needed safeguard for autocratic Russia. The general diplomatic situation thus remained highly favorable for further Prussian moves.

The Russian option for Prussia in central Europe received another confirmation when in March, 1868 the assurance was given that Russia would station troops on her border with Austria should war break out with France. Russia would in this manner perform for Berlin the service that she had rendered Paris in the Franco-Austrian War of 1859. Although no written engagement was made at this time, Bismarck could assume that Russia would not join with France. In addition, the Russian government used its influence with the southern German states to encourage them to co-operate with Prussia. Russian influence and military power were thus in effect put at the service of Bismarck in the last stage of German unification.

By 1870 both Prussia and France were ready for a decisive trial of strength. Although the Prussian diplomatic position was at this time undoubtedly superior, her military power was still in question. France, because of her great past and her military traditions, was usually judged the stronger, but neither power had tested its armies on a major battlefield since 1814. After that date Prussian military strength had not been rated highly; she was regarded as the weakest of the major powers, if not as a state of the second rank. Russian and British statesmen had in the past been principally worried lest a war between the two states result in such a severe defeat of Prussia that France would again be able to dominate central Europe. The final conflict was provoked by

French mishandling of the candidature of Prince Leopold of Hohenzollern-Sigmaringen to the Spanish throne. Although Napoleon III had been willing to accept the prince's brother as ruler of Rumania in 1866, he chose to make a major issue of the question at this time. Although neither William nor the prince's father would consider the acceptance of the Spanish invitation, Napoleon insisted that the German king issue a statement renouncing the candidacy for all time. In the conversations that followed, both Napoleon and Bismarck showed themselves willing to allow the question of French and Prussian power to be settled on the battlefield. The final French declaration of war on July 19 reflected the desire of both governments to determine in this manner the question of continental supremacy.

Once the fighting commenced it soon became apparent that the three other powers, Russia, Britain and Austria, would remain passive. The British attitude was reinforced when Bismarck published a draft treaty that indicated clearly Napoleon's previous attempts to annex Belgium. The Russian position had been determined by the promises of 1868 and by an additional assurance given in the previous June that Russia would cover the Austrian border with 300,000 men. This move allowed Moltke to concentrate an extra 100,000 troops against France. Throughout the war Russia exercised strong pressure on Austria to prevent her from beginning military preparations. The tsar promised to guarantee Austrian territorial integrity as long as that country refrained from warlike moves. Although Russia considered proposing a conference and European mediation, the idea was dropped after the Prussian victory at Sedan. Thereafter the Russian government concentrated on securing some advantage from her efforts on behalf of Prussia.

At the beginning of the war the Russian statesmen had not expected that the independent existence of the southern German states would be at issue, but the magnitude of the Prussian victories soon led them to abandon any hope that the division of Germany could be maintained. The Prussian desire to annex Alsace-Lorraine and the encouragement given by Bismarck also influenced her decisions. In October, 1870 at a meeting of his council of ministers, Alexander II declared his intention of denouncing the Black Sea clauses of the Treaty of Paris. On October 31 Gorchakov issued a circular note to the powers announcing the unilateral Russian action. Although this move aroused widespread protests, particularly on the part of Britain, little could be done. France had been defeated; Prussia had promised her support in 1866 and 1870. Britain could not act alone. Finally, a conference of seven powers was held where in effect the Russian action was approved and a new Straits settlement was drawn up. In the new agreement of March, 1871 the principle of the closure of the Straits was again affirmed, but the Sultan was allowed the right "to open the said Straits in time of peace to the vessels of war of friendly and allied Powers, in case the Sublime Porte should judge it necessary in order to secure the execution of the stipulations of the Treaty of Paris of the 30th of March 1856." The chief advantage that Britain had received from her victory in the Crimean War was thereby annulled. Both Russia and Turkey were free to build arsenals and maintain fleets on the Black Sea.

THE THREE EMPERORS' LEAGUE

Germany was thus united under Prussian leadership with Russian support. The event was concluded on a high note of friendship between the two countries. At the end of the war William telegraphed the tsar: "Prussia will never forget that she owes it to you that the war has not taken on extreme dimensions." Alexander II replied: "Let the friendship which unites us assure the happiness and glory of our two countries."[2] Despite the optimistic tone of this exchange, Russia now faced an entirely new situation in central Europe; she could no longer play between three political elements. The Habsburg Monarchy had also been drastically altered in its fundamental composition. The question

2. *Ibid.*, p. 355.

EUROPE IN 1871

remained whether Russian hopes would be fulfilled and the new Germany would remain the loyal friend that Prussia had been in the past—whether the empire would indeed save Russia from the dangers of a European coalition and offer support in the east.

After 1870 it did initially appear that the unification of Germany would make possible the reformation of the Holy Alliance on new and stronger foundations. Although no formal treaties were signed, the three emperors in a series of visits placed their relations on a co-operative basis and agreed upon the principles to be followed in foreign policy. In August, 1871 William I and Franz Joseph met at Ischl; in June, 1872 officers of the Habsburg armies visited St. Petersburg. In September, 1872 the tsar and Franz Joseph came to Berlin. In April, 1873 the German emperor traveled to St. Petersburg, and in June Alexander II was in Vienna. In February, 1874 Franz Joseph completed the round by visiting the tsar in St. Petersburg. Although the monarchs were now clearly on close terms and the Austro-Russian breach had been at least temporarily healed, no true alliance treaty was negotiated between the eastern powers. In 1873, when the German emperor was in Russia, a military convention was drawn up between the staffs, but Bismarck later refused to countersign the document. During the visit of the tsar to Vienna, in the same year, a general consultation agreement, the Convention of Schönbrunn, was drawn up, which was little more than a restatement of the common conservative convictions of the rulers. William I adhered to this pact in October, 1873. The bonds of union between the members of the Three Emperors' League were thus extremely vague. However, a return had been made to the classical conservative alliance system.

Although Prussia had won a real military triumph over France in 1870, the antagonisms and fears of the previous period were not easily healed. Until the end of his career Bismarck's principal concern in diplomacy was the protection and preservation of the united Germany that he had created. The German Empire was a new political creation in Europe; what had been so recently built up could also be destroyed by a coalition of hostile powers.

Like Russia, Bismarck too became a victim of the "nightmare of coalitions." To meet this danger he concentrated upon the isolation of France and the creation of systems of alliance that would assure that Germany would always be one of three in the constellation of the five great powers of Europe. France, in particular, caused him increasing concern since it was apparent that after the loss of Alsace and Lorraine her participation in any enemy coalition would be a matter of certainty. Moreover, her unexpectedly quick recovery and the strong feelings of *revanche* everywhere apparent showed that she might take the opportunity to strike back sooner than expected. In 1875 a combination of circumstances led to a war scare, which showed the uneasiness of the entire situation.

In order to test the general diplomatic situation, the French foreign minister, Decazes, in April, 1875, circulated among the capitals a report of his ambassador in Berlin concerning the possibility of a German preventative war against France. In answer the British government made representations in Berlin and, more important, Alexander II in a visit to Berlin, accompanied by Gorchakov, made it quite clear that Russia would not remain passive in such an event. Bismarck, who had not been contemplating aggressive action, reacted violently to this outside intervention. The episode demonstrated that, first, the era of adventure was over and Germany could no longer move freely in foreign relations and, second, combined French, British, and Russian co-operation against Germany was possible. The incident did, moreover, provide Gorchakov with the welcome opportunity to play the arbiter of Europe and to balance between the two rival powers.

Therefore, in the first years after the unification of Germany it did seem as if the Russian hopes and expectations would be fulfilled. Russia had used the occasion of the Franco-Prussian War to secure the abrogation of the Black Sea clauses of the Treaty of Paris; thereafter she had been able to join again in the Three Emperors' League with her former partners of the Holy Alliance. In the war scare of 1875 Gorchakov had seen the conformation of his expectation that Germany and France would remain permanently estranged and that Russia could play between them. In addition, in the years when affairs in Europe were dominated by the German question, Russia had been able to conquer great stretches of territory in Asia. The real test of Russian policy, however, had yet to come. It was only in the revival of the eastern question after 1875 that the Russian government was to learn the diplomatic consequences of its support of the consolidation of central Europe.

THE ASIATIC FRONTIERS

Although Russia in the first twenty years of the reign of Alexander II adopted a passive role in the affairs of the continent and the Near East, this same period was characterized by a recommencement of Russian expansion in the Middle and Far East. As a result, by 1885, in the reign of Alexander III, the Russian eastern boundaries had become stabilized, with a few small exceptions. The ease with which Russia accomplished the rounding of her Asiatic borders despite her military weakness was due to the poor quality of her opponents. China, from whom she won territory along the Amur, was also under pressure from the western powers; in the Middle East Russia faced only disunited, semi-barbarous states. Although she eventually came into conflict with Britain on the borders of Afghanistan, both governments were forced to seek a compromise because of the impracticability of contemplating a war in a remote area under the diplomatic circumstances of the time.

1. The Far East

The great Russian expansion over the Urals and across Siberia to the Pacific was accomplished before the reign of Peter the Great.

A fortress was constructed at Okhotsk in 1647 and Kamchatka was occupied in the 1690's. Expansion southward was limited when Russia signed the Treaty of Nerchinsk with China in 1689. In this agreement, the first concluded by a European power with Peking, the Russian government accepted a boundary that excluded it from the Amur valley. Chiefly interested in participating in the wealthy China trade, the Russians preferred to concentrate on the establishment of a profitable commercial relationship. Thereafter a mutually advantageous exchange of goods was indeed inaugurated, with the Russians specializing in the disposal of their Siberian furs, but they also offered leather, hides and cloth from Europe and Russia, as well as glassware. In return, they received silk, cotton cloth, tea, porcelain, sugar, and other luxury items. In this commerce China always had more valuable goods to offer than did Russia. In 1727 the Treaty of Kiakhta allowed the Russians to send a caravan of not more than 200 camels to Peking every three years and to establish an Orthodox mission of four priests and six students of the Chinese language in the capital city. These agreements, providing for the settlement of the boundaries and for commercial relations, lasted until 1858.

Excluded from the Amur valley, Russian activity in Siberia and the northern Pacific remained of necessity limited. The government supported and equipped voyages of discovery and exploration in the region, but little was done to develop or to settle the vast and inhospitable territory. As in the earlier period, the initiative for the extension of Russian activity came from private individuals, traders, soldiers, and adventurers. In 1799 Alaska was reached, and subsequently expeditions were sent down the Pacific coast of North America. In every case only a very limited number of men participated in these operations, which, because of the nature of the territory, involved little more than the occupation of lands that were either uninhabited or occupied by extremely primitive tribes. The Russian government, although willing to accept lands and sources of income that were offered without cost or danger to its European policies, was nevertheless extremely reluctant to take any steps that might lead to international complications, particularly in an area where it had no vital interests at stake.

The further development of the Siberian lands was, throughout the eighteenth and nineteenth centuries, limited by three factors: the lack of adequate communications, the bitter climate, and the difficulty of acquiring sufficient provisions. These problems led to a consideration of the advisability of acquiring the Amur river valley, despite the treaties with China. It was hoped that communications with the Pacific could be improved and that food for future settlements could be grown. The inauguration of an energetic, aggressive policy began with the appointment of Nicholas Muraviev in 1847 as governor-general of eastern Siberia. Without consulting his government, Muraviev proceeded to establish posts along the Amur on what was legally Chinese territory. He also sent an expedition to the island of Sakhalin. His activities met with little approval in St. Petersburg. Nesselrode did not want to involve his country in complications in the Far East. However, in moving against China at this time Russia was in fact paralleling the imperial policies of the western nations. In 1842, after the Opium War, the Chinese had been forced to open their trade to the European powers.

After the Crimean War the renewed conflict of the British and French with China in 1857 and 1858 allowed Russia the opportunity of legalizing and extending her conquests. In 1858 Muraviev signed the Treaty of Aigun with a local Chinese commander, who was in fact not authorized to conclude such an agreement. This treaty gave Russia territory on the north bank of the Amur and provided for a joint occupation of the Ussuri region. At the same time Admiral Putiatin negotiated the Treaty of Tientsin with the Chinese government, which extended to Russia the same commercial privileges that had previously been extorted by the British, French, and American governments. In 1860, N. P. Ignatiev, who was the Russian representative in

ASIA (RUSSIA AND CHINA) IN 1860

Peking, used the desperate situation of the Chinese government to gain the highly advantageous Treaty of Peking. Here the territorial provisions of the Treaty of Aigun were confirmed and, in addition, Russia received the enormous stretch of territory between the Amur, the Ussuri, and the Pacific Ocean. New trading privileges were also granted. With the acquisition of this land the Russian government proceeded with the construction of Vladivostok, which, since it was frozen only from December to March, allowed them more favorable port facilities on the Pacific. With the opening of the Suez canal in 1869, the voyage from Odessa to Vladivostok was reduced to forty-five days.

The acquisition of the Amur territory and the extended trading rights did not, however, result in an immediate development of the Siberian region. The great problems of food and transportation remained unsolved. The middle course of the great river remained covered with ice an average of 173 days of the year; the land did not prove suitable for the growing of adequate provisions. The government, moreover, showed little interest in promoting the colonization of the land or its real economic development. The long journey overland remained an immense obstacle. Because of the extreme hardship of travel by land, trade and passenger service between Russia and her Pacific lands remained primarily by sea.

Although the Amur question was settled peacefully and to the Russian advantage because of western pressure on China, a second dispute involving another sector of the long and turbulent Russo-Chinese border, threatened to end in war between the two countries. In 1862 a revolt broke out among the Mohammedan tribes in Chinese Turkestan where the peoples were of the same racial stock as those in Russian Turkestan. Their able leader, Yakub Beg, was able to establish a regularly organized state. The British government sent a mission to his court and his troops received training from British and Polish officers. The inability of the Chinese government to control the situation alarmed the Russian government because of the possible effect of the movement on its own tribesmen. The strategic importance of the area, the Ili valley, was immense, since this was the great "Gateway of the Peoples" through which the early invasions of Russia had flowed. In 1871 Russian troops entered the territory and occupied Kuldja. At the same time they assured the Chinese government that the move was only a temporary measure. In 1877-1878 the Chinese troops were able to put down the rebellion, and they then requested that the Russian armies withdraw.

In the winter of 1878 the Chinese delegate, Chung-hou, arrived in Russia for nine months of negotiations. On September 15, 1879 the Treaty of Livadia was signed, which constituted a major Russian triumph. Russia received most of the territory in question, including control of the passes through the Tien Shan mountains, an indemnity of 5 million roubles for the expenses of the occupation, and increased commercial privileges. When the Chinese diplomat reached home with this unfavorable document, he was promptly imprisoned and condemned to death. Although the sentence was subsequently commuted after widespread protests abroad, China did not accept the treaty and prepared for war. At the same time a new delegate, Marquis Tseng, was sent to St. Petersburg to negotiate a revised settlement.

The crisis over the Kuldja territory placed the Russian government in a difficult position. The primary Russian interests were, as always, clearly in Europe and at the Straits. The Russo-Turkish War of 1878 had just been concluded, and again Russian military weaknesses had been exposed. Although the possession of the Kuldja territory would give Russia a welcome strategic advantage, she was not in a condition to go to war over the question. Therefore, in the negotiations that now commenced, considerations of prestige and commerce were placed first. In the final Treaty of St. Petersburg of February 24, 1881, Russia accepted a much reduced territory, but received instead an increased indemnity of 9 million roubles as well as added commercial privileges. The entire incident, despite the final Chinese victory, embittered the relations of the two nations for the next years. Moreover, the Chinese, having now apparently imposed their will upon a European power, became more confident. They had, it seemed, as the British ambassador in St. Petersburg concluded, in fact achieved much: "China has compelled Russia to do what she has never done before, disgorge territory that she had once absorbed." [3]

During the reign of Alexander II, the Russians also attempted to come into closer commercial and political relations with Japan. In 1855 in the Treaty of Shimoda, which was patterned after the pact made between the United States and Japan of the previous year, they did receive the right to trade at three ports. The agreement also provided for a division of the Kurile Islands and a joint occupation of Sakhalin. In 1875 this treaty was modified, and Japan surrendered her claims to Sakhalin in return for full control of the islands. In general at this time the relations of the two countries remained good, although limited in extent.

The gains in territory made in the Far East were to an extent balanced by the liquidation of the Russian possessions on the North American continent with the sale of Alaska in 1867. The American settlements had been set up and administered by the Russian-American company, which had been chartered in 1799 in order to exploit the fur trade of Alaska and the North Pacific. In the reign of Alexander I, the company had extended its activities down the California coast. The establishment of Fort Ross in 1812 marked the furthest point of extension. The Pacific undertakings of the company had first met with the opposition of the Spanish government, later with that of Britain and America. Not only did these activities threaten international complications, but the affairs of the company itself did not prosper. Fort Ross was finally sold in 1841.

The Russian government, which at no time showed much interest in the North American territories, after the Crimean War decided that the possessions could not be defended. During the war a Franco-British squadron attacked Petropavlovsk, and it was quite apparent that the weak Russian Pacific fleet could not protect Alaska. Moreover, Russian-American relations were quite good, due principally to the fact that at the time both the United States and Russia were in conflict with Britain. The

3. Demetrius C. Boulger, *The Life of Sir Halliday MacCartney* (London: J. Lane, 1908), p. 351.

Russian government thus entertained the hope that the sale of Alaska would both increase the friction between Britain and the United States and also win Russia a friend on the Pacific. Negotiations, which commenced in 1854, ended in 1867 with the purchase of Alaska by the United States for $7,200,000.

2. The Middle East

Parallel to the Russian expansion in the Far East, the 1860's also witnessed the inauguration of an active policy of conquest and annexation in Central Asia. In contrast to those in the Far East, these conquests involved military operations. Moreover, in this field the Russian foreign office and the military stood in direct conflict. The military commanders in the field, usually with the support of their superiors in St. Petersburg, favored an aggressive, forward policy, but they were usually opposed by the foreign ministry, which saw clearly the dangers of such activities for its policy in Europe and, in particular, for its relations with Britain. The chief military problem for Russia in the area remained what it had always been—the difficulty of controlling a border territory inhabited by nomadic, semi-barbarous tribes. In 1864 in an attempt to enclose the Kazakh steppe, two forces were sent out, one from Orenburg and another from Semipalatinsk. In September the two columns finally joined in an assault on Chimkent. The entire area was then joined to Russia under the governorship of General Cherniaev. With the conquest of the steppe, the Russian forces now found themselves confronted with the three relatively settled communities of Khiva, Bokhara, and Kokand. In an effort to calm foreign apprehensions of future Russian actions, Gorchakov on November 21, 1864 issued a statement intended to pacify the powers. He explained that the Russian actions had been made necessary by the need to acquire a settled frontier, and he gave assurance that further advances would not be undertaken because the assimilation of territory occupied by "more regularly constituted states, would exact considerable efforts and would draw us from annexation to annexation into infinite complications. . . ."[4]

This policy, however, proved impossible to maintain. Not only were the ambitious Russian generals on the scene difficult to control, but the political leadership of the three khanates also proved unstable. Further advances were embarked upon almost at once. In 1865 Cherniaev took Tashkent; three years later General Kaufmann captured Samarkand. By 1869 both Bokhara and Kokand had become Russian protectorates. In 1873 a large expedition under General Kaufmann was sent against Khiva, and that state too became a Russian protectorate. In 1876, after an uprising, the territory of Kokand was formally annexed to Russia.

With the subjugation of the khanates, the attention of the Russian commanders next turned to Transcaspia, a territory also inhabited by nomadic peoples, the Tekke Turkomans. Again the chief intention of the action was to achieve a settled, stable boundary. In 1877 serious operations were commenced in the region, and in 1881 the Turkoman capital, Geok Tepe, fell to General M. D. Skobelev, who was to become one of the great popular military heroes. The subsequent extension of Russian military conquests and the fall of Merv in 1884 brought the Russian armies closer to the Indian border and to the buffer territory of Afghanistan. From this time onward relations with Britain became increasingly tense, and in 1885 a major crisis developed between Britain and Russia over this area.

The period when the official Russian policy was, therefore, that of *recueillement* had thus in fact resulted in the acquisition of great stretches of territory in the east. It is to be noted, however, that during the reign of Alexander II these advances were made only when they involved no danger of a war with a major military power. Territory was taken from China when that state was pressed by the west; when Peking threatened to fight over Kuldja, Russia backed down. The middle eastern khanates, mili-

4. Richard A. Pierce, *Russian Central Asia, 1867-1917* (Berkeley: University of California Press, 1960), p. 20.

CENTRAL ASIA IN 1895

tarily extremely weak, were conquered, but Alaska was sold when it was judged indefensible. The Russian policy of maximum acquisition with minimum risk was also shown in the attitude taken toward the unauthorized actions of individual Russian commanders. Undoubtedly, Russian officers did often violate instructions in their activities on the frontiers. When their actions, although contrary to orders, were successful, the government was not hesitant about taking advantage of the gains. Since medals and promotions went to the successful, the general or officer in command in a territory was certainly encouraged to press forward. Russian conquest and the occupation of disputed territory thus proceeded without a definite plan or pattern and with little constructive direction from St. Petersburg.

With the conquest of the khanates and the Transcaspian lands Russia acquired what was in fact a colonial area adjacent to her own territory. Although great hopes were held for the possibilities of the economic exploitation of the area, particularly as a source of raw cotton to avoid the British monopoly, these expectations were not immediately fulfilled. The reluctance of the ministries of foreign affairs and finance to become enthusiastic over the eastern conquests is quite understandable under the circumstances of the time. The new lands in the Middle and the Far East, all of Siberia in fact, were difficult to defend and were economically unprofitable for the government unless further huge sums were invested in their development. Since finance was the major problem of the Russian government, the treasury had difficulty enough providing for internal needs and the defense of the vital western frontiers without acquiring new burdens in Asia. The outer fringes of the Russian Empire could thus never play the major role in Russian policy that, for instance, India played in the determination of British actions. The colonial areas thus had a relatively minor place in the formulation of general policy.

In addition, in the nineteenth century the eastern frontiers never succeeded in engaging the interest of the politically significant sections of the Russian public as did the west and the Near East. The defense of the Russian western frontier was vital to the very existence of the Russian state; official Russia felt itself, and, indeed, was, a part of European civilization. The Near East also attracted Russian attention and interest not only because of the power considerations of the area but also because of the pull of past Byzantine and Orthodox tradition. Constantinople, rather than Samarkand, Delhi, and Peking, held the imagination of the Russian and awakened his passionate enthusiasm. For this reason, the wars and the conquests of the east, although they did make military heroes of the generals involved, did not balance in the Russian mind the humiliation of the defeat of the Crimean War or the extension of Prussian power in northern Germany. Russian prestige, severely shaken by the events of 1856, thus demanded a victory in the Near East or continental Europe, not the acquisition of additional eastern territories.

THE RUSSO-TURKISH WAR OF 1877-1878

Although the Russian government did secure much new land in Asia and the abrogation of the Black Sea clauses of the Treaty of Paris, it was also quite clear by 1875 that Russia had for almost twenty years played the role of a bystander in the great events of Europe. Leadership in continental policy had been assumed first by Paris and after 1870 by Berlin. The great accomplishment of the past decade, the unification of Germany, had been carried out with Russian approval, but without the control of events shown in 1849 and 1850. Moreover, although Gorchakov was able to play the role of arbiter in 1875, it had become apparent that the united Germany under Bismarck was not the compliant Prussia of the earlier period. The faithful friend and true ally of the days of Alexander I and Nicholas I had become the greatest single military power of the continent.

Russia had originally adopted the policy of *recueillement*, as has been emphasized, in order to concentrate on domestic reform. Although great changes were accomplished in the internal organization of the state and in the status of the majority of the people, these events had brought in their train severe dislocation and discontent. Since criticism of internal affairs was judged dangerous to the government, more freedom of comment on foreign policy was allowed as a safety valve. Public attention was then drawn away from failures at home, and popular feeling could find expression in attacks on other governments and not direct its attention to the methods and policies of the autocratic regime.

Those who disliked the policy of abstention from European affairs, therefore, were able to express their views in print. The Russian foreign ministry thus found itself increasingly under open attack from those in the Russian public and government who wished the resumption of a glorious national policy.

The program of Gorchakov and the foreign ministry remained after the unification that which it had before—the policy of *recueillement*. Gorchakov's chief assistant during the major part of his career as foreign minister, A. G. Jomini, summarized this policy in 1876: "Russia has been unified for a long time in her greatness and her national unity. Her territorial security is perfectly in order due to her defensive resources and to the lessons she has given invaders. What is now necessary is the development of her internal life, her productive resources, her prosperity, her culture, her commerce, her industry—all things which require peace. Her foreign policy should thus be purely preventative and defensive." [5] Although this course of action was indeed the wisest for Russia, the problem remained whether it could be maintained. The danger lay in what Jomini described as "*l'affreux chaos oriental*," where Russian prestige, historical tradition, and national power were alike involved.

During the reign of Alexander II the moderate policies advocated by the foreign ministry were often under attack by many nationally minded groups and individuals, but the place of prominence, certainly in foreign eyes, was occupied by the Panslavs. Although this term was used to designate men of widely varying beliefs, the Panslavs all reacted strongly against the negative role that had been previously played in foreign affairs and called for the resumption of an active program in which Russia would exploit her position as the greatest of the Slavic nations. In the reign of Nicholas I, the Slavophils, with their emphasis on the unique qualities of Russia in comparison to the west, had been precursors of the movement. Their ideas received little sympathy from

5. *Russia in the East, 1876-1880: the Letters of A. G. Jomini to N. K. Giers*, edited by Charles and Barbara Jelavich (Leiden: Brill, 1959), p. 44.

official quarters since both Nicholas I and Nesselrode could not well support a doctrine that would threaten the continued existence of the Holy Alliance. Russia also in their opinion was part of, and not apart from, Europe, and they could not favor an idea having revolutionary implications.

The defeat of the Crimean War, with its severe blow to the Russian national pride and the resultant reaction against the predominance of the German element in the administration, provided a good background for any program that would emphasize Russian power and leadership. The goal of all the Panslavs, although their individual programs differed, was the assumption by Russia of the leadership of the Slavic peoples; their liberation from foreign, that is Habsburg and Turkish, control; and their organization into political units closely allied to St. Petersburg. In 1858 the Moscow Slavic Benevolent Society was founded. Its aim was to assist the southern Slavs of the Ottoman Empire to achieve their freedom from Moslem control. This organization brought to Russia students from the Balkans, chiefly from Bulgaria, and carried on activities of a publicist and educational nature. Branches were later opened in St. Petersburg and Kiev. In 1867 the Moscow branch held a Slavic Ethnographical Exhibition which attracted attention in the west. The goals and general beliefs of these and related groups won the interest and support of influential individuals in the Russian court and society. Moreover, gifted and influential writers and journalists were drawn into the service of the cause.

In addition, the program of the Panslavs did correspond well with the Russian actual position in the Balkans. After the Peace of Paris Russia could no longer pose as the sole protector of Orthodox Christianity since the treaty specifically assigned that role to the powers together. Moreover, by 1870 the major non-Slavic Orthodox peoples, the Greeks and Rumanians, had been freed from Turkish rule. The next territories in question were those inhabited by Serbian, Bulgarian, and Montenegrin peoples —all of whom were Slavic. Although religious unity remained a consideration of policy, the emphasis could now be shifted to the racial tie with Russia. A program calling for a common policy among the Slavic peoples could also be used by Russia as a practical foreign policy weapon against both Austria-Hungary and Britain.

The ideas of the Panslavs naturally aroused the fears of the other powers. The British could not allow the establishment of a great Slavic state; the Austrians saw the program quite correctly as directed toward the destruction of the Danubian Monarchy. The two writers who obtained the widest public attention, R. A. Fadeev and N. Ia. Danilevsky, did indeed express opinions that were bound to arouse apprehension. In his book, *Opinion on the Eastern Question*, published in 1867, Fadeev argued that Russia should seek the destruction of both the Ottoman and the Austrian empires—that the road to Constantinople lay through Vienna. He emphasized the eternal enmity of Slav and Teuton and prescribed a solution by force. Danilevsky, in *Russia and Europe*, which appeared in the same year, pictured the great struggle of Roman-Germans against the Slavs. He too favored Russian leadership in the liberation of the Slavs and he called for a great Slav federation with Constantinople as the capital. Two of the foremost Russian journalists, I. S. Aksakov and M. N. Katkov, also joined the ranks of the Panslav publicists. Through the writings of these and other men the ideas of Panslavism received a wide audience in Russia and commanded the respect especially of those who believed that Russia should embark upon a glorious national policy.

The outbreak of a revolt among the peasants of Hercegovina in 1875 once again opened the eastern question and created conditions in which the nationalist and the Panslav could exert a strong influence on foreign relations. Although the new eastern crisis was in many ways similar to those in the past in that it was again caused by the revolt of the Balkan Christians against Moslem misrule, the general European diplomatic situation had profoundly changed. Austria-Hungary, now excluded from central Europe, showed a greater interest in Balkan affairs and a willingness to acquire new territory and influence. Moreover, well aware that the program of the extreme Panslavs would result in the breakup of their state, the Austrian and Magyar statesmen regarded St. Petersburg with renewed suspicion and distrust. In addition, contrary to the hopes of the Russian government, Prussia-Germany after 1870 proved a worse and not a better ally in the eastern question, due principally to the altered relationship of Vienna and Berlin after 1870. Since with the incorporation of Alsace-Lorraine into the empire, it could be assumed that, henceforth, France would remain a national enemy, Germany could not afford to estrange Austria because of that nation's strategic position. For the same reason Germany also could not allow a severe defeat or weakening of the Habsburg Monarchy that would eliminate that state from the ranks of the great powers since such an occurrence, given the French position, would put Berlin at the mercy of St. Petersburg. German policy in the Balkans, which was thus determined by considerations of general European interest, led her in the future to aid Austrian attempts to confine Russian power and to prevent the acquisition by Russia of significant gains in the area. This was not the role that Russia had envisioned for the unified Germany.

In the face of the new uprising of a Slavic Christian people, the Russian government, as in past crises, had two alternatives of action—it could follow a policy of co-operation with other governments, or at least with its allies in the Three Emperors' League; or it could seek to deal with Turkey alone. In this situation Alexander II, who made the final decisions, received conflicting advice. The foreign ministry, under the increasingly feeble and senile leadership of Gorchakov, the ministry of finance under Reutern, and also the ministry of war under Miliutin, throughout the crisis all advised caution. These men were chiefly concerned with the progress of the great reforms, and being in responsible offices they saw that Russia was in no condition to launch a war or adopt dangerous courses of action. They were opposed within their own departments and in the government in general by those with nationalist and Panslav convictions who wished Russia to resume an active policy. Of particular importance was Ignatiev because of his position as ambassador at Constantinople; his policies also received the strong endorsement of the tsar's brother, Grand Duke Michael. At the beginning of the crisis the moderate elements were able to maintain control, and Russia entered into negotiations with Germany and Austria-Hungary to attempt to solve the Balkan problem by peaceful mediation.

From 1875 to 1877 the powers therefore made repeated attempts to calm the revolt by compromise and by advocating programs of reform. The situation was further complicated by the attitude of the British minister Disraeli who wished to exploit the crisis in order to break the Three Emperors' League. As long as this coalition existed, he recognized: "There is no balance, and unless we go out of our way to act with the three Northern Powers, they can act without us, which is not agreeable for a state like England." [6] The British attitude tended to encourage Turkish resistance and therefore to make a negotiated settlement more difficult. The initiative for reform came always from the conservative powers.

The first of a series of reform proposals was drawn up by a consular commission in August, 1875. When these failed to secure acceptance, Andrassy, in December, 1875, issued with Bismarck's approval a program providing for land and tax reform and religious equality. Although the Porte accepted the note, the insurgents did not. In May, 1876 Gorchakov, Bismarck, and Andrassy together formulated the Berlin Memorandum. Here the conditions of the Andrassy note were restated, and an armistice of two months was suggested. France and Italy also accepted these terms, but Britain rejected them. Disraeli, wishing to make use of the crisis, then ordered the British fleet to Besika Bay. These British moves were interpreted in Constantinople as signifying support, and an intransigent attitude was maintained. Meanwhile, however, the internal situation in the Turkish capital deteriorated. In May, 1875 Sultan Abdul Aziz was replaced by Murad V under circumstances that appeared to foreshadow the breakdown of

6. William Flavelle Monypenny and George Earle Buckle, *The Life of Benjamin Disraeli* (New York: Macmillan, 1920), VI, p. 13.

the state at the center. The events in Constantinople naturally affected the decisions of the leaders of the subject nationalities.

Of the Balkan states Serbia had been most deeply concerned with the ultimate fate of the revolt in Bosnia-Hercegovina, since the declared aim of the insurrectionists was union with their neighbor. Although the Serbians received no official encouragement from the Russian government, they were given enthusiastic support and material assistance by the Russian Panslav circles. The Slavic Benevolent Committee collected funds throughout Russia, and volunteers streamed into Serbia to aid in the liberation of a brother Slavic people. In May, 1876 General Cherniaev, the hero of Tashkent, arrived to take command of the Serbian armies. The entrance of both Serbia and Montenegro into war with Turkey in June and July was thus initially welcomed with hope and approval by those in Russia with strong national or Panslav views. Unfortunately, the first feelings of exhaltation were soon replaced by bitterness and recrimination when it became apparent that the Russian volunteer groups contained a high proportion of misfits and incompetents. Moreover, the Serbian armies soon proved themselves incapable of defeating the Turkish forces. In October, 1876 Russia was forced to intervene to save Serbia by imposing an armistice upon Turkey. Meanwhile, Russian attention and patronage was turning increasingly to another South Slav nation, the Bulgarians. Henceforth it was to be on these peoples, and not on the Serbs, that the Russians were to base their Balkan policy.

In the period after the Crimean War the Bulgarians, even more than the Serbians, had enjoyed the particular attention of the Panslavs. The Moscow Slavic Benevolent Committee had been most active in educational efforts on their behalf; with Russian support the Bulgarian church was able in 1870-72 to separate from the Greek-dominated Patriarchate of Constantinople and to form its own national ecclesiastical organization, the Bulgarian Exarchate. The Bulgarians, like the Serbs, were thus encouraged to look to Russia for aid against the Ottoman Empire. In 1876 the Bulgarians joined in the insurrection, but with little success. In their effort to repress the revolt, Turkish irregular troops committed a series of atrocities, which aroused all of the powers; over 10,000 Bulgarians were reported killed. The massacre greatly increased the pressure on the Russian government to assist the Balkan Slavic people. A similar reaction took place in London after the publication in 1876 of Gladstone's pamphlet, *Bulgarian Horrors*, which denounced Turkish misrule in eloquent terminology.

During this period, when the uprising against the Porte spread through the Turkish lands, the powers had continued to negotiate. Since the attitude of Austria-Hungary remained of crucial concern for Russian policy, Gorchakov again sought to come to terms with that power. In the Reichstadt Convention of July, 1876, it was agreed that should Serbia be defeated in the war with Turkey, the two powers would intervene to restore the *status quo* and to try to obtain administrative reform. Should, however, the Turkish armies be defeated, a real partition of the empire was to be effected, but no large Balkan state was to be erected. Bulgaria, Rumelia, and Albania were to be established as autonomous states; Constantinople was to be a free city. Russia was to acquire southern Bessarabia and territory in Asia Minor; Austria-Hungary, for its share, would receive Bosnia-Hercegovina. Greece would be given Thessaly and Crete.

Despite this agreement the Russian government remained unsure of its diplomatic position. Its two principal opponents in eastern affairs remained the Dual Monarchy and Britain. The Crimean War had shown that Vienna could not be relied upon. Moreover, Bismarck at this time made it quite clear that if a war should occur between Austria and Russia, he would not allow Habsburg power to be crushed. Germany thus would not return in kind the Russian favors of 1866 and 1870. The Russian option for Prussia in central Europe would not be repaid by support for Russian policy in the east at the expense of the Danubian Monarchy.

Meanwhile, the diplomatic negotiations continued, although few concrete results were obtained. In December, 1876 a conference of ambassadors in Constantinople produced yet another reform proposal, which the Porte again rejected. The attitude of the Porte and the failure of powers increased the pressure of those in Russia who favored a war with Turkey. The circumstances of 1828 were thus again in effect; since the great powers could not bring about a settlement by negotiation, the only alternative appeared to be a solution by force and a Russo-Turkish war. To provide for this event the Russian government concluded two more agreements with the Dual Monarchy. In January, 1877 the Budapest Convention was signed, which provided for the maintenance of an attitude of benevolent neutrality by Vienna in return for the provinces of Bosnia and Herce-govina. In March a further agreement was concluded, which, in general, reaffirmed the provisions of the Treaty of Reichstadt. Despite these documents, which cleared the way for a Russian conflict with the Ottoman Empire, relations between Vienna and St. Petersburg remained tense and suspicious. After a final attempt by the powers to find a peaceful solution met with failure, Russia on April 24 declared war on Turkey.

Throughout the war the chief danger for Russia came from Britain, the power with the greatest interest in the maintenance of the Ottoman Empire and the possible organizer of a coalition against Russia. Certainly Disraeli and many in Britain were eager and willing to accept another open trial of strength. The central question at issue between St. Petersburg and London remained, as it had been throughout the century, that of the control of Constantinople and the Turkish Straits. On June 30, 1877, when the Russian armies crossed the Danube, the British fleet was ordered to Besika Bay. A condition of acute tension existed between Russia and Britain from the beginning of the crisis until the Congress of Berlin, which met one year later.

Because of the general diplomatic conditions, the Russian government, when embarking upon the war, expected and hoped for a quick victory in their campaign in the Balkans. An agreement was signed with Rumania in April, 1877, which provided for the Russian transit across the country in return for a guarantee of

Rumanian territorial integrity. Although the Rumanian government offered supporting troops, Russia only accepted their use later in the war and after military failures of its own. With the outbreak of the fighting the direction of policy in Russia became divided and confused because of the conditions under which the war was fought and the split of the government into three sections. The tsar accompanied his army into the field, where he soon fell under the influence of the nationalist and Panslav military groups as well as of Ignatiev, who joined him there. Gorchakov, too old and feeble for camp life, remained in Bucharest, largely excluded from affairs of state despite his official capacity as foreign minister. Routine business was handled by N. K. Giers in the foreign ministry in St. Petersburg.

Despite initial optimistic hopes, the Turkish campaign brought no triumphant progress toward Constantinople. As in the Crimean War and the Russo-Turkish War of 1828, grave faults were soon apparent in the organization and conduct of the campaign. A real disaster was suffered at Plevna in July and September. Nevertheless, the Russian forces were finally able to defeat the even less efficient Turkish army. In December Plevna fell, and on January 20 Adrianople was taken. Once again, as in 1829, Russian armies stood at the gates of Constantinople, and a decision had to be taken concerning the fate of the Ottoman Empire. The issues remained what they had been in the previous eastern crises: how far Russia could extend her power and control in the Near East without provoking the formation of a hostile coalition and a major war?

On January 31, 1878 an armistice was signed between Russia and Turkey and negotiations for a settlement commenced. Britain, apprehensive over the fate of the Porte, in February despatched her fleet into the Dardanelles. On March 3, 1878 the belligerent states finally agreed on the terms of peace. The Treaty of San Stefano, whose content was largely influenced by the ideas of Ignatiev, created conditions in the Balkans that appeared to assure future Russian control of the Ottoman Empire. Although Russia did not take either the Straits or Constantinople, the agreement provided for the creation of a great Bulgarian state extending from the Black Sea to the Aegean and dominating the Straits. It was assumed by the powers that this Greater Bulgaria would be a Russian vassal state. The new Bulgaria was to be given an elected prince and an assembly and to be allowed to maintain a militia. A Russian army of occupation was to remain in the country for two years. Other stipulations in the treaty provided for territorial gains for the other Balkan states, but no mention was made of the Austrian acquisition of Bosnia-Hercegovina, despite the treaties that had been concluded before the war. The peace thus both violated previous international agreements, and it signified an upset of the power balance in the Balkans, which neither Britain nor Austria-Hungary could accept.

The reaction of the powers to San Stefano made it apparent to the Russian government that insistence on its maintenance could lead to a war against a hostile coalition. The attitude of Germany was made clear through previous statements on the necessity of maintaining the Danubian Monarchy. Although there was in March and April much enthusiasm for resistance, Alexander finally allowed himself to be convinced, by arguments emphasizing Russian military and financial weakness, that Russia must retreat. In the second half of May, Ignatiev left office, and his influence was replaced by that of the conciliatory and moderate Peter Shuvalov, who represented the views of the foreign ministry. It was he, therefore, who was sent to London to try to arrange terms with the British government. In the Protocol of May 30 the major problem was settled by the Russian abandonment of the scheme of the establishment of a great Bulgaria. The British government simultaneously scored a second diplomatic triumph. Using the extreme weakness of the Porte, Britain forced upon that government, on June 4, the Cyprus Convention, which compensated London for the Russian gains in the war. In return for a pledge that Britain would guarantee its Asiatic territories, the Ottoman Empire ceded the strategic Mediterranean island. In prep-

aration for the forthcoming congress, Britain also made an agreement with Austria to the effect that both would co-operate at
the meeting. It was thus Britain, not Russia, that held the highest
cards in the coming weeks.

On June 13 the third great European congress of the century
opened in Berlin under the presidency of Prince Bismarck. The
great powers were again represented by their chief ministers:
Disraeli and Salisbury for Britain, Andrassy for Austria-Hungary,
Waddington for France, and Corti for Italy. Although Gorchakov
went as the chief Russian delegate, the burden of the negotiation was taken by Peter Shuvalov. The final agreement, signed
one month later, restored the balance of power in the Near
East. Since the main lines of settlement had been drawn by
private arrangements prior to the congress, the delegates did
little more than implement the previous agreements. The principal question of concern, the fate of Greater Bulgaria, was
met by a division of the territory into three sections. The first,

Bulgaria proper, became an autonomous principality; the second, Eastern Rumelia, was placed under a Christian governor and was to be semi-autonomous. The third section, the Macedonian lands, was returned to Turkish rule. It was assumed by the powers that Russia would dominate the autonomous Bulgaria but that her influence would only be equal to that of the other powers in Rumelia. Russia received, in addition to her right of preponderant influence in Bulgaria, southern Bessarabia, Kars, Ardahan, and Batum, which was to be made into a free port. To compensate for the Russian acquisitions, Bosnia-Hercegovina was handed over to Austro-Hungarian occupation and administration. If Vienna had at the time pressed for the annexation of the provinces, her wishes would undoubtedly have been met. Andrassy, however, reflecting Magyar views, was not eager to secure the inclusion of more Slavic peoples in the Danubian empire.

The Berlin settlement also brought about other great changes in the map of the Balkans. Although each state received some increase in territory, these gains were satisfactory to none, and therefore led to further minor conflicts. Montenegro, Serbia, and Rumania received additional lands along with full independence from the Porte. Montenegro was almost doubled in size, and in 1881 received access to the sea with the acquisition of the port of Dulcigno. The assignment of two purely Albanian districts to Montenegro resulted in an uprising in the area and a return of the districts to Moslem rule. Rumania, deprived of southern Bessarabia in direct violation of the Russo-Rumanian agreement of 1877, received in consolation the poorer, non-Rumanian territory of Dobrudja. Greece, who was promised a border rectification in the treaty, eventually acquired Thessaly and a part of Epirus. Serbia, now abandoned by Russia, turned to Vienna for diplomatic support. Blocked from expansion westward by the Austrian occupation of Bosnia-Hercegovina, her aspirations were directed southward and she was given Pirot and Niš.

Although the engagements of 1856 and 1871 in regard to the Straits were reaffirmed in the Treaty of Berlin, the congress witnessed a major development in the question. On July 11 Salisbury made this statement: "The obligations of Her Britannic Majesty relating to the closing of the Straits do not go further than an engagement with the sultan to respect in this matter His Majesty's independent determinations in conformity with the spirit of existing treaties." The exact meaning of the declaration was vague, but it did signify that Britain would honor the closing of the Straits at her convenience. The determination of whether the sultan was acting independently or under Russian influence would be made in London. The Russian delegate immediately responded that the closure of the Straits was a European principle, binding on all, and that it was not subject to unilateral interpretation. The British action, which nullified the security that Russia had gained through the international agreements, caused great concern in Russia. Thereafter it was necessary to seek additional diplomatic support to maintain the Russian position on the problem.

Despite the fact that Russia had indeed gained much in the treaty with the establishment of a satellite Bulgaria, the reannexation of southern Bessarabia, and the acquisitions in Asia Minor, the final treaty was interpreted in Russia as a great defeat. When compared with the wilder aspirations of the Panslavs, it was certainly not a diplomatic victory, but it is doubtful if more could have been achieved under the circumstances. Gorchakov, sensing the popular reaction, pushed as much of the responsibility on Shuvalov, his fellow delegate, as possible. The chief scapegoat, however, for the anger of the Russian public became Bismarck, the "honest broker" of the Berlin Congress. Although he had usually voted with Russia at the meetings, Germany, under his leadership, had not played the role that Russia wished her to play. Berlin had not been the firm and faithful ally of Russia against the other powers in the eastern question; the unification of Germany had not freed Russia from the nightmare of a hostile coalition. Also, instead of Gorchakov playing arbiter between France and Germany, Bismarck had sat as judge in a contest between Russia and her opponents. Thus, after the Congress of Berlin, there occurred much the same shift in opinion that had taken place after the previous congress at Paris. Russian animosity became directed not at Britain, the chief competitor, but at a German power which had previously been regarded as a friend and ally. The Russian reaction against Berlin was expressed in a press war in the spring of 1879 and in a series of minor incidents. In August, 1879 the tsar wrote the kaiser an angry letter, but the two rulers subsequently met and patched up the quarrel. However, the basic theme of the Panslav, the inevitable conflict of Slav and German, appeared to receive justification. Although the Panslavs as a body of opinion were never to exert the same influence on the formulation of foreign policy, the Balkan crisis left bitter feelings behind and helped establish a frame of mind that later was to have unfortunate results.

The Congress of Berlin and the eastern crisis had thus accomplished Disraeli's objective of the breaking of the Three Emperors' League. Gorchakov and those with similar convictions in the foreign ministry now called for a return to the policy of *recueillement* and noninterference in European affairs. They wished to ally with no power, but to maintain a program of "free hands" and isolation. This proud policy appealed to the nationalist, but it was not practical under the circumstances. The Russo-Turkish War, like the Crimean War, although it ended in victory, again demonstrated Russian military weakness. Moreover, two immediate dangers faced the Russian government after the congress. In the treaty, the Porte had been given the right to send troops into eastern Rumelia. The Russian government feared that if this action were carried out, it would precipitate another Balkan revolt and a reopening of the eastern question. In addition, the British declaration at the Congress of Berlin brought up again the problem of the closure of the Straits. However, although Russia could ill afford to stand alone, her choice of allies remained limited. Republican France was unacceptable both from a military and an ideological standpoint; Britain as before could not be considered. There remained only the two German courts, Berlin and Vienna, despite the fact that the conservative alliance had not functioned to the Russian satisfaction in the crisis of the 1870's.

Although Gorchakov continued to oppose any agreement with

Austria and Germany, Shuvalov, Giers, and P. A. Saburov, who was to become the Russian ambassador in Berlin, now advocated a renewal of the former diplomatic alignment. The tsar supported the negotiations with the central powers in order to avoid a condition of isolation and also to gain support for the Russian interpretation of the Straits agreements. It was decided at the same time that Russian policy would, thereafter, remain defensive and that the chief concentration would be on the solution of the Russian internal problems. Adventurous actions, such as the Russo-Turkish War had been, were, in the future, to be avoided. The Russian government, therefore, accepted in principle the renewal of the Three Emperors' League. The subsequent negotiations, nevertheless, proceeded slowly because of the hesitant attitude of Austria-Hungary who saw few advantages for herself in the arrangement. The final agreement was not signed until 1881, after Alexander II had been assassinated by a terrorist organization.

*   *   *   *   *

The reign of Alexander II thus witnessed a major re-drawing of the map of Europe and a revolutionary readjustment of the power relationships of the large states of Europe. These years also saw the extension of the Russian boundaries to enclose huge stretches of land in the Middle and Far East. In the Treaty of Berlin, Russia, in addition, reacquired southern Bessarabia and won lands in Asia Minor as well as a protectorate over the new Bulgarian state. In internal affairs a period of major reform and domestic reorganization had been inaugurated. The age of Alexander II was therefore an active and a creative period. Despite the difficulties of readjustment, very substantial gains had been achieved in both foreign and domestic politics. It is interesting to note, however, that despite these obvious successes, the general feeling at the conclusion of the reign of Alexander was not optimistic, particularly in regard to foreign policy. Perhaps the principal cause of the relative disillusionment was the discrepancy between Russian hopes and what had actually been achieved. The great reforms provided no final answer to the domestic crisis; with the rise of radicalism it appeared that more problems had been created than solved. The Russo-Turkish War had again demonstrated that in comparison with the other powers Russia was not in a financial and military sense the equal of her competitors. Moreover, the single great national enthusiasm of Alexander's reign had been the crusade in the Balkans for the Christian Slavs. Instead of achieving a victorious and glorious peace, the Russian government had been called before the powers to account for her actions and had been forced to abandon her maximum program, an act humiliating for a major power.

The profound significance of the major event of these years, the unification of Germany, was slow in dawning upon the Russian awareness. This miscalculation, however, was shared by other governments. It was only in the crisis of 1876 to 1878 that it became evident that the new Germany was not the old Prussia. Russia now found on its doorstep a nationally minded, militarily powerful state with an economic, political, and social system far stronger than that of autocratic Russia. The industrialization of Germany, which commenced around 1865 and became fully apparent in the 1890's, increased the military differential between the two states. Central Europe, which in the days of Alexander I and Nicholas I had been a virtual power vacuum, could now no longer be controlled from St. Petersburg. As long as Bismarck directed German policy, the consequences of the change were not wholly detrimental to Russia. Educated in the Prussian tradition and fully aware of the need for Russo-German friendship, Bismarck endeavored throughout his career to maintain the old conservative alignment. It was thus only during the reign of Alexander III that the full significance of the new situation was finally realized.

V

Alexander III

Alexander III, who ascended the throne in 1881, ruled for the relatively short term of thirteen years. Nevertheless, his reign was to bring about a basic realignment in Russian foreign policy. Influenced by the horrible events of his father's assassination, Alexander III, in his internal policies, abandoned further reform and returned to the reactionary system of Nicholas I. The last of the Russian autocrats, the tsar, upon assuming power, rejected the draft of a constitution that had been approved by his father, thus blocking the further immediate political evolution of the country. In foreign affairs, he did, however, favor the continuation of the negotiations that led to a re-formation of the conservative alliance with Vienna and Berlin.

Born in 1845, Alexander III was the second son of Alexander II. When his brother Nicholas died of tuberculosis in 1865, he became the heir to the throne. He also later married his brother's fiancée, the Danish Princess Dagmar, the daughter of Christian IX. Of only moderate abilities and retiring in manner, Alexander preferred to live a life of calm and retirement with his family at Gachina away from the world of politics in St. Petersburg. Because he was not expected to inherit the throne, his training had not been as intensive as that of his brother, but he had in the persons of the historian Soloviev and his tutor Pobedonostsev two able teachers. Pobedonostsev, in particular, influenced the formation of the tsar's political ideas in a strongly conservative direction. He repeatedly urged Alexander to consider his role as tsar in the paternalistic tradition of that of the father of a family and not to be misled by demands for constitutional reform, which, he argued, was not the true desire of the mass of the people.

To his conservative convictions Alexander III also joined a strong Russian nationalism. In the 1870's he was believed to share the ideas of the Panslavs, but later as tsar he quite obviously did not adhere to their full teachings. Like the Russian nationalists in general he maintained a strong dislike of Austria-Hungary and Britain. In April, 1881 he commented: "I understand only one policy. . . . To exact from every situation all that is needed by and is useful to Russia, to disregard all other considerations, and to act in a straightforward and resolute manner. We can have no policy except one that is purely Russian and national; this is the only policy we can and must follow." [1] Although such remained his intention throughout his reign, it was not always easy to determine what was best for Russian interests. He obviously shared in the enthusiasms of the nationalists. He read with particular interest the articles of the gifted journalist, Katkov, who called for a strong and assertive national policy. His chief advisors, in contrast, were against any adventures abroad. His reign, unique in the annals of the tsars, to the end remained an unbroken period of peace despite the occurrence of severe crises in the Near and Middle East. This condition was made possible by the realization

1. Florinsky, *Russia,* II, p. 1088.

within Russia of her military impotence and by the general desire of all of the powers in the 1880's to avoid armed conflicts.

Throughout his reign Alexander III was associated in foreign policy with one principal minister, N. K. Giers. Although the tsar inherited Gorchakov from his father, that statesman, now in his eighty-third year, was clearly senile and incapable of administering his office. Despite the fact that many expected Alexander III, because of his nationalist leanings, to appoint Ignatiev, he finally in 1882 officially named Giers to the position he had actually held since the Congress of Berlin. The son of a frontier postmaster and of Lutheran, Swedish-German ancestry, Giers rose to high office chiefly through diligent work and moderation of character. His career was immensely aided by his marriage in 1849 to Olga Cantacuzino, a Rumanian and a niece of Gorchakov. He served first in the Danubian Principalities, Egypt, and Persia; later he was the Russian representative in Bern and Stockholm. In 1875 he returned to St. Petersburg as Gorchakov's deputy and Assistant Foreign Minister. In character and training he proved an excellent second for his impulsive and overbearing master. Faced throughout his career by constant opposition, particularly from the nationalists, he was able in general to maintain his position and to keep his country from involvement in conflicts for which it was ill prepared. In foreign policy he favored the program adopted at the end of the reign of Alexander II of the emphasis on internal development and the remaking of the alliance with the conservative powers.

THE REVIVAL OF THE THREE EMPERORS' LEAGUE

Alexander III faced, at the time of his assumption of power, an international situation that, although more favorable than that which his father had met in 1855, had, nevertheless, been profoundly altered by the creation of the united Germany. Berlin, not St. Petersburg or Paris, was now the center of continental diplomacy. Moreover, in Bismarck, the diplomatic genius of the age, the Russian statesmen found a formidable opponent. Fortunately for the tranquillity of central Europe, Bismarck, as one of the chief pillars of his policy, favored the continuation of the close ties between St. Petersburg and Berlin that had characterized Russian-Prussian relations throughout the century. Although the links between the courts were never as strong under Alexander III as they had been during the reign of his father, Bismarck, as long as he remained chancellor, tried to maintain the atmosphere of the Holy Alliance. He continued to insist upon the necessity of co-operation between the conservative powers against the revolution, although these arguments in an era of increasingly competitive nationalism tended to take on a hollow ring.

The treaty marking the renewal of the Three Emperors' League was finally signed on June 18, 1881. The pact obligated the partners to maintain an attitude of benevolent neutrality should one of them become engaged in a war with a third power. In the eastern question they agreed upon a policy of consultation and agreement should changes take place. The three states also declared their adherence to the principle of the European and mutually obligatory character of the Straits settlement. Austria gained the right to annex Bosnia-Hercegovina when an advantageous moment should arise; the three powers agreed not to oppose the eventual union of Bulgaria and Eastern Rumelia. The agreement thus offered advantages to each of the contracting parties. Germany gained the assurance that Russia would not join France should war break out on the Rhine. Russia could now depend on the support of her allies for her interpretation of the closure of the Straits and, in addition, for the eventual unification of the Bulgarias. Austria-Hungary received confirmation of her domination over Bosnia-Hercegovina.

Although the three courts of the Holy Alliance were once again joined by a specific agreement, the basic relationships between the powers had greatly altered. In the 1880's the difficulty experienced in the revival of the alliance was chiefly caused by the changes in the Danubian Monarchy that had been brought about by the unification of Germany and the transformation of the internal structure through the *Ausgleich*. Under the Holy Alliance the three powers had clearly enjoyed a community of interest in central Europe and in their sharing of the lands of partitioned Poland. Moreover, prior to the era of the national unifications each power had primary interests in geographic areas which did not directly conflict with the other partners and where they needed the assistance of their allies. Prussia wished to guard her position and lands on the Rhine against France; Austria was interested in maintaining her domination over the Italian peninsula; Russia had her eastern policy to protect against Britain. However, by 1870 Austria had been expelled from Italy and Germany was dominant on the Rhine. Although Russia still needed allies in the east, she had less to offer in return. Moreover, the Dual Monarchy, who now turned southeast and whose policy was greatly influenced by the Magyar views, had adopted courses of action in the Balkans that would inevitably conflict with those of Russia. The former community of interest of the three northern courts was, therefore, by the reign of Alexander III not what it had once been. The balance of strength between the partners had shifted and the number of issues on which they could render each other assistance had sharply diminished.

In addition, the old bonds of common conservative ideology had lost much of their significance and validity. It is interesting to note that as the tide of revolutionary activity in Russia rose, the role which the prevention of such movements played in Russian foreign policy became submerged. In the period between 1814 and 1854 the Russian support of the principle of intervention in the internal affairs of other states to prevent the overthrow of the legitimate ruler had been predicated on the assumption that it would be Russian armies that would march into other countries in support of their rulers. In that period the Russian government itself was never in the position of having to consider that foreign armies might be called upon to enter St. Petersburg to save the tsar. By the reign of Alexander III it was, however, the Russian ruler who was in danger, but it is certainly impossible to imagine that the tsar would have put his signature to a treaty that would have allowed the armies of Germany and Austria-Hungary to invade Russia in order to suppress a revolution. Yet this basis was the only practical foundation for a real conservative alliance designed for the protection of the monarchical system. By the end of the nineteenth century it was quite clear that the principle of nationalism had triumphed over that of political ideology even in that state which was the one most directly menaced by revolutionary agitation.

It was indeed the power of the national idea that first divided and then broke the alliance of the conservative courts. The belief of the Panslavs in the inevitability of final conflict between Slav and Teuton has already been discussed. Even the moderate Russian nationalists now recognized that Russia could not regain her former position in Europe without a reversal of 1870. Although the unification of Germany had been the right solution for the German people, it had obviously been wrong for the Russian state. The assumptions of the Panslavs of the basic rivalry of Russia with the central powers was shared by influential circles in both Germany and Austria-Hungary. In the Habsburg capital many, particularly among the military, foresaw and prepared for what they were certain would be a great war with Russia over the Balkan and Slavic questions. In Germany, too, similar groups wished a continuation of the active policies of the 1860's and the acquisition of additional territory and power by the new German Empire.

Despite the desire of Bismarck to preserve the lines to St. Petersburg, the position of Germany within the framework of the Three Emperors' League was quite different from that of Prussia in the Holy Alliance. As we have seen, before the Crimean War and the unification of Germany, Berlin had accepted the lead and direction of St. Petersburg in matters of vital importance because of the apparent vast military superiority of Russia. After 1870 united Germany was obviously the stronger power, certainly as long as Russia was not in alliance with France and had not come to terms with Britain. Russia could thus not dictate to

Germany after 1870 in the manner that she had dealt with Prussia in 1850. In addition, although Bismarck supported a Russian alliance, his primary interest was in the preservation of the Habsburg Monarchy. He feared two possibilities: first, that if Austria were defeated in a war that involved Germany, she would then join with France. Russia could thereafter dominate the situation by threatening to join the enemies of Germany in a new Kaunitz coalition. Second, he foresaw that if Russia went to war and defeated Austria, thus removing her from among the states of the first rank, then Germany would be in an equally dangerous position. Thereafter, she would be placed between France and Russia and without a real ally to the south. Isolated on the continent, she would be at the mercy of her neighbors. Bismarck saw quite clearly that the dangerous issue in European diplomacy was that of the eastern question. He would have preferred that Russia and Austria-Hungary simply partition the territory into spheres of influence. When this proved impractical, he attempted to keep his two neighbors in some sort of an alliance arrangement and to restrain both from adventurous policies.

The maintenance of peace in the first part of the reign of Alexander III was immeasurably aided by the determination of the two principal statesmen in Germany and Russia to try to avoid open conflicts and to mediate disagreements. Both Giers and Bismarck shared the belief that the main task for their respective governments was the concentration on internal consolidation and development; they were both opposed by those in their own countries who wished a greater emphasis on foreign policy. Giers in particular had a difficult time because of the strong reaction against Germany after the Congress of Berlin. Even men such as Peter Shuvalov, who had been sympathetic to the German cause, now regretted the French defeat. The Russian attitude was expressed also in the adulation and attention shown those who adopted an openly warlike attitude. The popularity of General Skobelev, the hero of Geok Tepe, who supported a war of Russia against Austria in aid of an uprising that had broken out in Bosnia in 1881, was an example of the popular feeling. The maintenance of a policy of co-operation between the two countries thus became increasingly difficult, despite the basic interest of both states in the maintenance of peace and the preservation of the conservative alliance.

Throughout the duration of the Three Emperors' League, which was renewed in 1884 but finally expired in 1887, Russia was part of a very complicated pattern of alliances devised by Bismarck to control the international situation. Primarily concerned with the protection of the gains of 1866 and 1870, he feared the formation of a coalition of those powers that had been directly injured by the unification of central Europe. Since after the annexation of Alsace-Lorraine France was to be reckoned as definitely in the enemy camp, he took steps to ensure that Paris would not become the center of diplomatic combinations directed against Berlin and would remain, if possible, isolated. The first alliance in what was to be an intricate network was concluded soon after the Congress of Berlin. The Dual Alliance of October 7, 1879 between Germany and Austria-Hungary was a defensive alliance directed against Russia. Should Russia attack either power, the other signatory must come to its partner's assistance. Should Germany become involved in war with France, Austria was obligated only to maintain a benevolent neutrality unless Russia entered. This treaty was renewed periodically and lasted until the outbreak of the war in 1914. It existed parallel with and was not replaced by the subsequent Triple Alliance. The partnership was of particular value to Austria-Hungary, who was now protected against an outright Russian aggression in the Balkans. Having secured its chief objective, the Dual Monarchy thereafter saw no need for extending its commitments. The negotiations for the Three Emperors' League were thus prolonged by the Austrian hesitations. As we have seen, this alliance was finally concluded in June, 1881. The agreement was strongly favored by Bismarck since it brought Russia into an alignment he could control. As long as Russia remained alone in Europe, the danger existed that she might join France. The alliance also served to moderate and contain the actions of the two Balkan rivals.

On May 20, 1882 a further combination, the Triple Alliance, was concluded, which brought Italy into the Austro-German camp. Since she too wished to be a colonial power, Italy was greatly disturbed by the French annexation of Tunis. The agreement that was signed at this time was thus directed primarily against France. Under its terms Germany and Austria were to assist Italy in the event of a French aggression; Italy would render similar aid to Germany. All the members of the alliance were obligated to join in a war should one of their number be at war with two great powers and to remain neutral if with only one. Thus Italy would be neutral in a conflict between Russia and Austria-Hungary, but would join should France and Russia fight Germany and Austria-Hungary.

In June, 1881 the network of alliances radiating from Berlin was lengthened by the conclusion of a treaty between Austria and Serbia. It will be remembered that although Panslav doctrines had called for assistance to all of the Slavs, practical military aid had been rendered only to the Bulgarians after the Serbian defeat of 1876. At the Congress of Berlin the Russian government had told the Serbs to turn to Vienna. As a result Prince Milan had been forced into a position of dependency on Vienna and the treaty of June, 1881 in effect made Serbia a vassal state. In return, Austria Hungary agreed to support Milan in his desire to assume the title of king and made vague promises of support for Serbian aspirations in Macedonia.

The final agreements in this pattern were concluded in 1883 by both Germany and Austria-Hungary with Rumania. Angered over the Russian seizure of Bessarabia in violation of the Treaty of 1877, the Rumanian government looked abroad for aid against further Russian encroachments. The agreements with the German powers, thus, promised support should Russia attack Rumania. In return, Rumania was obligated to assist Austria-Hungary in the same circumstances. The weakness in the partnership lay in the Rumanian national claims to Transylvania and the increasing policy of Magyarization practiced in the area by Budapest. However, as long as the Rumanian government saw its chief danger as coming from its northern neighbor, alliance with Vienna and Berlin was necessary.

This system of alliances joined four of the five powers of the continent of Europe but isolated France. Because of her imperial policies, Britain was also drawn into a policy of co-operation with the Triple Alliance. The wave of renewed imperial expansion after 1870 brought France and Britain into conflict over North Africa. With the French acquisition of Tunis in 1881, the fate of Egypt came next in question. The British involvement with France over this state and the rise of tension with Russia over Afghanistan made it impossible for the British government to pursue policies contradictory to those of the Triple Alliance.

Although the Bismarckian system of alliances was impressive, the question remained whether they could preserve the peace in a major crisis. The chief point of danger was still in the Balkans, but the situation in the Middle East was also becoming increasingly tense. The ability of the alliance network to fulfill its intention was to be tested in the next years when Britain and Russia came close to conflict over the Afghan border question and when Russia's satellite Bulgaria challenged Russian overlordship.

THE AFGHAN BORDER DISPUTE

The value to Russia of her renewed alliance with Berlin and Vienna and the support that she thus gained for her interpretation of the Straits agreement was soon to be demonstrated by the events in the Middle East. The steady pattern of Russian conquest and expansion in the area had been watched with care and increasing apprehension in London. Once again, as in previous periods, the alarmists in Britain saw in the Russian actions a carefully conceived plan designed to take India. The fact that these advances were made despite repeated official Russian assurances that such action would not be taken naturally increased the doubts felt concerning Russia's reliability and honesty. Even if this condition was the result of bad communications and disobedient commanders, the fact remained that Russian troops were approaching the routes to India. The Russian capture of Merv in 1884 brought Russia dangerously close to the border of Afghanistan.

Because of its location between India and the Russian possessions in Central Asia, the preservation of Afghanistan as a buffer state was undoubtedly to the interest of both Russia and Britain. The political instability of the state and the nature of the country as a whole, however, made his aim difficult to accomplish. At the time of the Russian advance into Kokand, the Amir of Afghanistan, Shir Ali, had requested British assistance, which was denied. After the conquest of Khiva, he again appealed to Britain, but was unable to obtain any direct assurances of aid. Under these circumstances he turned to St. Petersburg, and in 1878 he received a Russian mission in his capital. But, at the same time he refused to receive one from Britain. The British government, fearing that Russia would establish a protectorate, opened the Second Afghan War of 1878-1879, which ended in the deposition of Shir Ali. Although thereafter Afghanistan was in theory a neutral buffer state, it was in fact a British protectorate.

Because of the political shift in Afghanistan, Russia and Britain now stood face to face over a common border for the first time in the entire period under discussion. The issue in dispute between them was the line to be drawn between their empires, which met at this point. The exact border of Afghanistan was exceedingly difficult to establish because it ran through a wild region inhabited by tribes who were under the general jurisdiction of the Amir of Afghanistan. In 1884 the Russian government agreed to the formation of a boundary commission that was to investigate the question on the spot. In September a British representative was sent, but when he arrived in Afghanistan he found that his Russian counterpart was delayed, nor did he appear in the next months. In the meantime the Russian forces slowly pushed forward in the territory under dispute with the objective of occupying as much land as possible. By February, 1885 the situation had become critical. In January the British had suffered a major setback in the Sudan when General Gordon and his garrison were massacred at Khartoum. Faced by the double pressure in Egypt and in Afghanistan, the British government gave priority to the Russian threat and made preparations in India for war. A Russian move towards Herat was particularly feared. On March 30 an open battle occurred between Russian and Afghan troops at Penjeh, which increased the danger of the entire situation.

In this moment of crisis the value of the Three Emperors' League for Russia became apparent. Britain, who was without allies in the imperial conflict, could not hope to conduct a victorious war against Russia over Middle Eastern issues unless she could repeat the plan of the Crimean War, sail through the Straits, and initiate a campaign in the Caucasus. To prevent the opening of the Straits to British warships, Bismarck used pressure at Constantinople. He was supported not only by his allies, Austria and Italy, but also by France. Under the circumstances, both the British and Russian governments were virtually forced to arbitrate the conflict; neither was in a position to fight over the issue, and a real military engagement under the existing military and diplomatic conditions was virtually impossible. Although both powers agreed to arbitration, the question was finally settled by direct negotiation in the treaty of September, 1885, which set the Russian-Afghan boundary. Russia received the greater portion of the territory under dispute, but British predominance in Afghanistan was recognized in return. In March, 1895 a final settlement of the Pamir boundary was reached and a strip of Afghan territory was maintained between the territories of Russia and India to serve as a buffer zone.

Despite British fears to the contrary, there is no indication that Russia had any real designs for the conquest of India or that plans were ever made for the incorporation of that territory into the Russian Empire. The value of the land as a weapon against Britain was, nonetheless, thoroughly appreciated. Without adequate naval power to challenge British domination of the seas, Russia could only directly threaten British interests by pressure in the Middle East and in the eastern Mediterranean. Certainly,

Russian troops could never be landed on British soil the way British armies had been despatched to the Crimea. Therefore, in every major Russian-British crisis plans were made for an invasion of India, principally to exert pressure on Britain to aid in the accomplishment of Russian policy in other areas. The British sensitivity over the fate of the "jewel" of their empire made such threats effective. The Russian government during the period under consideration never had the military capacity nor the desire to carry out such a great undertaking.

THE BULGARIAN CRISIS

Although the Middle Eastern problem was thus solved in a manner acceptable to both sides, a major crisis followed in the Balkans in connection with internal events in Bulgaria which did not end in an equally satisfactory solution for the Russian government. After the Congress of Berlin the great powers had assumed that the autonomous Bulgaria under a foreign prince would be a Russian satellite and stand in a colonial relationship to St. Petersburg. The establishment of this state as a dependency had been the single great gain for Russia at the Congress of Berlin and the justification of the Russo-Turkish War. Control of the area was also most important from strategic considerations since the land formed a bridge to Constantinople. It was thus vital for the success of Russian policy in the Near East that a stable, friendly government be maintained in Sofia, which would look to Russia for instructions and would be a loyal ally in time of war.

The Russian government was also convinced that in its task of directing the administration of the new state it had to deal with a population that would welcome its benevolent, tutoring hand. Panslav enthusiasm for the Balkan Slavs had in the war concentrated itself on the Bulgarians; it was optimistically assumed that similar sentiments were felt in Bulgaria. And indeed after the liberation of the country from Turkish control there was a great fund of gratitude toward Russia, although it was not as much as Russia thought. The Bulgarians after the war expected to gain their freedom; they did not wish merely to change masters. They were therefore willing to accept direction and advice but not dictation. The Russian government thus met again in a liberated Balkan people a response it neither expected nor understood. Russia had, undoubtedly, in the case of Bulgaria, as previously in Greece and Rumania, expended large sums and had lost many men in wars against Turkey; and she expected to be repaid with eternal gratitude. The Balkan states, in contrast, recognized their debt to Russia, but they felt themselves independent political entities tied to no particular camp. They wished to remain free to align with whatever group best suited their interests and to regulate their internal affairs on the basis of purely domestic considerations.

The first years of the Russian protectorate over Bulgaria passed relatively smoothly. A new government was established under Russian direction with the Russian army in occupation. A draft constitution was drawn up in Bulgaria and then sent to Russia. This first document called for the establishment of a strong executive branch and was therefore conservative in form. The draft was examined by the ministries concerned and by a special commission and then it was returned to Sofia. In Bulgaria a constitutional assembly was summoned, which proceeded to examine this proposal. The constitution, which the Russian government offered only as a suggestion, was then subjected to thorough examination and debate. In this assembly the two political parties, the Liberals and the Conservatives, which together were to dominate the political life of Bulgaria, took shape. The issue that divided them was the balance between the executive and the legislative branches of government. The final form adopted for the constitution was extremely liberal in character, with the Liberals winning their demand for a strong legislature. The country was also to enjoy full civil liberties and the preponderant assembly was to be elected by universal manhood suffrage. It is interesting to note that the form of government adopted by Bulgaria was in great contrast to that in Russia. The Russian government stood sponsor for a regime whose people enjoyed rights far in advance of those of the Russians themselves.

Though the assembly altered the draft constitution presented by the Russian government, it did elect the prince designated by the controlling power. There were, in fact, few candidates available for the position. The final choice of Alexander of Battenberg was determined largely by the fact that he was acceptable to all of the powers. He was related to the British royal family, but he was also a nephew of the tsar. In selecting him the Russian government expected that he would follow its suggestions and directions. Alexander himself had little training for his future position as head of a Balkan state; in politics he was conservative, and he disliked the liberal constitution under which he was obliged to govern.

As had previously been true in the Danubian Principalities, Russian influence and control in Bulgaria was exercised through the Russian representatives in the state. In addition to the usual diplomatic agents, Russia had also a large number of military officials in the country. In the Bulgarian army all officers above the grade of captain were Russian; the Bulgarian minister of war was a Russian officer. These men were thus under the jurisdiction of the Russian war ministry, and they were expected to consult St. Petersburg on questions of policy. The diplomatic representatives, in contrast, were under the authority of the foreign ministry, and they sought their instructions in his office. Unfortunately for the success of Russian policy in Bulgaria, although the war and foreign ministries did often consult on common problems, adequate measures were not taken to ensure that the military and diplomatic agents in Sofia co-operated and co-ordinated their policies. Thus in time a difficult situation developed. Representatives of the two branches of the Russian service entered into competition with each other and joined opposite camps on domestic issues in Bulgaria.

The first major political issue involved the determination of Alexander of Battenberg to amend the new constitution. In this conflict the prince naturally allied with the Conservatives against the Liberal opposition. He was able to gain support for his views from the Russian consul, A. P. Davydov, a friend of Giers. However, General Parensov, the Russian minister of war in Bulgaria, in contrast, supported the Liberals and the constitution, with the approval of Miliutin and the Russian war ministry. In the end Prince Alexander resorted to a *coup d'état* to set aside the constitution, an action that he carried out without first notifying the Russian government. Thereafter, the Russian officials shifted roles. K. G. Ernrot, who was sent to replace Parensov, supported the prince and the Conservatives. Khitrovo, who became diplomatic agent, joined the Liberals.

Meanwhile, Alexander III had become tsar of Russia. Although he approved of the prince's action because of its conservative motivation, he was even more firmly determined than his father had been that Bulgaria should accept Russian direction. Moreover, although there had been a degree of sympathy and affection between the Bulgarian prince and Alexander II, no such feelings characterized the relationship of the new tsar and his cousin. Alexander III expected to be treated with the respect due the ruler of a great country, not as a relative. He also thought of Bulgaria purely in the terms of a satellite state. His stronger policies were to be introduced at a most inauspicious moment in Russo-Bulgarian relations. With time the Bulgarian political leaders had become increasingly resistent to Russian pressure and more eager to escape from Russian tutelage. Although the Bulgarians were grateful for past Russian military assistance and diplomatic support, they as a group had little admiration for Russian political life or its civilization. It is interesting to note that when the Panslav organizations brought Bulgarian students to be educated at Russian schools, these young men came primarily into contact with the elements of the Russian youth who were particularly dissatisfied with Russian autocracy. In Russia they also read and became acquainted with the western social and political philosophies that were the basis of the Russian revolutionary movement. Panslav educational efforts thus produced the opposite effect to that originally intended. Study in Russia had shown the degree to which that state lagged behind the west and not its capability of assuming the leadership of the Slavs. The Bulgarian political leaders, whether educated in the east or the west, thus turned toward western Europe for inspiration.

Before continued Russian pressure and interference in the political life of Bulgaria, Alexander adopted the only possible course of action by which he could maintain his independence. He joined with the two political parties to form a common front against Russian domination. He also restored the original constitution in order to win Liberal support. In reprisal, Russia withdrew two of her chief representatives, but she took no further action. Bulgarian defiance, however, lost for the new state Russian diplomatic support abroad. In its negotiations with other governments, Russia ceased in its efforts to further Bulgarian national interests. Whereas previously Russia had included the eventual unification of Bulgaria and Eastern Rumelia among its own foreign policy aims, this event was now firmly opposed. Alexander of Battenberg, because of his refusal to be a puppet ruler, had completely lost the Russian confidence.

The prince was able to resist Russian pressure on his state and to unite his people on this issue, but his position was not easy. It was extremely difficult for any Bulgarian government to withstand Russian pressure since it was impossible to obtain the support of any foreign government. Austria and Britain were sympathetic to the show of independence, but because of the general diplomatic situation they could not offer concrete assistance. Moreover, at the Congress of Berlin they had recognized that Bulgaria was within the Russian sphere. Bismarck, in particular, stood strongly behind the maintenance of the Berlin policy because he feared lest further Balkan complications should upset his delicate balance of alliances. In June, 1884 he commented bluntly that if Prince Alexander "would be something other than a Russian viceroy, then he has misunderstood his position."[2]

In September, 1885 a revolt broke out in Plovdiv, which

2. Stählin, *Geschichte Russlands*, IV/1, p. 528.

brought the entire issue of Russian control in Bulgaria again on the international scene. Despite the separation of the two Bulgarian provinces at the Congress of Berlin, the movement for national unification had proceeded in Eastern Rumelia after 1879, at first with the enthusiastic aid and assistance of the Russians. When the Russian officials subsequently reversed their stand, the Bulgarian nationalists continued their activities despite Russian opposition. On September 18, 1885 a group of revolutionaries deposed the governor-general of Eastern Rumelia and announced the union of their province with Bulgaria. Alexander of Battenberg was thus faced with a difficult decision. His position in Bulgaria demanded that he accept the leadership of the national movement. Like Cuza in Rumania and King Othon in Greece, he had found that it was only in the furtherance of national issues that he could unite his nation and gain support for his rule. If he refused to recognize the union, he could probably not remain as prince of Bulgaria. However, the international situation was clearly unfavorable for the event. Russia had made her negative attitude quite clear. Moreover, in August, 1885 Alexander had met with Giers at Franzenbad and apparently at that time gave assurances that he would not take steps to further the national cause. Russian disapproval of the revolt was expressed at once. On September 21, when it became apparent that Alexander would accept the headship of a united Bulgaria, the tsar ordered all of the Russian officers out of the country. He announced also that he would not recognize the unification as long as Prince Alexander and his government remained in office. Since the Bulgarian army was now deprived of all of its higher officers, it appeared that the Bulgarian state was militarily virtually defenseless.

The Bulgarian union was in fact saved by the thoughtless and ill-managed acts of King Milan of Serbia. Increasingly unpopular in his own country, he feared the effect upon his own position of the increase in power and prestige that the union gave his neighbor state. With the Bulgarian army apparently in a state of total disorganization, an ideal situation appeared to have presented itself. Milan therefore declared war on Bulgaria on November 13, despite an Austrian warning to the contrary. Because of the internal conditions in Bulgaria, the powers expected to witness a quick Serbian victory. To the surprise of all, the Bulgarian army not only defeated its opponents on its own soil, but it prepared to invade Serbia itself. In this crisis the Austrian government intervened to save its protégé and forced the conclusion of a peace between the states on a *status quo ante* basis. The Bulgarian victory, nevertheless, had saved the union.

Despite the intense opposition the Russian government felt towards the prince and the unification of Bulgaria, it was recognized that Russia could not afford to precipitate a major Balkan crisis over the event. Although Bismarck maintained his position of support of Russian control in the country, Britain and Austria-Hungary were openly delighted at this blow to Russian prestige and power. A compromise solution was finally agreed upon. Alexander of Battenberg was recognized as the governor-general of Eastern Rumelia, in theory only for five years, and the provinces were to remain administratively separate. The prince, however, almost immediately violated this agreement and joined the two assemblies. The united Bulgaria was thus created.

Although Bulgarian unification was achieved, the Russian government did not cease in its efforts to regain political control and if possible to oust the prince. Alexander III, who placed the entire question on a personal and emotional basis, was particularly bitter. The Russian leaders also appear to have held the illusion that the "Bulgarian people" were for them and that only the prince and his regime prevented a reconciliation. Conspiracies directed against the person of Alexander and against his government, therefore, received assistance from St. Petersburg. On the night of August 20, 1886, with the foreknowledge of Giers and the tsar, a band of conspirators entered the prince's room and forced him to sign a document of abdication. They then transported him out of the country and left him in Bessarabia. The provisional government established thereafter by the revolutionaries proved only of short duration. After three days the government was again taken over by loyal forces under the leadership of Stefan Stambolov, who then invited Alexander to return to his country. Thus only eleven days after the kidnapping, the prince again crossed the border. Here confused and exhausted, he made a disastrous mistake. Under the apparent impression that Russian support for his return might be forthcoming, he telegraphed the tsar: "As Russia gave me my crown, I am prepared to give it back into the hands of its Sovereign." [3] This message not only enraged the Bulgarian leaders, but it also gave the tsar the welcome opportunity of accepting this offer of abdication. When the Russian government in reply indicated its disapproval of his continuation in office, the prince appointed a regency and then left the country.

Russia now had the opportunity of once again establishing its influence; however, the mistakes of the past were repeated. General Nicholas Kaulbars, who was sent from Russia to deal with the situation, resorted to the same measures of pressure and violence that had alienated the Bulgars in the past. When the newly elected Bulgarian assembly proceeded with the choice of a new prince against Russian opposition, Kaulbars and the Russian officials all were recalled from the country; a complete break in diplomatic relations followed. In the next years the Russian government tried repeatedly to isolate and hinder the activities of the Bulgarian government in foreign affairs. This attitude accounted for much of the difficulty that the Bulgars met in attempting to find a new prince. Finally, in December, 1886 the name of Prince Ferdinand of Coburg was suggested, and in July, 1887 he was formally elected to replace Alexander of Battenberg. In the first years of his reign he was unable to obtain the recognition of any of the powers, and his tenure in office seemed indeed precarious. Nevertheless, the new Bulgarian state under the political guidance of Stambolov had shown the internal strength necessary to throw off the domination of Russia and to bring about the unification of the nation, despite the fact that it enjoyed the outright military support of no great power.

3. Charles Jelavich, *Tsarist Russia and Balkan Nationalism* (Berkeley: University of California Press, 1958), p. 258.

The tremendous blow to Russian prestige in eastern Europe resulting from the successful national revolution and again from the election of Ferdinand had strong repercussions within Russia. As a result Giers, personally, was forced to face the great crisis of his career as foreign minister because of the attacks launched on his policy by the nationalist press. The most effective opposition was offered by the publicist Katkov, whose articles in the *Moskovskii Vedomosti* (Moscow News) were read by the tsar. Katkov's position was also supported by Pobedonostsev and Saburov, of whom the latter now entered the camp of the nationalists despite his previous advocacy of alliance with Austria-Hungary and Germany. In March, 1886 Katkov made the error of publishing the terms of the agreement of 1884 of the Three Emperors' League. This document was secret, but its contents had been communicated by Saburov to the journalist. Alexander was greatly enraged over this breach of trust, and Katkov never again enjoyed similar influence. He died the next year.

Though Giers was able to withstand this storm, it was also apparent that a modification would have to be made in the policy of alignment with the northern courts. The Austrian attitude in the Bulgarian crisis made a continuation of the Three Emperors' League impossible, despite Giers' advocacy of its maintenance. Alexander III was now quite unwilling to co-operate with Vienna. He was, however, ready to continue close relations with Germany. The firm attitude taken by Bismarck against Alexander of Battenberg won general Russian approval; it was Vienna not Berlin that stood in the enemy camp. Alexander III himself commented:

Germany and Russia, closely associated, would put everything in order, would maintain tranquility and peace everywhere, would avert the revolution and be the masters of the world. Unfortunately Austria stands between us.[4]

In May, 1887 negotiations were therefore commenced with Germany alone by Paul Shuvalov, the Russian ambassador in

4. Stählin, *Geschichte Russlands,* IV/1, p. 548.

Berlin. During these discussions Bismarck, after communication with Vienna, read to the Russian representative the contents of the Dual Alliance with Austria. He argued that since the German position had consistently been that Austria must be upheld, this defensive alliance with Vienna did not preclude an agreement with Russia. Bismarck again emphasized in these conversations the old formula of the necessity of mutual support among the conservative powers. The Reinsurance Treaty, concluded on June 18, 1887, brought the German chancellor the assurance of Russian neutrality should France attempt to reverse the decision of 1870. In return, Germany agreed to support Russian interests in Bulgaria and at the Straits. The "preponderant and decisive" interests of Russia in Sofia were recognized, and Germany agreed not to allow the restoration of Alexander of Battenberg. Aid was also promised should Russia endeavor to re-establish "a regular and legal government" in Bulgaria. In regard to the Straits, Germany promised Russia assistance should the tsar "find himself under the necessity of assuming himself the task of defending the entrance of the Black Sea." Although Bismarck in this agreement apparently assured Russia of wide support in the east, he thereafter proceeded to create through a system of counter-alliances a general diplomatic situation that would make it impossible for Russia to carry out an active policy either in Bulgaria or at the Straits and thus benefit from the treaty with Germany.

The Reinsurance Treaty was only one in a wider framework of alliances encouraged by Bismarck in order to meet the double threat of the collapse of the Three Emperors' League in the east and the revival of French revanchism in the Boulanger movement in France. Before the conclusion of the agreement with Russia, Bismarck had already tightened his western alliances. With strong German approval Britain and Italy on February 12, 1887 signed the first Mediterranean agreement, which was devised to protect the *status quo* in the Aegean and the Black Seas. Later Austria-Hungary and Spain adhered to this agreement, which was directed primarily against the extension of French control in North Africa. Although Germany did not formally become a member of this combination, she was connected with it through her allies of the Triple Alliance. This later pact was renewed on February 20, and Italy was allowed further advantages. The Reinsurance Treaty, the third in the series, was, as we have seen, concluded in June. The further deterioration of the Balkan situation after the election of Ferdinand of Coburg in July led directly to German sponsorship of a fourth agreement. Since Bismarck had in the Reinsurance Treaty promised Russia German support in Bulgaria, he now needed a combination that would assure that these promises need never be kept. Using again the instrumentality of the Mediterranean agreements, in which Germany did not participate, he supported the conclusion of the second pact of December, 1887. Here Italy, Britain, and Austria-Hungary joined to preserve the *status quo* in the Near East and thus to block Russian moves against Sofia. With this agreement in existence, Bismarck could with safety publicly support Russia. Since the Russian government was faced with a front of the other powers in the eastern Mediterranean, she could not act, and henceforth the Bulgarian problem as an international issue slowly lapsed. It should be noted that although these agreements, as the later diplomatic arrangements, remained secret in detail, the existence of the alignments and their participants were usually known.

The Bismarckian system of alliances and counter-alliances thus brought Europe through the year 1887. It was a complicated pattern and perhaps unnecessarily complex. Peace was, after all, maintained not so much through the existence of the agreements as because of the fact that none of the major powers wished to, or was prepared to, enter a major war. The preservation of the system also depended on the continuation in office of Bismarck. His ability to control German diplomacy, let alone European, came seriously into question in 1888, the year of the three emperors. First, William I, under whom Bismarck had served for so long, died. He was succeeded by his son, Frederick III, who was expected to favor the liberal, pro-British trend in Prussian policy. When he died from cancer of the throat after only three months in power, his son William II succeeded to the throne. Although more conservative in politics than his father, the new emperor was also more intolerant, aggressive, and headstrong. It was perhaps inevitable that the young ruler, who wished to be more than a figurehead, should clash with the man who had been for so long accustomed to directing German policy unhindered.

Agreement and alliance with Russia had, as we have seen, always been a central theme in Bismarck's policies, although after 1870 St. Petersburg had been subordinated to Vienna. The maintenance of this friendship had also been the constant preoccupation of Russia, even when the lines to Vienna were down. It has been shown how in so many respects Russia and Prussia, and later Prussia-Germany, had complemented and paralleled each other. They had common interests in the partitioned Poland, in the upholding of the conservative order, and they were strategically necessary to each other as long as Russia remained in conflict with Britain and Germany with France. These conditions remained valid in 1888. Under the new regime Bismarck continued therefore to emphasize the stern necessity of Germany's friendly relations with her eastern neighbor, particularly in view of the attitude of France. He also saw that, even if Germany should win a future war against Russia, little would be gained since:

This indestructible empire . . . would after its defeat remain our natural and revengeful opponent just as France is today in the west.[5]

These convictions were initially shared by the new emperor, but Bismarck met increasing opposition within the German foreign ministry from those who felt that the Russian agreement conflicted with Germany's obligations under the Triple Alliance.

The entire question of German-Russian relations was reviewed at the time of the scheduled renewal of the Reinsurance Treaty in 1890. The negotiations were commenced in Germany in February by Shuvalov, who then went back to St. Petersburg. When he returned to Berlin in March, he found the situation entirely altered. Bismarck was no longer chancellor, and the emperor had

5. *Ibid.*, p. 569.

accepted the advice of those who opposed the renewal of the agreement. Alexander III received the news with indifference; he had never felt any great enthusiasm for the pact although he had understood its advantages for Russian policy. However, for Giers the German rejection was a bitter blow. Throughout his career as foreign minister he had always supported the alignment with Berlin even though this position had won him the dangerous opposition of those with Panslav and strongly nationalist beliefs. Although the German government would not now renew the Reinsurance Treaty, Giers sought to obtain some kind of substitute. He was willing to drop the sections concerning Bulgaria and the Straits; he also declared that he would be satisfied with a simple exchange of letters. He was primarily concerned with securing something on paper that would justify the continuation of his policy. The Russian proposals met with no response in Berlin, where Bismarck's successors were bent upon strengthening the ties with Britain. With great reluctance Giers and his associates were now forced to consider a complete change of policy and the formation of the alignment previously pressed by the nationalist opposition—that of alliance and co-operation with Republican France. The diplomatic situation that Bismarck had labored so long to prevent had thus been created. Russia and France both stood alone. Neither had any outstanding quarrel with the other, but both faced dangerous opposition from their neighbors. A policy of collaboration under such circumstances could not long be avoided.

THE FRANCO-RUSSIAN ALLIANCE

The formation of a Franco-Russian alliance had long been supported by the nationalists in both France and Russia; however, many considerations still hindered its accomplishment. The chief link between the states remained the fact that both were now diplomatically isolated and faced the danger of seeing their policies, whether offensive or defensive in intention, blocked by the combination of the Triple Alliance and Britain. France and Russia thus had the same potential enemies, but they did not have similar immediate aims and interests in foreign policy. Russian interests were still primarily concentrated in the Balkans, where the chief opponents were Austria-Hungary and Britain. Russia had no quarrels with Germany nor did she wish to antagonize that military giant. France, in contrast, had no important Balkan goals; she was thus unlikely to lend active or enthusiastic assistance to Russian projects in the east, certainly not as long as her principal enemy lay across the Rhine. She had certainly no interest in fostering Russian antagonism to the Danubian Monarchy over the fate of the small states of the Balkans where she had nothing at stake. French policy remained in this period divided in that the government sought to carry on an active continental policy against Germany and also a colonial program against Britain. Her chief opponent, however, always remained the German Empire. The strong nationalists wished to prepare for a war of revenge and to regain Alsace-Lorraine; the moderates feared that Germany would launch a preventive war for the purpose of eliminating French power once and for all. The chief aim of the negotiations with Russia in French eyes was thus to obtain the support of the Russian armies against Germany's eastern frontiers in time of war, although the French had few illusions about the actual military strength of Russia at the time. The Russian government naturally had no great enthusiasm about fighting Germany for French aims on the Rhine when no outstanding issues stood between St. Petersburg and Berlin.

The ideological issues of the past century also continued to hinder closer political relations. Certainly, the Third Republic and tsarist Russia stood poles apart. Despite her value as an ally, France remained for the conservative Russian the center of revolutionary movements of all colors and the patron of Polish nationalism. Little respect was felt for the reliability and stability of the French regime itself. The repeated scandals and internal crises in Paris did nothing to alter this view. The incompatibility of the two systems of government was chiefly a matter of concern to the Russian officials; the French, with nothing to fear from tsarist autocracy, were interested chiefly in securing the assistance of the Russian armies, less in the ideological implications of the question.

In both France and Russia, as has been mentioned, the strongest support for an alignment came from the extreme nationalists. Neither group had much sympathy or interest for the aims of its counterpart, but they recognized that they needed each other. If the immediate issues were put aside and only general long-range questions were considered, then Germany too was the principal enemy of Russia as well as of France. It was clear that Russia too had lost by the decision of 1870 and that the new Germany threatened the claims of both Paris and St. Petersburg to continental supremacy. The Russian Panslav, foreseeing an inevitable clash of Slav and Teuton, realized that a French alliance was necessary to secure the realization of his dream of a great Slavic empire; the French nationalist, bent on a policy of *revanche*, saw that France could only regain its former role as the great nation of the continent with the destruction of Germany, a project feasible only with Russian co-operation. Both nations thus had the common aim of the reversal of the achievements of Bismarck. Alexander III in 1891 uttered these convictions:

In case of war between France and Germany we must immediately throw ourselves upon the Germans in order not to give them time to defeat France at once and then turn against us. We must correct the mistakes of the past and crush Germany at the first opportunity.[6]

Despite these considerations, the negotiations between France and Russia were initiated because of the actions of Germany, which left the Russian government no other alternative. At the time of the dropping of the Reinsurance Treaty, the advisors of William II had not believed that a Franco-Russian alliance was possible because so many issues separated the two countries. They were chiefly concerned with tightening the connections between Germany and Britain through the Triple Alliance. When on July

6. V. N. Lamzdorf, *Dnevnik, 1891-1892* (Moscow, 1934), p. 299.

1, 1890 an agreement was signed in which Germany received Heligoland in return for the abandonment of claims to lands in Africa, it appeared as if the policy of co-operation with Britain was well under way. At the same time the German government undertook measures to ameliorate the position of the Poles who were under German domination. It thus appeared that German policy had taken the course that had caused so much concern in other periods, that of co-operation with liberal England and the adoption of measures in support of Polish nationalism. A liberal and pro-Polish Prussia in alliance with Britain had always been recognized as a danger to Russian policy; Germany following the same course made the maintenance by Russia of a diplomatically isolated position impossible. The existence of ties between Germany and Britain were underscored at the time of the renewal of the Triple Alliance. The Italian premier, Rudini, in a speech in June, 1891 implied that Britain had joined the combination of the central powers. If this were indeed true, then both France and Russia were faced in Europe and overseas with a solid block of preponderant military and diplomatic power. Thus, although Russia and Germany had no outstanding immediate differences between them, it appeared that Berlin was firmly attached to the camp of the Russian opponents.

Even before 1890 the groundwork had been laid for Russo-French co-operation in the financial field by an ill-advised act of Bismarck made before he was forced out of office. In 1887, in reprisal for action taken against German interests in the Russian Baltic provinces, he made it impossible for the Russian government to secure loans in Berlin. Russia, thereafter, turned to Paris, a far better money market, and the necessary funds were readily obtained. This economic relationship, which the French government manipulated for political ends, remained until the fall of the tsarist regime when the French were left with much worthless paper on their hands. Nevertheless, the loans strengthened the relations between the two governments and gave France a large stake in the Russian economy. It also took the financial weapon out of the hands of the German government and gave it to the French.

The actual negotiations for an agreement were, nevertheless, slow in initiation and in completion. In July, 1891 the improved relations between the two countries were demonstrated during the visit of a French squadron to the Russian naval base of Kronstadt. On this occasion the tsar stood at attention during the playing of the Marseillaise, the hymn of the revolution, the ban on its performance in Russia having been lifted for the occasion. The first written agreement between the two powers was contained in an exchange of letters in August, 1891. The stipulations reflected the hesitancy of the Russian government to accept really effective obligations in regard to France. It was merely agreed that the two signatories would "confer on every question of a nature to threaten the general peace." Should either power be endangered by aggression "the two parties agree to come to an understanding on measures which the realization of that eventuality would make it necessary for both governments to adopt immediately and simultaneously." These statements, the first stage in the Franco-Russian alliance, were thus quite limited in extent. The agreement could also be directed against Britain as well as against Germany.

The significant and central agreement for the alliance was not negotiated until a year later. Since the chief bond between France and Russia was the military assistance that they could render each other against Germany, it was proper that the chiefs of staff should be primarily concerned with the drawing up of the arrangement. In August, 1892 General Boisdeffre and his Russian counterpart, General Obruchev, agreed upon a far-reaching military pact, which, after its ratification, was to form the basis of the Russo-French alignment that brought both nations into the First World War. In the conversations concerning an agreement the French showed they were primarily interested in ensuring that at the commencement of hostilities the Russian army would immediately launch an attack upon Germany's eastern frontier and not simply remain on the defensive. The French government feared a military situation in which the German armies would enter Paris while the Russians concentrated on the Balkans and Austria-Hungary. The final agreement, which was directed clearly against Germany, met the French demands. It was stipulated that if France were attacked by Germany, or by Italy backed by Germany, Russia would come to the aid of France. France assumed similar obligations towards Russia in case of a German attack or an Austrian aggression backed by Germany. Mobilization by any member of the Triple Alliance obligated both Russia and France immediately to call up their troops. It was further agreed that at the outbreak of hostilities France would immediately employ 1,300,000 men in action against Germany while Russia should enter with 700,000 to 800,000 in order "that Germany will have to fight at the same time in the east and in the west." The duration of the agreement was to be the same as that of the Triple Alliance.

This pact, initialled by the two chiefs of staff, still required the approval of the tsar and the French government. The ratification was long delayed because of continued hesitation in Russia, particularly on the part of Giers, to enter into an openly anti-German agreement. Throughout the negotiations the alliance received the strong support of the Russian ambassador in Paris, Mohrenheim, who did all he could to promote good relations between the countries. The tsar's distrust of the French regime was strengthened again by the Panama Canal scandals of 1892, when it was shown that members of the government were involved in financial irregularities in connection with the construction of the waterway. In this period Giers again tried unsuccessfully to initiate some kind of discussions with Berlin. In October, 1893 a Russian squadron visited Toulon amid scenes of enthusiasm and rejoicing. The renewed friendship with Russia had won the strong acclamation of the French public, which felt that their country had won a strong ally against Germany. Finally, in December Giers was able to notify France that his government accepted the agreement. On January 4, 1894, with the French approval, the Franco-Russian alliance was established.

This agreement has received much study and much adverse criticism because it contributed to the creation of the alliance system that eventually brought the European states into a major war over a relatively minor Balkan incident. However, it is difficult to see how such an alignment could have been avoided in the early 1890's. Russia could not afford to stand alone, particularly in the face of the Triple Alliance working in co-operation with Britain. It should also be emphasized that the agreement was a strictly defensive alliance, and it was certainly not followed by any immediate attempts by Russia to turn it into an offensive weapon. In fact in its first years the agreement caused France to join Russia in a policy of peace and the maintenance of the *status quo* in the Near East. Nor were there any indications that the alliance would remain firm and lasting; other similar engagements had been terminated, and the international situation was to take many turns before 1914.

The alliance did, however, divide the continent into two camps, Triple Alliance against the Franco-Russian alliance. As before, the two danger areas remained the Rhine, where French and German interests clashed, and the Balkans, where Russia and Austria stood in opposition. Although the next years were to be dominated by imperial rivalry, these two areas never lost their significance. It is also interesting to note that in the long view in the formation of both alliance systems it was the stronger power that saw its freedom of action ultimately hampered. Under the relatively firm rule of Alexander III, Russian policy in the east remained under control. When this situation changed during the reign of Nicholas II, the French government found itself allied to an unstable government, whose balance and wisdom in a time of crisis could not be relied upon. France in 1914 went to war to defend Russian Balkan policy over an issue in which she had no direct interest and one that was certainly not worth the risking of her national existence. In the same manner Germany after the conclusion of the Dual Alliance became increasingly dependent upon her Austrian ally, but that power underwent a process of disintegration and division similar in degree to that in Russia.

Because of this relationship it was to be the Balkans and not the Rhine that was to be the area of chief significance. The danger in the situation increased after the turn of the century when, because of their failures in internal policies, neither Russia nor Austria-Hungary could afford to suffer humiliations abroad. The alliance relationship thus forced both France and Germany to support their allies, even when the latter pursued dangerous and provocative policies.

＊   ＊   ＊   ＊   ＊

Despite the fact that the reign of Alexander III lasted but a short time, it perhaps constituted the most significant period of the century in regard to tsarist diplomacy. Although the unification of Germany had occurred previously, the policy of alliance with Berlin had been continued through the Three Emperors' League and later through the Reinsurance Treaty. The dropping of that agreement by William II in 1890 marked the end of the policy of co-operation and friendship that had been maintained by Berlin and St. Petersburg almost without interruption since the reign of Catherine the Great. The importance of this realignment was as great for Germany as for Russia and for the same military and strategic reasons. The area of greatest significance for Russia was that occupied by Prussia and partitioned Poland. It was from here that Europe could effectively launch an invasion of Russia that could endanger the existence of the state. Thus in comparison to central Europe, the Near, Middle, and Far East always remained sideshows. The great achievement of 1814 had been the securing of the conditions of maximum security through the control of Congress Poland, the tripartite division of the German lands, and the maintenance of military superiority in eastern Europe. The Holy Alliance had aided Russia in that it joined together the three conservative monarchies for the preservation of the system established by the Congress of Vienna. This highly favorable situation was changed in 1870 with the emergence of the united Germany; but as long as the diplomatic ties were kept between Berlin and St. Petersburg, the Russian western frontiers were safeguarded. This entire structure fell in 1890 when Germany not only abandoned the line to St. Petersburg but also sought a policy of exclusive alignment with the Russian adversaries: Britain and Austria-Hungary. The Russian government then faced the possibility that conflicts in Asia and in the Balkans could result in a direct invasion of Russia. It was not the Crimea that was now in danger but St. Petersburg and Moscow.

The decision to abandon the Reinsurance Treaty was made in Berlin, not in St. Petersburg; the Russian foreign ministry had wished to keep it. The Russian government thereafter followed the obvious course when it with reluctance concluded the agreement with France. Even with the alliance with France Russia was still at a disadvantage in relation to her neighbor, since behind Germany stood the Triple Alliance in co-operation with Britain. In the next years this superiority of Germany over Russia was to increase at a steady pace. The enormous advantages that the accelerating tempo of industrialization offered the German military establishment were not paralleled in Russia. Although Russia too entered a period of industrialization in the 1890's, her internal structure, in contrast, rapidly deteriorated. Economic change led to social and political unrest and not to an increase of national power. It was this combination of military weakness and political maladjustment that was to lead in 1917 to the collapse of the regime.

The reign of Alexander III marks, thus, the end of the great period of Russian diplomacy in the nineteenth century. Four rulers, Alexander I, Nicholas I, Alexander II and Alexander III, together with their three chief statesmen, Nesselrode, Gorchakov, and Giers, had, despite inevitable mistakes, nevertheless kept Russian prestige high and her policy on an even keel. In the next reign, under Nicholas II this continuity and direction were lost. Instead, the negative elements of the preceding years joined with the growing internal chaos to lead Russia into adventures for which she was not prepared.

VI

Nicholas II

Nicholas II succeeded his father, who died of a kidney disease, and came to the throne at the age of twenty-six. Like Alexander III he had been educated under the guidance of Pobedonostsev, and, in the tradition of his predecessors, he accepted the basic policies and principles of Russian autocracy. With only a limited education, his preparation for his office also suffered from the fact that he had not been adequately initiated into the conduct of state affairs and had himself not held important positions in the government. In 1890-1891 he made a long journey, accompanied by his brother George and his cousin Prince George of Greece, to Greece, Egypt, India, China, and Japan, then home through Siberia. His subsequent interest in the east was thus influenced by his travels. A firm believer in autocracy and in the divine origins of his own power, he was to prove a bad constitutional monarch. He was, however, in temperament in no way suited to the role of an absolute ruler. Well-meaning, but weak, unstable, almost childish in his reactions, he fell too easily under the influence of the last person who talked with him. This lack of determination was to prove especially unfortunate in the field of foreign policy, where the tsar had to make the final decisions.

Throughout his reign Nicholas II was always open to the influence of those around him but particularly to that of his wife, Princess Alice of Hesse-Darmstadt. A granddaughter of Queen Victoria, the empress was brought up in England, and her manner was that of an Englishwoman. She and her husband always corresponded in the English language. Stronger in character than the tsar, she interfered increasingly in state affairs, where her influence was always in the direction of the strengthening of the conservative forces.

The greatest tragedy in the lives of the couple centered on the health of the heir to the throne. After a succession of five daughters, a son was finally born in 1904, but it soon became apparent that he had hemophilia, inherited from his mother's family. Both Nicholas II and his wife often associated with adventurers and even outright charlatans, but it was through their child's sickness that the most disastrous of these advisors, the monk Rasputin, gained a dominating position in the Russian government. The fundamental weakness of character of the tsar and his inability to keep order in his own house reflected itself in the foreign and internal policies of the empire until the destruction of the regime in 1917.

In foreign affairs Nicholas II inherited from his father the French alliance, of whose existence he learned only after his accession. During the first years of his reign he not only maintained, but even tightened the bonds of this agreement. In 1896 he travelled to France; in 1897 the French president Faure returned the visit. In 1899 the alliance was strengthened through the provisions that the military agreement should be of indefinite duration and that the pact in general should be extended to cover the "maintenance of equilibrium" rather than only "the maintenance of peace." The existence of this alliance, however, in no way hindered Nicholas II from considering and discussing agreements with Germany or Austria-Hungary. Like the previous tsars, Nicholas II felt a strong sense of dynastic kinship with the court of Berlin, despite his dislike for William II. In his meetings with the German emperor and in their correspondence, Nicholas II showed himself personally willing to accept a policy of co-operation, even when such an agreement would have meant a violation of the French alliance.

This reign also witnessed the Russian initiative in an event that must be recorded here since it falls outside of the subjects discussed in the following pages. In August, 1898 the Russian government called upon the other states to meet in a conference to limit armaments. Like the proposals of Alexander I, this summons was greeted with much suspicion and derision. Russian actions in the Far East at the time seemed to indicate that Russia herself was following anything but a peaceful policy; the weak economic structure of the country obviously made it advantageous for her to seek to limit the weapons of her neighbors, since she could not hope to rival their capacity for arming. Nevertheless, a meeting was held at The Hague in 1899. Although no disarmament agreement was reached, the governments attending did attempt to regulate the conditions of warfare and, more significant, an international court of arbitration was established. A second meeting in 1907 also failed to result in a limitation of arms, but problems of international law were more successfully handled.

It is extremely unfortunate that the tsar with the least capabilities of real leadership should also have been backed by the weakest of foreign ministries in the century. If Nicholas II had been associated with a statesman of the caliber of Bismarck, or even Giers or Nesselrode, Russian foreign policy might have taken an entirely different course. Instead, the conditions of the past century were in fact reversed. We have seen how, since the Congress of Vienna, four tsars were served by three chief ministers. Each of these had been trained thoroughly in his duties by his predecessor and had enjoyed considerable experience in diplomacy before assuming the office of foreign minister. This system had provided continuity and unity of policy. In contrast, Nicholas II was served by seven different ministers before his fall in 1917. None of these were men of unusual capability. Giers, who remained in office after the death of Alexander III, died in 1895. A. B. Lobanov-Rostovsky, who followed him, was an experienced and able statesman, but he died after little more than a year in office, to be succeeded by M. N. Muraviev, a man of much less ability, who served until 1900. His successor, V. N. Lamzdorff, who served from 1900-1906, was a sober, hard-working administrator, but he lacked experience in service abroad. The next minister, the ambitious Izvolsky, who was in power from 1906-1910, adopted a more active policy but, as we shall see, suffered a humiliating defeat. He was followed by S. D. Sazonov, in office from 1910-1916, who owed his position to his relationship to Stolypin and who proved to be unable to maintain control of the affairs under his jurisdiction. B. V. Sturmer (July-November, 1916) and N. N. Pokrovsky (1916-1917) held office during the difficult final years of the reign.

The Near East in the 1890's

In the 1890's Russia, like the other great powers, entered upon a period of imperial expansion in the Far East. The shift of emphasis from the Near East and Europe to Manchuria and the Pacific was made possible because of the interest of all of the powers in similar enterprises and also their common desire to maintain the *status quo* in the area that had formerly been the center of dispute: the Ottoman Empire. Although a series of crises arose here, all of the governments showed a determination to settle matters peacefully and not allow an upset of the balance. In this endeavor, the lines between the Triple Alliance and the Franco-Russian alliance tended to disappear since no power now felt it could benefit by independent action. This policy of agreement was best represented by the Russo-Austrian understanding of 1897 in which the former opponents agreed to co-operate to maintain the *status quo*. The Russian desire to remove the Balkans from the field of diplomatic conflict had been shown already in the reconciliation that took place with Bulgaria in 1896. In this question, as in the concurrent Armenian and Cretan crises, the Russian government thus followed a course of action that was to contrast with its later policies in the Far East.

As we have already seen, a period of highly strained relations followed the accession of Ferdinand of Coburg to the Bulgarian throne. Despite the fact that diplomatic relations between the two countries had been broken, the Russian government continued to try to exert pressure on the country; and it also encouraged activities of a violent and illegal character against the new regime. Thus Ferdinand and his influential minister, Stefan Stambulov, were in constant danger of overthrow or assassination because of the actions of groups that enjoyed at least unofficial Russian support. Since none of the great powers had yet recognized the new ruler, the position of the Bulgarian government was most precarious. Under these circumstances, it became of utmost importance that Ferdinand marry. If he had an heir, there would be less temptation for his rivals to assassinate him. However, because of the stipulations of the Bulgarian constitution, which required that the heir be of the Orthodox faith, the prince had great difficulty in finding a bride. Finally he secured the acceptance of Marie-Louise of Parma, but only on the condition that their children be brought up as Catholics. Against strong Russian opposition, Ferdinand and Stambulov were able to amend the constitution. Subsequently, the prince married, and soon a son was born. Relations with Russia during this period remained tense and dangerous. A change, however, came in 1895 when Nicholas II became tsar and after Stambulov had been forced out of office and later assassinated. Ferdinand recognized clearly that Bulgaria could not continue indefinitely in a condition of diplomatic isolation. Moreover, she needed the support of a great power for her national aspirations for the acquisition of lands still in the control of the Porte. Because Bulgaria lay by common agreement in the Russian sphere, it was unlikely at the time that any other major government would lend assistance. For these reasons, Ferdinand finally decided to seek a reconciliation with St. Petersburg. As a first step, and against the strong opposition of his wife, the prince saw the necessity of meeting the Russian wishes on the conversion of the heir. As had previously been the case in its relations with Greece under King Othon, the Russian government now placed the first emphasis on the religious issue. Ferdinand, therefore, had his son, who had been christened a Catholic, re-christened in the Orthodox church. With this major obstacle removed, Russia then recognized the government of Prince Ferdinand, and relations returned to normal after the long break. Russia, however, was never again able to exert the predominating and dictatorial influence in Bulgarian internal affairs that had characterized the first years of her protectorate over the new state.

The change of attitude of Bulgaria toward Russia and the recognition that a reconciliation would have to be sought was at least partially occasioned by the development of the Macedonian problem in the 1890's. Bulgaria clearly could not afford to lose Russian support in an issue where previously she had enjoyed the patronage of St. Petersburg. For it was only with Russian assistance and pressure on the Porte that the Bulgarians in 1870 had obtained the right not only to establish a Bulgarian exarchate but also permission to extend the jurisdiction of that organization over any Macedonian territories in which two-thirds of the population voted for their inclusion. With these rights the Bulgarians had launched a highly successful educational and cultural offensive. Russian support of the Bulgarian claims had also been shown in the provisions of the Treaty of San Stefano where Macedonia had been a part of the Greater Bulgaria provided for in that agreement. Thereafter the boundaries of the Bulgaria of San Stefano became the national aim of the subsequent Bulgarian governments.

Naturally the maximum program of San Stefano and the Bulgarian cultural offensive in Macedonia met the opposition of both Greece and Serbia. The Bulgarian gains had been chiefly won at the expense of the Greeks whose influence was exerted through the Patriarchate at Constantinople. Greek interest in the area was also increased when with the acquisition of Thessaly and part of Epirus in 1881 their national territories approached those of the disputed area. Serbian claims were also reinforced after the disappointments of the Congress of Berlin. Forced by Russia to acquiesce to the Austrian occupation of Bosnia-Herce-govina and to accept a position of subservience to Vienna, the Serbs could only direct their ambitions and salve their national pride in Macedonia.

In order to fortify their own position and to win converts to their cause, the opposing parties in the Macedonian dispute pro-ceeded to organize. In the early 1880's the Bulgarians formed the Cyril and Methodius Society; the Serbian Society of St. Sava was organized in 1886 in answer. Those who sought an inde-pendent Macedonia established in 1893 the Internal Macedonian Revolutionary Organization (IMRO). Thereafter in 1895 the Bulgars set up the External Organization whose intention was the annexation of the area by Sofia. In 1894 the Greeks entered the scene with the formation of their Ethnike Hetairia. The first and perhaps the chief result of the rise of national feeling in Mace-donia was thus to destroy any hope of Balkan unity. Instead of concentrating on a policy of common opposition to the Ottoman government, the three states now engaged in bitter rivalry over this territory.

In addition to Macedonia, another section of the Ottoman Empire, Armenia, was also in the 1890's subject to violent na-tional agitation. Here, as among other subject nationalities of the Porte, revolutionary committees were organized with the aim of securing independence or at least autonomy for their people. Unfortunately, in this case, the Armenian revolutionary leaders made a grave miscalculation. They believed that if they com-mitted acts of violence against individual Turks, the Porte would reply with such extreme measures that the powers would be forced to intervene to rescue the Armenians as they had in similar cases come to the aid of the Balkan peoples. The plan worked only so far. Atrocities committed by Armenian terrorists did provoke a violent Turkish reaction; from 1894 to 1896 massacres were repeatedly reported. The powers, however, failed to react as expected. Although the British public proved sympathetic, the government did not act. Moreover, Russia, the upholder of the rights of Balkan nations, proved less receptive to the idea of Armenian freedom. With a large Armenian population of its own, which was also subject to national influences, the Russian government could not support a movement in the Ottoman Empire that might eventually react to its own disadvantage, particularly at a time when a strong Russification program was being pursued in regard to the Russian minorities. At this time also Russian influence had increased in Constantinople and Russia could gain no advantage from a further weakening of the empire. Although no serious crisis occurred over the question, the Armenian incident did lead to the formulation of plans to seize the Bosphorus should Britain take action. These were strongly supported by the Russian ambassador in Constantinople, Nelidov. In the end the powers did nothing for the Armenians beyond the usual recommendations to the Porte for reform. The entire question ultimately merged into the more serious problem of the Cretan uprising of 1896.

Although Greek in nationality, the island of Crete had not been joined with free Greece in 1830 because of British opposition. From 1824 to 1840 the island was under the control of Egypt; it then returned to direct Ottoman rule. The same condition of Turkish maladministration and national unrest developed here as in the rest of the Ottoman lands. Uprisings of the restive Christian population occurred in 1841, 1858, and from 1866 to 1868. These revolts were met, as ever, with the usual sequence of the formulation of reform programs by the powers, the acceptance of these plans by the Porte, and the subsequent failure of the Ottoman authorities to implement the measures agreed upon. However, even with the best will the Ottoman government would have had great difficulty in pacifying or conciliating the Cretans. They, like other national minorities, wished not reform, or even autonomy, but union with Greece. They naturally received a great deal of moral and material support from the mainland, although by the 1890's the Greek nationalist was more interested in Macedonia, where his claims were disputed by other states. Crete was clearly Greek and would inevitably one day join free Greece.

In February, 1896 the question was reopened when another rebellion broke out, which was supported strongly from the Greek mainland and by the Ethnike Hetairia. In February, 1897 the Cretan rebels declared their union with Greece. Although the Greek government was well aware of the international aspects of the situation, it was forced to send aid because of the great enthusiasm within Greece for the revolt. Prince George, the second son of King George I of Greece and, incidentally, the former companion of Nicholas II on his travels to the east, was sent to the island with an expedition of 1,500 men. This reopening of the eastern question and the new threat to the Ottoman domains was received very unfavorably in St. Petersburg, despite the support the Russian government had previously offered the Cretans in the crisis of the 1860's. The continental powers also favored the Russian position on the maintenance of the *status quo*. The enforcement of this policy was rendered impossible by the lack of co-operation from Britain. The Cretan rebellion could only be checked if the flow of supplies from Greece were halted, an action that could only be carried out with the assistance of the British navy. When this could not be obtained, no positive action was possible. Meanwhile, political pressures in Greece mounted. Although entirely unready for war, the Greek government in April, 1897 launched an invasion of Turkish territory. The Turkish troops, better prepared than in previous years, soon inflicted a decisive defeat upon the Greeks. At the same time Russia took steps in both Serbia and Bulgaria to prevent them from joining with Greece. The powers then put pressure on both Greece and Turkey and compelled the belligerents to conclude an armistice. In September a final peace treaty was signed, which allowed the Ottoman Empire only a few token gains despite its military victory. Although the Greek armies were defeated, the Cretans lost little from this disaster. Instead they won the fulfillment of much of their program. They were not allowed to join Greece, but they received an autonomous status and, more significant, through the support of both Britain and Russia, they obtained the appointment of Prince George as their governor. The separation was thus largely a fiction, and it could be expected that the island would soon be integrated into the kingdom. The Cretans, in contrast to the Armenians, had thus been able to win great power intervention and had achieved most of their national aims.

With the settlement of the Cretan question a condition of comparative calm characterized the diplomacy of the Balkans for the next ten years. The desire of Russia for the maintenance of the *status quo* in the area had been shown in her attitude toward Bulgaria and in her co-operation with the continental powers in the Armenian and Cretan questions. A similar policy of inactivity was also now to the interest of Austria-Hungary, whose government faced grave internal political problems. Since both powers had primary interests in other directions, Russia and the monarchy were able to come to an understanding. In April 1897, during the Greek crisis, Franz Joseph, with his foreign minister, Goluchowski, visited St. Petersburg where an agreement was concluded that put the Balkans "on ice" for the next decade. Both powers agreed to co-operate to preserve as far as possible the *status quo* in the area and to maintain the closure of the Straits. The problems raised by the possibility of the further disintegration of Ottoman rule in the peninsula were also discussed, but no definite plans were made beyond the mutual recognition of the fact that the balance should be preserved. In October, 1903, the two rulers met again at Mürzsteg. Here they discussed the new outbreaks that had occurred in Macedonia, and they drew up a reform program. Although their co-operation did little to settle the Macedonian problem, it did signify a continuation of a policy which removed the Balkan area from the international diplomatic arena until 1908. With her southwestern front secured through an understanding with her opponent, Russia was then free to turn her attention to the Far East. Without the agreement of 1897, the Russian government would not have been able to embark upon the adventurous and dangerous course that was now to be followed. The pact that brought peace to the Balkans thus led to war in the Far East.

THE FAR EAST TO 1905

Although Russian activities in the Near East thus showed a desire to retain conditions as they were and to co-operate with other powers, the policy adopted in Far Eastern affairs was to lead in an entirely different direction. For the first time in the century under consideration, the problem of China and the Far East in general were to occupy the central position in Russian diplomacy. Here Russian activities paralleled those of the western European states, who, after 1870, entered upon a new era of overseas conquest directed towards Asiatic and African lands. At the end of the eighteenth century European imperialism as a movement had slackened. Of the two major powers concerned, France had become absorbed by continental affairs, and Britain was at least partially disillusioned with colonial conquest after the American Revolution. Despite this weakening of interest, the powers had, nevertheless, continued to protect and enlarge their colonial possessions. Concern over the approaches to India was, as we have seen, a determining aspect of British policy as directed toward Russia. French expansion in North Africa, involving chiefly assistance to Egypt and the annexation of Algeria in 1830, signified the continued imperial interests of France, which were also reflected in other parts of the world. The attitude of all the powers toward the Ottoman Empire and Russia's conquests in Central Asia were also examples of imperial policies. The shift after 1870 was thus one of intensity and commitment; the states involved embarked upon more active programs of expansion aimed at the control or annexation of great stretches of territory in Asia and Africa. The character of the movement was also strongly stamped by the influence of the industrial revolution. The advanced technology of the industrialized states not only gave them the facility to subdue more easily backward nations, but it also widened the difference between the civilizations of the conqueror and the conquered. In addition, the new economic development made colonial areas more attractive as places of investment, of trade, or as sources of raw materials. Much of the former disillusionment with colonies had been that they did not pay. Now it appeared that indeed a highly profitable relationship could be developed between the industrial nation and its dependencies. The intense competitive national pride that characterized the nations at the end of the century could also find expression in this field. National glory often provided sufficient incentive when economic gain was not immediately apparent. The actions of Europe in Asia and Africa, thus, reflected, and indeed became, an extension of European politics—its industrial civilization and its competitive state system.

The chief power who participated in this new movement was again the greatest of the imperial states, Britain. But others followed close behind. France, Belgium, Holland, Germany, Italy, and Spain all joined in the competition. The United States and Japan, despite the fact that they at one time had been the objects of colonial domination, now also sought to expand overseas. In this complex Russia occupied an interesting position. In Asia, as we have seen, she was herself an imperial power, but in her relationship to western Europe she was in a sense a semi-colonial dependency because of the character of her trade, German investments and French loans. By 1914 approximately $2,000,000,000 in French money was in Russian hands. It has already been mentioned how France used the money market to ensure Russian support for her policies. Nevertheless, the Russian government now joined the other powers and also tried to extend its control over peoples and regions whose economic and political organizations were inferior to her own.

Excluded because of her geographic position from a real share of the African cake, Russia naturally concentrated on expansion in Asia, where she enjoyed certain advantages over the other great powers because of her long history of dealings with the Oriental peoples. Moreover, at this time Russia could follow an expansionist or imperialist policy only in the Far East. Her borders in the Middle East had been settled by agreement with Britain; the pact of 1897 with Austria closed that area for further gains. In addition, even if she had not wished to adopt a forward policy in China, it would have been difficult to maintain her former attitude once the other imperial states commenced their attempts to control China. Russia could afford to neglect her eastern frontiers and territories only as long as the area as a whole remained a power vacuum. When Britain, France, Germany, the United States, and Japan entered the scene, the situation was entirely altered. The Russian opponents in Europe and the Near East now appeared on the Pacific. Therefore, although in fact the Russian actions were to be offensive, not defensive, in intention, it was virtually impossible for her to remain passive once other states threatened Chinese independence.

The general diplomatic situation was also very favorable to the commencement of an active policy. The French alignment gave Russia security in Europe and a ready money market. The Austrian pact of 1897 closed the dangerous eastern question for a period. Germany was most anxious to encourage the Russian government to turn east and away from the Balkans, where renewed rivalry between Russia and the Austrian Empire could again place Berlin in a difficult situation. William II, in his letters to the tsar, repeatedly pressed his cousin to take up the sword of Europe against the "Yellow Peril." It was certainly to the interest of Germany to encourage the Russians to involve themselves deeply in Chinese affairs, because they would there inevitably run up against British opposition. The Germans believed that they would then be in a position to play between the two and to make gains to their own advantage.

The growing problems arising from the necessity of defending Siberia and the Pacific possessions also played a large part in the Russian decision to press forward in the east. The old difficulties concerning the provision of adequate food supplies and communications still hampered the development and settlement of Siberia. The advantages to be gained from the securing of a port that would be ice-free all year were obvious, although it could be gained only at the expense of Korea or China. The great weakness of the Russian Siberian communications, from a military and strategic viewpoint, became, of course, far more significant once the European great powers and Japan commenced a policy of expansion in Asia.

In addition, certain economic considerations influenced the Russian attitude. It has already been shown that in its relations with China the Russian government had in the previous two hundred years been more interested in the development of trade relations with Peking than in territorial conquest. The 1890's witnessed the spread of the Industrial Revolution to Russia. Russian merchants, realizing that their industrial goods were not of sufficiently high quality to compete on the markets of the west, wished to find customers in the Middle and Far East. It was hoped that these eastern markets could be captured and secured before the British arrived. With only goods of a relatively inferior quality to offer, the Russians had little interest in promoting free trade policies in their colonial areas. They were more concerned with establishing spheres of control where they would enjoy a monopoly and not face the competition of industrially more advanced nations. The amount of influence, however, that these economic interests could exert upon the decisions of the government is debatable. Although, as has been emphasized, commercial questions had always played a part in Russian policy in China, economic considerations at this time probably played a secondary role to those of political and military advantage.

Certainly, expansion in the east as an idea alone had a great appeal; Nicholas II himself was open to such influences. Many who were close to the tsar, such as Prince E. E. Ukhtomsky, believed in the Asiatic Mission of Russia. The colonial gains of all of the powers were justified by high-sounding claims about civilizing missions and the white man's burden; Russia was no exception. It is interesting to note, nevertheless, that the concept of Russian expansion in the Far East never won the real support of large sections of the Russian public. Only the Balkans, with the ultimate goals of the acquisition of the Straits and Constantinople, the Byzantine imperial city, greatly stirred Russian enthusiasm. The Far East remained more the concern of individuals and cliques, not a matter on which the Russian government could hope to win the same great popular approval with which such imperial activities were greeted in Britain or Germany.

The inauguration of an active policy in the east was largely due to the actions of the influential and able minister of finance, Witte, who thought of the question largely in terms of economic gain. Throughout his career in office, he advocated Russian expansion in Asia, but he favored a policy of gradual economic penetration. He thus came into conflict with those who wished to pursue the same goals quickly and with military means. Witte's first concern involved the construction of a trans-Siberian railroad. The need for such a line had been recognized in the 1870's, but it was only in 1891 that its construction was finally decided upon. Both Giers and Alexander III strongly supported the project, and it was the chief financial preoccupation of the government during the administration of Witte. Although the finance minister favored the line principally because of its economic advantages, he was not averse to drawing wider pictures for the impressionable tsar: "From the shores of the Pacific and the heights of the Himalayas Russia would dominate not only the affairs of Asia but those of Europe as well." [1] In 1891, as has been mentioned, the heir Nicholas, who was also accompanied by Prince Ukhtomsky, travelled through the east. At Vladivostok he was able to participate in the ceremonies inaugurating the commencement of the building of the railroad.

In the Far East, the chief areas of concern for Russia were Manchuria and Korea. Manchuria, whose territory extended as

1. B. A. Romanov, *Russia in Manchuria, 1892-1906,* translated by Susan Wilbur Jones (Ann Arbor, Mich.: J. W. Edwards, 1952), p. 47.

a salient into the Russian lands, was of particular interest after the decision was made to build the railroad to the Pacific. Quite obviously an immense advantage would be gained if it were possible to run the line directly across Manchuria to Vladivostok rather than to follow the curve of the border. Korea attracted Russian attention because of its warm water ports. In both of these areas the chief Russian competitor for control was not to be either Britain or the nominal owner, China, but the rising new great power, Japan. Korea, strategically of vital concern for the island nation, brought about the first open duel of Japan and Russia. In the 1870's the powers had been able to extract commercial treaties here as well as elsewhere in the Far East. Although Korea was in theory an autonomous kingdom under Chinese sovereignty, the predominant influence was in fact divided between China and Japan. In 1884, a reform movement, which was pro-Japanese in direction, caused disturbances that led to the sending of troops by both controlling powers. In 1885 the two governments agreed to withdraw their troops and henceforth to act together should further intervention be needed. After a decade of continued rivalry between China and Japan, another rebellion occurred in 1894, this time pro-Chinese, and both Peking and Tokyo again dispatched troops. When the revolt was put down, Japan refused to recall her soldiers and war broke out. The Japanese victory in this conflict resulted in the conclusion of the Treaty of Shimonoseki in April, 1895. In this agreement Japan gained control over areas where Russia had a strong interest and which were coveted by the groups that favored an aggressive eastern policy. At this time Korea was declared independent; Japan annexed the Pescadores Islands, Formosa, and the Liaotung peninsula with Port Arthur. Commercial concessions were also gained. The Japanese victory, which completely upset the balance of power in the east, affected adversely the other European powers.

In this new situation the Russian government had a choice of action: the integrity of China could be protected, which would require the revision of the Treaty of Shimonoseki, or compensation could be demanded to balance the Japanese gains. The general situation in regard to China was thus reminiscent of that in regard to the Porte. Russia could either follow a policy calling for the protection of Chinese territorial integrity but at the same time attempt to dominate the government and expel the influence of other powers, or she could favor outright dismemberment in co-operation with other nations. Witte at this time still favored peaceful penetration and thus the adoption of the first alternative. Russia, he argued, should oppose partition until she was militarily stronger and could therefore gain more. Instead she should seek to obtain the dependence of China upon her and win concessions in this manner. In contrast, other ministers, including Lobanov-Rostovsky, preferred to secure immediate compensation in the form of a port in Korea and rights in northern Manchuria. In this first instance, the advice of Witte won out. Russia thus joined with Germany and France to force Japan to accept a revision of the treaty. Consequently the Liaotung peninsula with Port Arthur remained under Chinese jurisdiction. Britain, who did not join in this pressure upon Japan, now began to see the island as a possible ally against the combination of Russia, Germany, and France in the Far East.

With this diplomatic victory against Japan secured, Russia turned towards implementing the policy of establishing domination over the Chinese government under the guise of protection. The Russian government enabled China to pay her war indemnity to Japan by supplying her with funds obtained through French loans. In 1895 the Russo-Chinese bank was chartered, with Prince Ukhtomsky as chairman, and again French money formed the basis of Russian policy. The greatest gains, however, were made when in May, 1896 the Chinese statesman, Li Hung-Chang, visited St. Petersburg for the coronation of Nicholas II. In the secret Li-Lobanov Treaty of June, 1896, Russia and China joined together in a defensive pact against Japan. In return for this protection, China was to allow a railroad to be constructed across Manchuria, which would shorten the route to Vladivostok by about 450 miles. This line, called the Chinese Eastern Railway, was to be controlled by the Russo-Chinese Bank because the Chinese refused to grant the concession directly to the Russian government. However, since Russia in fact owned the bank, it therefore really had the railway. The concession, which included some very unusual privileges, was to be for eighty years, when the line would revert to Chinese ownership without further compensation. The Chinese government also had the option of purchasing it after thirty-six years.

Despite the fact that this agreement on the surface dealt with railway matters, it established virtual Russian domination in Manchuria because of the conditions attached. The railroad company was allowed to maintain a police force, ostensibly to protect the line. It had administrative authority over the strip of land through which the line ran. Under the cover of this agreement, Russian soldiers were introduced into Manchuria, and the Russian government held practical jurisdiction over Chinese territory. Russia thus had established the basis for a possible future annexation of the entire province. With her interests in Manchuria now secured, the Russian government turned to Japan, and in 1896 the two powers established a condominium over Korea and agreed to co-operate to exclude other powers.

The Russian policy of seeking to maintain the territorial integrity of China proved difficult to uphold because of the activities of the other European great powers in the Pacific. In 1897 two German missionaries were murdered in Shantung. Using recompense for this incident as a pretext, the German government demanded Kiaochow and concessions in Shantung. The German action precipitated a round of outright landgrabbing by all of the powers. Despite the strong opposition of Witte, who continued to believe in the wisdom of the old policy and who did not wish to antagonize Japan, it was decided that Russia too would demand territory. Muraviev, now foreign minister, wished to take Port Arthur, and he secured the approval of Nicholas II for the move. In the spring of 1898 Russia was thus able to extract from the powerless China a twenty-five-year lease to the Liaotung peninsula and the right to build a naval base at Port Arthur and a commercial port at Dalny. Permission was given for the construction of another railroad, the South Manchurian Railway, to run from Dalny to Harbin, where it would link with the Chinese Eastern Railway. France and Britain at this time also used the opportunity to make gains at the expense of China. The policy of partition was accepted by all the great powers.

The absorption of the Liaotung peninsula by Russia, which had previously been denied to them, naturally was strongly resented by the Japanese. They were, nevertheless, willing to make an agreement that would signify their recognition of Russian domination in Manchuria in return for Russian acceptance of Japanese control over Korea. The reluctance of the Russian government to abandon all claims in Korea made such a pact impossible. However, in 1898 an agreement was made in which the particular position of Japanese commercial interests in Korea was recognized. The question of the political domination of the peninsula still remained unsolved.

The imperialist policies of the European powers finally provoked a strong Chinese nationalist reaction. The Boxer Rebellion of 1900 was suppressed by the European powers, who co-operated to meet this threat to their special privileges. The outbreak gave the Russian government the opportunity to send in troops to occupy Southern Manchuria and to increase its forces assigned to the Manchurian railroad. This strengthening of Russian military power in Manchuria and the subsequent threat that it offered to the interests of the other powers aroused chiefly the apprehension of Britain and Japan. France, the Russian ally, and Germany, who always encouraged Russian expansion, were less concerned. Britain, therefore, had to look outside the European political complex for an ally to aid in the halting of Russian penetration into China.

Britain, however, did first attempt to secure the co-operation of Germany, since obviously that power would provide the most effective counterweight to Russian expansion. Russia could not well devote her national energies or expend military strength in

China if she were threatened on her vital western front. Moreover, negotiations were in process between London and Berlin on the possibility of reaching a more general agreement. The German government proved unwilling to fight Britain's battles in the east and believed that it could only gain advantages for itself from the Russo-British antagonism. With the negative German attitude, Britain was left with another alternative, that of seeking the support of Japan. Here she was successful in finding a government with similar interests in regard to Russia. Britain needed in particular an ally with a land army. The potency of the Russian threat lay in the fact that Russia did have territory adjacent to China and she could occupy Chinese territories with large forces. The British fleet could obviously not meet the Russian armies. The problem facing the British government was thus exactly like that she had met in the Middle East and at the Straits. She needed the support of a power like Japan with an army in Asia, or one like Germany who could threaten Russia on another front.

Like the Russian government, the Japanese statesmen were divided among themselves on the policy to be adopted. Repeated attempts had been made and were to be made to obtain an agreement with Russia on the basis of the Korea-for-Manchuria bargain. In 1901 the Japanese former premier, Prince Ito, travelled to St. Petersburg to attempt to make a Russo-Japanese agreement, but he was unable to gain a clear recognition of Japanese predominance in Korea. The Japanese government, therefore, finally decided upon the conclusion of an alliance with Britain. During the initial discussions over the terms the inclusion of Germany was considered; but when the wider conversations between Berlin and London failed, this combination was abandoned.

The British-Japanese alliance of January, 1902 was a major diplomatic event for both powers, and it signified the abandonment by Britain of the policy of "splendid isolation" that it had so long followed. She now signed a pact of a general nature, whereas before she had consented only to join in agreements designed to solve specific problems. The pact, a defensive alliance, obligated both partners to preserve a position of neutrality should one of them be engaged in a war with a third power, but to join in the conflict should another state enter. Through this agreement Britain gained an ally against further Russian expansion in China; Japan received support for her claim to domination in Korea. The joining of the two principal Russian opponents in the east should have warned the Russian government of the necessity of adopting a moderate policy. Instead, Russian actions became increasingly irresponsible.

The lines of division on policy within Russia remained, meanwhile, much as they were before, except that Witte was supported by the foreign ministry, now under Lamzdorff, in his desire for the adoption of a gradual extension of control in China. In opposition, the war minister, Kuropatkin, although recognizing the dangers to Russian policy in Europe caused by the eastern adventures, supported measures leading toward the eventual annexation of northern Manchuria. The position of the regular officials of the government was, unfortunately, at the time being challenged by the influence exerted upon the tsar by a small clique that stood for an outright aggressive policy in the Far East. Of particular significance was Alexander Bezobrazov, whose most interesting exploit concerned the organization of a company for the exploitation and development of a timber concession on the Yalu river. This undertaking, far from being a purely economic move, was to be an instrument for the penetration and eventual control of Korea. Although the obvious significance of such a venture for Russo-Japanese relations was clear, the tsar nevertheless provided the money for the undertaking. Nicholas' involvement in the Orient always also received the strong encouragement of William II, who took every occasion to emphasize the support that Germany would lend to the Russian "great task" in Asia. Russia's destiny, wrote William II in 1895, was "to cultivate the Asian continent and to defend Europe from the inroads of the Great Yellow Race. In this you will always find me on your side ready to help you as best I can . . . the great future for Russia [is] in the cultivation of Asia and in the Defense of the Cross and the Old Christian European culture against the inroads of the Mongols and Buddhism . . ." [2] Later he commented: "Therefore it is evident to every unbiased mind that Korea must and will be Russian."

Meanwhile, the diplomatic negotiations among the powers in the Far East centered around the question of the Russian forces that had entered Manchuria during the Boxer Rebellion. Under pressure from the other governments, Russia finally agreed to withdraw her troops in three stages. With the completion of stage one, the operation was brought to a halt. By 1903 the adventurers and those who wished an aggressive policy had in fact taken over the direction of Russian policy. The defeat of Witte and the moderates was greatly aided by the support given the opposition by the minister of interior, V. K. Plehve, a bitter opponent of the finance minister. In May, 1903 Plehve stated his convictions: "Russia has been made by bayonets not diplomacy . . . and we must decide the questions at issue with China and Japan with bayonets and not with diplomatic pens." [3] The minister also thought that "a little victorious war" with Japan would do much to calm the revolutionary agitation within Russia. In May Bezobrazov was made a state secretary and thus assumed much control in eastern affairs. At the same time Admiral Alekseev was appointed regent over the districts of the Amur and Kwantung. He received with this post powers that previously had belonged to the responsible officials in St. Petersburg. With the clear victory of his opponents, Witte was forced to resign.

Although negotiations continued between Japan and Russia in 1903 and 1904, it was apparent that no agreement could be reached. Both states prepared for war. Faced with a constantly increasing buildup of Russian military power, the Japanese in

2. William II, *Letters from the Kaiser to the Czar,* edited by Isaac Don Levine (New York, Frederick A. Stokes, 1920), pp. 10-13.
3. B. H. Sumner, *Tsardom and Imperialism in the Far East and Middle East, 1880-1914* (London: Humphrey Milford, n.d.), p. 14.

ASIA (RUSSIA AND CHINA) IN 1904

February, 1904 opened the conflict with a surprise attack on Port Arthur. The imperial policies of both governments had now reached their logical conclusions.

The Russians at the outbreak of the war felt few misgivings, mainly because of their contempt for the Japanese, whom they referred to as "baboons." They, like the Japanese, were not averse to a trial of strength over the fate of Manchuria and Korea.

Despite the hopes of both belligerents, the events of the war did not unfold as expected. From the beginning the Russian military effort was hampered by bad leadership and by strong conflicts between those in charge of the operations. Although the trans-Siberian railroad was completed for most of its length in 1903, a section across Lake Baikal remained unfinished. The entire line was also only single track. Moreover, the Russian government was never able to make this war a popular one with the Russian people. It remained a war of the officials, and it never captured the imagination of the public. The Japanese met with similar disappointments. In order to achieve victory they recognized that they must engage and annihilate the Russian forces in Asia in a short time. A long war would allow the Russians to organize and mobilize their potentially superior resources and to bring men and equipment from Europe via the railroad. With more men and matériel on the spot in fighting condition, the Japanese forces did achieve initial great successes, but they did not attain their real objective.

The major battles on land and sea were, nevertheless, won by the Japanese. At the beginning of the war they had the advantage of a superiority in numbers of about 180,000 men to the Russian 130,000. They also were fighting much closer to their home base and their centers of supplies. Both Britain and the United States were sympathetic with Japan; the Russian ally, France, could do little to aid her. The war in the Far East centered on the Japanese attack on Port Arthur and on the campaigns in Manchuria. In January, 1905 after an unimpressive resistance the port city surrendered. The battles in Manchuria were of particular significance because of the relatively large number of troops involved. After a series of engagements in which the Russian armies were gradually forced back, the war in Manchuria came to a climax in the great battle of Mukden in February and March, 1905. Here the forces were about even, with about 300,000 soldiers engaged on either side. Once again the Russian troops met with a decisive land defeat.

The course of the conflict at sea was equally unfortunate for Russia. Much of her Far Eastern squadron was either sunk, damaged, or immobilized at Port Arthur at the beginning of the war. Later, Admiral Togo inflicted a defeat on the remaining ships. With the virtual destruction of its Pacific fleet, the Russian government was forced to bring its Baltic squadron to Asiatic waters; the closure of the Straits to warships prevented the use of the ships in the Black Sea. On the night of October 21, 1904, at Dogger Bank in the North Sea, the Russian officers mistook some British fishing boats for Japanese battleships and fired on them. This episode resulted in a major crisis between Britain and Russia. The British government in the war was naturally sympathetic to its ally. In contrast, the German government did all that it could to assist the Russian fleet, and it aided in the fueling and supplying of the vessels. After a nightmare voyage the Russian ships did manage to arrive in May in eastern waters only to meet with a naval disaster, the battle of Tsushima.

Russian naval power was thus erased and the armies beaten, but Russia had certainly not been rendered incapable of continuing the war. The military situation was, in fact, unsatisfactory to both sides. The financial burdens of the conflict weighed heavily in each country. The rise of revolutionary activity in Russia showed that troops might soon be needed to quell civil disturbances. Under these circumstances the proposal of President Theodore Roosevelt to mediate the war was accepted by the two powers. A final treaty was therefore signed at Portsmouth, New Hampshire, on September 5, 1905.

Agreement upon satisfactory terms was made difficult by the instructions given the Russian delegates, Witte and Baron Rosen, requiring that they surrender no Russian territory and agree to pay no indemnity. The Japanese government expected both. Finally a compromise was accepted, by which Russia, although not paying a money indemnity, did surrender rights in China equivalent to a high monetary compensation. She also was forced to agree to the surrender of half the island of Sakhalin. Japan received, in addition, the Russian lease of the Liaotung peninsula, along with Port Arthur, Dalny, and the Southern Manchurian Railroad, which had formerly been under Russian control. Manchuria was restored to Chinese jurisdiction; Korea, the point of contention, was declared independent, but was generally recognized to be within the Japanese sphere. In 1910 Japan formally annexed the peninsula. Thus, with the exception of Sakhalin, Russia did indeed surrender none of her national territory, but she did lose almost all that she had gained in the past decade of intense diplomatic and military activity in the Far East. Her armies had suffered humiliating defeats, and the peace, like that in connection with the Kuldja crisis, was a blow to Russian prestige. Asiatic armies and an Asiatic power had been able to overcome a European state.

After the defeat by Japan and with the concentration on internal reform after 1905, Russian policy again became limited and realistic in the Far East. In addition, since after the war Russian diplomacy was again to shift to the Near East, Russia was led by general considerations to seek a policy of agreement with her former enemies, Britain and Japan. A peaceful settlement of the remaining issues in the east would allow a full concentration on the other problems. Having failed to defeat each other, both Japan and Russia saw the wisdom of co-operating, this time to the detriment of the interests of China. In 1907 and 1910 agreements were concluded, which, if they had been signed in 1904, would have prevented the war. The Russian government now, with far more respect for Japan, agreed to a partition treaty. Japan retained full control in Korean affairs and in southern Manchuria and Inner Mongolia; Russia for her share was given domination over northern Manchuria and Outer Mongolia. In 1911, Outer Mongolia, with Russian support, declared itself independent of China and thereafter became a clear Russian dependency. A further treaty confirming and delimiting these spheres of influence was concluded in 1912. By collaborating with Japan in the partition of China, Russia thus made great gains of territory at no cost. The policy of co-operation with Japan at this time fitted well into the general Russian pattern of alliances that had meanwhile developed in Europe. On the eve of the First World War, Russia, Japan, France, and Britain formed a common front in an alliance that operated to the Russian advantage in Europe and Asia.

Although Russia therefore lost in the end comparatively little in the peace, the public reaction to the loss of the war helped precipitate events that led to a major change in the political structure of the empire. Once again, as in 1854-56, defeat in battle had brought to light the grievous faults and failures in the civilian and military apparatus. In 1905, however, in contrast to 1856, reform was forced upon the government by the active agitation of the people. Throughout the reign of Nicholas II discontent with the autocratic regime had spread widely among the population. Opposition stemmed not only from among the rural classes but also from among the social groups whose numbers had been greatly increased by the industrialization of the country—the workers and the middle class. In Russia, as in other European countries, both radical and liberal first joined together in a common effort to change the conservative regime of the tsar. Here, as elsewhere, liberal leadership and the classical program of that political philosophy, with its emphasis on constitutional government and civil rights for all classes, were first predominant. Internal agitation and the demand for reform were given impetus by the reports of the humiliating defeats and failures in the war against Japan. The revolutionary year 1905 commenced with the events of the "Bloody Sunday" of January when soldiers shot down workers who had come to petition the tsar. This disaster was followed by a wave of strikes and of peasant uprisings in the country. Although in March the tsar agreed to the summoning of an elective legislature, the disorders and violence increased during the summer. The revolutionary activity culminated in the great strike of October. Faced by this rebellion Nicholas II in the same month issued a manifesto, drawn up by Witte, which answered in essence the liberal demands. Russia was to receive a popularly elected legislature (the Duma), whose approval would be necessary for the passage of laws. Full civil rights were also guaranteed. With these changes, Russia now became a constitutional monarchy. In the next years, as in the period after the Crimean War when the great reforms were introduced, the prime attention in Russia was again concentrated upon the internal scene. The new regulations were not successful in meeting the domestic problems. In this situation of political instability and unrest at home, it was thus advisable that Russia be part of a strong external alliance system, which would provide protection at a time of internal crisis.

THE FORMATION OF THE TRIPLE ENTENTE

During the years when Russian attention was concentrated in the Far East, the other European powers went through a period of changing relationships. In the west, colonial questions centering upon Africa and the Mediterranean held the center of the stage. In this field, similar to the situation in the Near and Far East, the continental alliance lines of Triple Alliance and Franco-Russian alliance did not hold firmly. The tendency shown by the continental imperial powers to co-operate overseas was, of course, a great disadvantage to the one nation that had remained outside of either grouping, Britain. This power now conflicted with France in Africa and with Russia in the Middle and Far East. The Near East, it will be remembered, remained out of the international limelight for about a decade. Like Russia and Germany, Britain also always had to face the danger that the other states might unite to partition her possessions. The idea of a continental coalition against the British Empire, which Napoleon had in fact tried to form, was always a possibility. The existence of this state of tension between Britain and the alliance of France and Russia in the imperial field was of particular value to Germany, who hoped to be able to play between the rivals. Because of the apparently irreconcilable divisions between them, the German government never gave sufficient weight to the danger that Russia, France, and Britain might reverse this situation and combine against Berlin.

The most interesting of the diplomatic negotiations of the end of the century were those carried on at the time between Germany and Britain in an attempt to settle the terms for an alliance. The desire of the German government at the beginning of the reign of William II for such a combination has already been discussed. Certainly at this time the two powers did have many interests in common, and no great disputes divided them before the launching of the German naval program. They had much to offer each other; their combination in an alliance would join the greatest seapower with the strongest landpower. They were also the two most highly industrialized states and each other's best customers. However, in many issues they did not have common interests. In the 1890's Britain, as has been mentioned, was anxious to acquire an ally who could exert pressure on Russia and limit her expansion in Asia. The British, with their military strength concentrated on the seas, could not render equal service to Germany. Germany might find her army fighting Britain's battles for her empire. Moreover, Germany expected to gain by Russian conquests in China, and she had done her utmost to encourage Russian efforts in the East. At the end of the century Germany's embarcation on a policy of overseas expansion and, in particular, her decision to build a "risk" navy provided a specific source of great friction between the governments. The rise of German competition in the overseas markets to the detriment of British trade also contributed to the increase of the conflict. Nevertheless, negotiations were directed towards an alliance. The British colonial secretary, Joseph Chamberlain, was a particular supporter of what he regarded as a "natural alliance." The first discussions in 1898 reached no definite conclusion. When the outbreak of the Boer War in 1899 clearly demonstrated to the British the danger of their isolated position, they made another attempt in 1901 to reach an agreement with Berlin. The negotiations this time centered entirely on the Asiatic question. Germany, averse to entanglements with Russia and feeling that under the circumstances Britain was bound to act with her in any given diplomatic situation, refused to accept terms that might eventually engage her in a war with the allied France and Russia for the sake of Britain's eastern possessions. With this refusal Britain turned, as has been explained, to the east to find an ally against Russia. In 1902 Britain concluded the alliance with Japan.

The French government, meanwhile, also reassessed its position. France too had no desire to face Germany in a war started by the Russian-British disputes over the control of China. Moreover, unlike Germany, France had a clear view of its own primary interests and major aims. Whereas Berlin now attempted to pursue an active policy both overseas and on the continent and finally gained the enmity of three of the five great powers, France gave a clear first priority to its continental position and to the German frontier. The French government was thus willing to compromise on its maximum colonial program in order to strengthen its continental position. From 1898 to 1905 Théophile Delcassé directed French policy; under his leadership a slow and gradual rapprochement was undertaken with Britain and Italy. In 1899 an agreement over the Sudan was reached with London. In 1900 a deal was made with Italy by which French rights in Morocco were recognized in return for French acceptance of the Italian claims in Libya. This pact with France lessened the dependence of Italy on the Triple Alliance for support for its colonial endeavors. In an even more significant agreement, signed in November, 1902, Italy further gave the assurance that she would remain neutral should France "as the result of direct provocation . . . find herself compelled, in defense of her honor or of her security, to take the initiative of a declaration of war." The Italians had thus for all practical purposes left the Triple Alliance.

The most significant of the French negotiations were, however, those begun with Britain who now had no hope that a German alliance could be completed. The successful conclusion of these discussions produced the Entente Cordiale of 1904. In the agreement made at this time, Britain and France settled between them all of their outstanding colonial disputes. The heart of the pact was the recognition that Morocco should fall to France and Egypt to Britain. Other points of conflict in Newfoundland, Africa, and Siam were simultaneously settled. In 1904 Spain and France made a similar agreement delimiting their respective spheres of influence in Morocco. These colonial settlements profoundly altered the diplomatic scene. Through the instrument of these pacts, France was now linked with Britain, Spain, and Italy, the latter having in reality withdrawn from the alignment with the central powers. The French government also had the alliance with Russia, which had been strengthened in 1899; its new partner, Britain, was linked by a firm agreement with the great power of the Far East, Japan. Therefore, by 1904 France had succeeded in reversing the conditions that had existed in Bismarck's time; it was Paris and not Berlin that was the center of European diplomacy. It was naturally to the interest of France to round out her diplomatic system by drawing her two partners, Russia and Britain, into some kind of a combination. The danger of their continued antagonism had been clearly shown in the Russo-Japanese War. If France could end this contradiction in her alliances by bringing both powers into agreement, she would have regained the continental position that she lost in 1870.

By 1905 Russia, weakened by a lost war and an internal revolution, was also ready to negotiate. The Russian leaders recognized that they would need a period of peace and that a policy of retrenchment in foreign affairs would be advisable. The extreme financial distress in which the Russian government found itself naturally made it increasingly dependent on French loans, which Paris always used as political weapons. By this time Russia, as Britain had done previously, had conducted unsuccessful negotiations with Germany. With the exception of the issues involved in the Russian-Austrian quarrel in the Balkans, Russia and Germany had even less cause to disagree than did Britain and Germany. Certainly, as long as the Russian government had Britain as its chief opponent, it could not afford to antagonize Berlin.

Moreover, in the Near East and in China in the 1890's the three powers, Russia, France, and Germany, had co-operated with success. There was always the temptation for the continental powers to continue this policy and to combine in a coalition directed at the destruction of British world power. With the failure of the British conversations, William II, in reversal of his policy in 1890, sought actively to obtain an agreement with Russia. Since the German government was averse to the inclusion of France in preliminary discussions, the German emperor attempted to use his influence over the weak tsar to gain the type of agreement favored in Berlin. Two attempts were made in 1904 and 1905 by William II to negotiate a defensive alliance of the two countries; both failed because of the opposition of the Russian and the German ministries to the conditions formulated by their rulers.

After the Dogger Bank incident William II in October, 1904 sent to Nicholas II the draft of a defensive alliance. Article 2 of this agreement provided for the eventual adherence of France. Although the tsar approved the pact, both Witte and Lamzdorff insisted that it was in contradiction to the French agreement; Paris should first be consulted and not merely be asked to adhere later. When Germany refused, the two countries signed a limited agreement promising mutual assistance if war with Britain should break out as a result of the German fueling of the Russian Baltic fleet during its journey to Asia.

The second attempt at an alliance brought similar negative results. During a meeting on a yacht at Björkö in July, 1905 the two emperors placed their signatures on a treaty much like that suggested in 1904. Its clauses provided that: "If one of the two Empires is attacked by a European power, its ally will aid it in Europe with all forces on land and sea." When Nicholas II finally disclosed its contents to his ministers, they again rejected it as incompatible with the French alliance. They were not averse to a tripartite agreement, but they did not want a tie with Berlin alone. As a result the Björkö pact simply faded out of the diplomatic picture. The German government, calculating that a Russo-British agreement was not probable, was not greatly concerned over this failure. It did, however, mark the last chance before the outbreak of the war for the re-creation of something like the old alliance of the three northern courts. It must be remembered that Russia at the time was linked to Vienna through the Balkan agreements of 1897 and 1903. The conclusion of a pact between Russia and Germany would have signified that ties of a kind again bound the former allies. The possibility of the formation of a continental coalition died, of course, with the establishment of the British-French entente of 1904.

Although the Russo-Japanese war had increased the tension between London and St. Petersburg, relations improved rapidly after the peace. In fact, it is interesting to note that the major Russian animosity appears to have again been directed against Germany, who had encouraged Russian activities and who many, such as Witte, believed had "pushed" Russia into the battle. In 1907 and 1910 the major differences with Britain's ally, Japan, were settled. There were therefore no more points of conflict in Asia. At the same time, with enthusiastic French approval, relations were improved with Britain. Although in the past century Britain and Russia had often joined in pacts of a limited and definite nature, conflict and rivalry as we have seen had more often characterized their attitude toward each other. Both nations now had a common interest in bringing an end to their traditional antagonism. In Britain King Edward VII and his foreign minister, Sir Edward Grey, were anxious to make an agreement, largely because of the increasing competition of Germany in the naval field. The conversations were also enthusiastically supported by the British ambassador in St. Petersburg, Sir Arthur Nicolson. Alexander Izvolsky, now Russian foreign minister, strongly favored the policy, but he did not wish the understanding to have an anti-German direction. He notified the German government of his intentions, and he received its approval.

Finally, on August 31, 1907 an agreement was concluded, which settled the outstanding colonial disputes of the two signatories in Asia. The most significant section of the treaty involved the tripartite division of Persia, the area where British and Russian interests most directly conflicted. It was agreed that Russia would dominate in the north, Britain in the south, and that a neutral zone would be established as a buffer in the center. In addition, Tibet was recognized as under Chinese sovereignty, and both powers were to withdraw. Afghanistan was to remain under British control, but it was not to be annexed. Although the Russian government sought to obtain a statement on the Straits, the British refusal to consider this question postponed it for the future.

Despite the fact that this agreement dealt only with imperial questions, it, like the Franco-British agreement of 1904, had far wider political significance. Russia was now part of a block of states, including France, Britain, Japan, Spain, and even Italy, which were linked by treaties of varying kinds. She also had the agreement with Austria-Hungary. With this defensive alliance pattern were created the basic conditions that would allow her a period of peace in which to concentrate on internal reform. If adventures in foreign policy were avoided, Russia had nothing to fear from foreign pressure. The danger area remained, as throughout the entire century, the eastern question. The situation here was also affected by the new grouping of powers and the heightened importance that the maintenance of the Habsburg Monarchy was now to have for the German Empire.

Russia had not intended that the British pact have an anti-German significance, but the event profoundly disturbed the German government. The visit of King Edward to Reval in June, 1908 increased its fears of the degree of co-operation that actually existed between Britain and Russia. The new friendship of these two former enemies appeared to close the last link in the chain that the Germans believed was encircling their country. Instead of following the examples of the wise French and Russian governments who, when pressed, simply cut their foreign commitments and retreated where necessary, the German government instead tended to react with increasing vigor and to extend rather than to limit its fields of activity. Germany challenged France in the two Moroccan crises of 1906 and 1911 and lost. The naval program, which contested British rule of the seas, was also pushed. An active policy was maintained in the Near East and relations between Germany and the Ottoman Empire became more cordial. Under these circumstances the fate of Germany's sole major ally, Austria-Hungary, took on a new significance; less than ever could Germany afford to see the monarchy collapse from inner strife or from foreign war. The progressive weakening of the real power of that state because of its increasing national disintegration was, therefore, to have a major effect on international relations. Unfortunately for the peace of Europe, after 1908 both the Dual Monarchy and Russia again turned their attention to the Near East. Neither power, because of its weak internal condition, could afford a setback in diplomacy; both attempted to seek major advances. A new crisis was now to test the Russian diplomatic alignment and also the relations of Vienna and Berlin. The Balkans thus again became the center of European diplomacy and were to remain so until the outbreak of the First World War.

The Revival of the Eastern Question

Neither Russia nor Austria-Hungary could well afford a strong foreign policy; however, both states acquired foreign ministers who favored such a course of action. In 1906 Alexander Izvolsky replaced Lamzdorff; in the same year Aehrenthal took the same office in the Dual Monarchy. The relations of the powers had hitherto been determined by the agreements of 1897 and 1903, which called for the maintenance of the *status quo* in the Balkans. During the decade in which this policy was in effect, a major change had occurred in the diplomatic balance in the Near East. Germany had in the meantime become deeply involved in Ottoman affairs and had acquired a direct interest in the fate of the empire.

It has already been explained how throughout his career Bismarck had remained well aware of the perils involved in the eastern question for the united Germany. The Balkan area, which he declared was not worth "the bones of a Pomeranian grenadier," he would have preferred to see partitioned between Austria and Russia. Under no circumstances did he wish Germany to become involved in a war over Balkan questions. In his alliances with Austria-Hungary and Russia he attempted to restrain the competitive powers and to keep the balance between them. This careful and moderate policy was reversed by William II, and the German government embarked upon a course of action that brought it directly into the problems of the Porte and made it a rival in Constantinople of Britain and Russia for dominant influence in the Ottoman Empire. The significance of German involvement in the question of the control of the empire was, thus, not only that it was a new departure in policy but that it also was bound to involve increased hostility with the states having traditional interests in Constantinople. German penetration before the war was both economic and political in direction. In the 1890's the chief German interests centered around the construction of a railroad that was to run from the Persian Gulf to Konia; the line would then join with the Turkish railways in Anatolia, which were already under German control. The "Berlin to Bagdad" railroad remained a point of diplomatic dispute until the eve of the First World War. It affected German relations with both Russia and Britain, whose interests in Persia were thus challenged. In addition to furthering these concrete plans in order to achieve an economic advantage, William II contributed to the suspicion with which the German moves were met through a series of singularly unwise statements concerning Germany's relations with the Moslem world. Most inept from the point of view of international relations was his declaration in 1898 at Damascus in which he proclaimed his friendship for the 300,000,000 Moslems of the world, a needless annoyance to Britain and Russia, both of whom had large populations of Moslem subjects, whereas Germany had none. The activities of Germany in the Near East, although she certainly had as much right to exploitation and political control as did her rivals, naturally resulted in the increase of the political importance of the Anglo-Russian entente of 1907.

Pressed by Germany in yet another field, the British government became more ready to strengthen the military ties with Russia and to overlook obvious Russian violations of the agreement concerning Persia.

Of far greater significance for the future course of events in the Near East was the process of weakening that the state structure of the Habsburg Empire was undergoing through the rise of national feeling among the Slavic populations. Although the Czech-German struggle was of major importance for the internal history of the monarchy, it was the South Slav question that was to have the strongest repercussions upon foreign policy. This problem was influenced by the successful conclusion of the national liberation movements of the Balkan peoples against the Porte. By 1900, as we have seen, the Rumanians, the Bulgarians, the Serbians, and the Greeks had all obtained independent or autonomous status, even though some of their people still remained under foreign rule. Only Albania, the most primitive and disorganized of the Ottoman regions, was yet without a separate political organization. These great victories of Balkan nationalism were bound to have an effect upon the nationalities of the Habsburg Empire, with, of course, the exception of the Germans and Magyars who enjoyed a privileged status. Although all of the peoples went through a period of similar national agitation, the South Slav movement alone will be discussed here since it involved Russian policy in the Balkans and led eventually to the great war of 1914.

The South Slavs in the empire were divided into three groups and lived in territories in both halves of the Dual Monarchy. The Slovenes, who inhabited chiefly the provinces of Carniola, Gorizia, Carinthia, and Styria, were governed from Vienna, and of the three South Slav peoples remained most loyal to the Habsburg dynasty. The Croatians lived both in Dalmatia, which was under Austrian control, and in Croatia and Slavonia, which were part of the Hungarian lands. The Serbs, the least numerous, were chiefly to be found in the Voivodina, under Magyar administra-

NATIONALITY MAP OF AUSTRIA-HUNGARY

	Croats and Serbs		Italians		Rumanians
	Czechs		Magyars		Ruthenians
	Germans		Poles		Slovaks
			Slovenes		

tion. The occupied provinces of Bosnia-Hercegovina were inhabited by both Croats and Serbs. Although many political programs were formulated to deal with the question of the position
of these national minorities within the empire, two in particular
threatened the existence of the entire structure. The first involved
the separation of the Croats and Serbs from the Habsburg Em-

pire with the subsequent formation of an independent Croatia and the annexation by Serbia of her nationals and their lands. The second, far more significant because of its grander aspects, was the Jugoslav movement, which called for the union of the Serbs, Croats, and Slovenes of the monarchy to form a great Balkan state with free Serbia and Montenegro. Despite the fact that the Serbs were separated from the Croats and Slovenes by religion, past history, and general culture, this idea of Jugoslav unity held the greater appeal and was therefore of the greatest danger to Vienna.

To meet the problem of South Slav agitation, two practical courses of action were open to the monarchy, both of which involved the Kingdom of Serbia. As the stronger of the two free South Slav states, Serbia naturally exerted a great attraction on the subjects of the Dual Monarchy, particularly those under Magyar control. Like the other Balkan governments, the Serbian state had as its chief foreign policy aim the acquisition of all of its national lands still under foreign domination. Both the Serbian and the Jugoslav programs of the South Slav minorities of the empire, thus, received constant encouragement from Belgrade, although the accomplishment of these plans would result in the dissolution of the Dual Monarchy. To counter this danger the first possibility open to Vienna was the path of attraction and conciliation. Under the program of trialism, associated primarily with the name of the heir to the throne, Franz Ferdinand, the Slavic minorities were to be brought into the administration of the monarchy on an equal basis with the dominant nationalities. The logical extension of this plan would be to then bring Serbia, willingly or unwillingly, into the union, which would now include almost all of the peoples of the three South Slavic groups. The empire would then be firmly based on the geographic unity of the Danube basin and also upon a political balance of its three component peoples. Ultimately, of course, because of the population ratio, the empire would have become a Slavic rather than a primarily German and Magyar political entity. The chief weakness of this solution was that which had previously plagued all of the reform proposals for the Ottoman Empire. The privileged peoples, in particular the Magyars, were no more willing than the Turks had been to surrender their position; the other nations wanted not a share in the government but autonomy or even a separate political status.

The second possibility, the solution by violence, thus appeared to many the only possible way to preserve the Empire. This alternative, which involved the forceful maintenance of the *status quo*, brought up inevitably the question of the disposition of the neighboring nation. An independent Serbia, following an irredentist program, would always form a center of leadership for dissident South Slav groups. Unless that land were either conquered and annexed or made a vassal, the Dual Monarchy would have on its borders a state whose national efforts were devoted to its destruction. From the point of view of Habsburg internal interests, the conquest of Serbia was a clear advantage; from the diplomatic standpoint it was a question of the gravest concern because of the links between Belgrade and St. Petersburg and the historic role of Russia as the protector of Balkan Orthodox Christendom.

Parallel to the increase in South Slav agitation in the monarchy, a new movement, Neoslavism, earned growing popularity in Russia, in particular among the liberals. This doctrine was especially relevant to the Slavs of Austria-Hungary who were primarily Catholic. In contrast to the Panslavs, those who supported this program called not for a Slavic federation under Russian control but a true league of independent, constitutional Slavic states. Since this plan would lead ultimately to the political liberation of the Russian-controlled Ukrainians and Poles, Neoslavism as such received little sympathy among conservative political circles. The dissolution of the Habsburg Empire was one matter, that of the Russian another. After 1910 the emphasis returned to the basic Panslav idea that Russian military power should be used where possible to free the Slavic, particularly the Orthodox Slavic, peoples. The Neoslav idea, however, was significant in that it showed that the Slavic question as such, and the liberation of Slavic peoples engaged the interest of Russian political circles from the left to the far right. This issue was thus one in which the government could ill afford to suffer defeats abroad.

Under these circumstances the relations of Vienna and Belgrade were of first importance to Russia as well as to Germany. This was the witches' cauldron that was to brew the First World War because it faced the four governments concerned with problems that were virtually insoluble by peaceful means. It could not be expected that the South Slav peoples, any more than the Poles, Irish, Bulgarian, Greek, or other peoples under alien political authority, would give up their endeavors for independence; in the given situation it was inevitable that the Serbian government should help them whenever possible. On the other hand, the Habsburg government could not remain inactive, nor could one expect the German and Magyar peoples to surrender their position without a good fight. It has already been explained how Germany, by the beginning of the new century, found herself with only Austria-Hungary as a loyal ally. Her own security thus demanded that this state remain intact and with little diminution of its military power. At the same time, events in Russia brought that government into closer relations with Serbia than it had enjoyed at any time in their previous history.

After the establishment of Serbian autonomy at the beginning of the nineteenth century, Serbo-Russian relations had varied in their degree of closeness and cordiality. The low point was reached when at the Congress of Berlin the Russian government abandoned Serbia to the Dual Monarchy in return for the control of Bulgaria. During the next period Serbia became in fact a vassal state of the monarchy. After the defection of Bulgaria from the Russian camp, relations between Belgrade and St. Petersburg became closer. In 1903 a particularly bloody revolution brought about the overthrow of the Obrenović dynasty and the accession of Peter Karadjordjević. Although a change of policy was not at once evident, the new king did bring his country closer to Russia; and, more significant, he subscribed to the Greater Serbian program, calling for the assimilation of all of the Serbs into the state.

Under the brilliant leadership of the king's chief minister, Nikola Pašić, who wished to make Serbia the Piedmont of the Balkans, Belgrade naturally became a point of attraction for the dissident South Slavs in the Dual Monarchy. The national program also won the enthusiastic support of the Serbian people, who looked as in 1876 to Russia for practical assistance. The accession of the new dynasty and its adoption of a program of national advancement added to the already dangerous situation. Now in both Austria-Hungary and Serbia strong parties existed which believed that their own desires could only be fulfilled by the destruction of their neighbors. In both cases the support of an additional outside great power was needed. Without the firm backing of St. Petersburg, Belgrade could not stand up to or advance against the Dual Monarchy. Without Germany, Austria-Hungary could neither defend its own position nor move forward in the Balkans. This perilous game of four powers was played twice. In 1908 Austria-Hungary made a move to the detriment of the South Slav idea, obtained the support of Berlin, and inflicted a real humiliation on St. Petersburg. In 1914 a similar action brought about war, the destruction of the empire, and the eventual victory of the Jugoslav idea. The Bosnian crises of 1908-1909 thus offered a preview for the chain of events that were to lead to the catastrophe in 1914.

Relations between Vienna and Belgrade after 1903 became, as could be expected, increasingly difficult. As the first step in his foreign policy, King Peter of Serbia attempted to establish closer ties with Bulgaria. In 1904 a treaty was concluded between the two states, which aimed at the accomplishment of a customs' union by 1917. Viewing this pact as inimical to her own Balkan interests, Austria-Hungary placed an embargo on Serbian exports and commenced the "Pig War" of 1906. (Pork was the chief item of Serbian foreign trade.) The Serbian government was able to withstand this pressure since it found other markets for its goods, notably in Germany. The chief point of friction between Serbia and the Monarchy was not, however, economic, but national. It concerned the provinces of Bosnia and Hercegovina. The Austrian occupation of these lands, which the Serbs regarded as their primary foreign aspiration, rankled. The extent of the Austrian investment in the area also showed that the monarchy did not intend to relinquish it again to the Porte. With every year Serbian hopes for its acquisition thus grew dimmer. Not only was it quite apparent that Austria-Hungary intended to retain the provinces permanently, but by 1908 that government had determined to change the status of the occupied provinces. The opportunity for such a move occurred after Izvolsky became the Russian foreign minister.

Immediately after his entrance into office, Izvolsky sought to embark upon a more active policy despite the obvious fact that Russia militarily was unprepared for such a course of action. He first made an entirely unsuccessful attempt to obtain the right to fortify the Aland Islands, and then he turned to the question of the Straits. The regulations that had been in force were in all probability the most favorable that Russia could hope to attain under the general circumstances of the time. The closure of the Straits did protect the Russian shores from invasion. However, the Russo-Japanese war had shown the difficulties that could be caused by the bottling up of the Russian fleet in the Black Sea. The long journey of the Baltic fleet to Asian waters had been made necessary because the Black Sea units could not be utilized. The ideal arrangement for Russia would be one that would allow Russian ships to sail freely in and out of the Black Sea but would deny equal access to other powers. It was precisely this unequal bargain that Izvolsky now sought to obtain. He was also under the impression, gained from the Reval meeting, that Britain would not oppose a change in the status of the Straits. France as an ally would not block his wishes. It therefore remained for him only to make an arrangement with Vienna.

Like Izvolsky, the Austrian foreign minister, Count Alois von Aehrenthal sought to commence his period in office with real accomplishments. His first action broke, in spirit, at least, the agreements of 1897 and 1903. Without consulting Russia he announced in 1908 the building of a railroad that was to run from

Sarajevo through the Sanjak of Novipazar to Mitrovica, where it would join with the Turkish lines of Macedonia and thus eventually lead to the Aegean. The plan was regarded in St. Petersburg as a violation of the previous arrangements concerning the maintenance of the *status quo*. In answer the Russian government announced a plan of a railway to run from the Danube to the Adriatic.

The Sanjak railroad thus caused friction between the governments; but the two ministers were chiefly concerned about the questions of Bosnia-Hercegovina and the Straits, and here they could co-operate to their mutual benefit. Although they had previously discussed the possibility of acting in these matters, their final agreement was considerably hastened by the Young Turk Revolution of July, 1908. At this time Sultan Abdul Hamid was forced to put into effect the Constitution of 1876, and the status of the territories still under the suzerainty of the empire came into question. Bulgaria as well as Austria-Hungary was affected by the events. Thus when Izvolsky met with Aehrenthal in Buchlau, Moravia, in September, he found that he could quickly come to terms on the question of the Straits. Although the exact decisions reached at this time became later a matter of controversy, the two ministers did agree in general that Russia would support the Austrian annexation of Bosnia-Hercegovina in return for the aid of the monarchy in securing the opening of the Straits for Russia. With the support of Vienna ensured, the Russian minister continued his trip to the other capitals of Europe where he hoped to secure a similar favorable reception.

Once Izvolsky had left, Aehrenthal quickly proceeded to collect his side of the bargain. He first consulted with Ferdinand of Bulgaria, and they agreed on common action. On October 5 the independence of Bulgaria was proclaimed; on October 6 Austria-Hungary announced the annexation of the provinces. Izvolsky learned about the event in Paris. The Austrian action precipitated an immediate international crisis. The status of the provinces had been set by the Congress of Berlin; in theory it could be altered only by another conference. In 1870 Russia had unilaterally denounced the Black Sea clauses of the Treaty of Paris, but this move had been confirmed by an international gathering. Izvolsky in particular was affected by the Austrian action. His visit to London, which had taken place in the middle of October had proved a complete failure. The British government had demanded reciprocal rights of entry into the Black Sea and had conditioned their acceptance on that of the Turks. Russia could therefore not hope to obtain its part of the Buchlau bargain. Russia then proposed that a conference be called to discuss the annexations. The monarchy agreed only on condition that all the arrangements be made prior to the opening of the meeting, which would then just register the *fait accompli*. Since no power wanted to go to war over the matter, the annexation was in the end confirmed by direct negotiations between Austria and Turkey. In February, 1909 Austria-Hungary agreed to return the Sanjak of Novipazar and to pay compensation for the provinces. In April, in another agreement, Ferdinand was recognized as the king of an independent Bulgaria in return for a similar payment.

Meanwhile, however, tension continued to mount in the Balkans, where both Serbia and Montenegro made military preparations. The Serbian government, deeply resenting this tightening of the Habsburg hold on a South Slav territory, hoped to obtain Russian assistance and appealed to St. Petersburg. Austria-Hungary, who had not consulted her ally about the annexation before the event, turned to Berlin and was able to receive full support for her policy. On March 21 the German government delivered what was regarded in Russia as a virtual ultimatum that the Austrian annexation be recognized. After consultation, the Russian government decided that it was not in a position to risk war, and the desired acceptance was given. Without Russian aid Serbia was powerless to resist. Not only was she forced to accept the annexation but also to subscribe to a statement that she "undertakes further to change the course of her present policy towards Austria-Hungary and to live henceforth with the latter on a footing of good neighborliness."

The entire Bosnian episode was on the face a triumph for the diplomacy of the central powers and a defeat for Russia. Izvolsky was in particular deeply embittered, since this event put the stamp of failure on his career as minister. In 1910 he was replaced in office by Serge Sazonov and sent to Paris as ambassador. In this position he retained his resentment against the central powers and he worked for the strengthening of the Triple Entente. At the end of this crisis Russian anger was directed primarily not at Britain, who had prevented the Russian acquisition of commensurate gains at the Straits, or even at Austria-Hungary, who had undoubtedly played a clever trick, but at Germany, who had backed up the stand of Vienna with a stern warning to St. Petersburg. The strong support that Germany gave at this time also had an effect on Vienna. It was now clear that in contrast to the policy of Bismarck, the German government would risk a major war to support the Balkan interests of its ally and on an issue in which it had not been consulted beforehand. In contrast, Russia had received no aid from her allies.

The Austrian victory over Serbia naturally intensified rather than calmed South Slav agitation. At the time of the crisis and in the years thereafter the Austrian chief of staff, Conrad von Hötzendorff, strongly pressed for the destruction of Serbia. The failure of the Habsburg government to have recourse to the solution of violence at this time probably removed the possibility that it could be carried through at all without unleashing a general conflict. In 1908 Russia was unprepared for war; she also did not have the backing of her allies should she have wished to come to the aid of Serbia. Although only a surmise is possible, given the general diplomatic situation we may assume that Austria-Hungary could have reduced Serbia at this time. Later in 1914, when with far more justification she launched an attack on Serbia, the position of the powers had so altered that a localized war was no longer possible.

Although the Bosnian episode embittered relations between Berlin and St. Petersburg, there was certainly no break between the governments. In November, 1910 Nicholas II with his new foreign minister, Serge Sazonov, travelled to Potsdam. There the two rulers discussed the question of the Near East, and the Russians withdrew their opposition to the Bagdad railroad in return for German recognition of Russian predominance in northern Persia. The agreement was a blow to Britain, who had previously refused to negotiate on the railroad without French and Russian participation. The German government was, however, unable to obtain the written declaration that they wanted, which would have contained a Russian promise not to join Britain in policies hostile to Germany in return for a German guarantee not to support expansionist Austrian actions in the Balkans. At the meeting the tsar did assure William II that he would not follow an anti-German policy.

The annexation crisis thus brought to an end the policy of co-operation and the maintenance of the *status quo* in the Near East, which both Russia and Austria-Hungary had supported in the previous decade. Although the Habsburg government did indeed revert to its former passive attitude, it could no longer act in close concert with St. Petersburg. In fact, now deeply distrustful of Vienna, Russia attempted to form a front against further expected aggressive moves on the part of Austria. Negotiations were first entered into with Italy, who was deeply dissatisfied with the failure of the central powers to give adequate attention to her claims for a share in the division of the Ottoman lands in the Balkans. The Italian government was interested primarily in the Albanian territories, but it had received no support from Austria for these claims. In October, 1909 Nicholas II and Victor Emmanuel, accompanied by their foreign ministers, met at Racconigi, where it was agreed that a policy of co-operation would be pursued in Balkan affairs. The Russian government also agreed to support Italian claims in North Africa in return for aid in the Straits question. In 1911 Italy went to war with Turkey and as a result annexed Tripoli.

The Russian desire to erect a counterweight against Habsburg penetration southeast affected principally her relations with the Balkan governments. Sazonov, personally a weak leader, had no desire to precipitate another eastern crisis; he knew well how ill-prepared his country was to meet further Balkan disturbances. Nevertheless, he did not have a clear policy of his own nor was he able to exercise control over the activities of his subordinates in the eastern capitals, who proceeded to implement programs of their own. The Russian representatives in Sofia, A. Nekliudov, and in Belgrade, N. Hartwig, were able to work actively to form a Balkan alliance, which they hoped would operate against Austria-Hungary but which in fact led to war against the Ottoman Empire.

Like the great powers, the Balkan governments were influenced by the Young Turk Revolution and the resultant Bosnian crisis. They looked upon the events as an opportunity for them to acquire the remaining territories of Turkey-in-Europe, in particular in Macedonia. The states thus welcomed the interest and encouragement given them by the agents of the Russian government, but they wished to exploit this support to expel Turkey from the peninsula and not merely to block further Austrian moves. Under Russian sponsorship the governments entered into negotiations among themselves and a series of agreements was reached. The first of these, concluded in March, 1912, joined Serbia and Bulgaria in a mutual assistance pact, which on the surface appeared indeed directed against the monarchy. In a secret annex, however, provisions were made for a war with the Ottoman Empire. All the territories to be annexed by each power were described, with the exception of a disputed area that was to be left to the arbitration of the tsar. In May a similar pact was completed between Bulgaria and Greece which provided for mutual assistance in a conflict with Turkey. Because of the clash of the claims of the powers over Thessaloniki, no territorial division was agreed upon. By October Montenegro had joined in agreements with Serbia and Bulgaria, and the Balkan League was completed. Since the Ottoman Empire was at the time involved in war with Italy, it seemed a propitious moment to begin operations.

Although Sazonov was kept informed on the course of the negotiations, he appears to have been singularly blind as to their real implications. When the French president Poincaré visited St. Petersburg, he recognized at once that these were war alliances. In face of this threat to the general peace the powers were consulted, and with general consent Austria and Russia, acting in the name of the other powers, warned the Balkan states not to start a war with Turkey. The declaration, sent on October 8, arrived too late. On that same day Montenegro declared war on the Porte, soon to be followed by the other allies. Russia, who had been instrumental in forming the Balkan association, thus saw it fall completely from her hands. She was unable to control the actions of the Balkan states once they had come into agreement with each other.

Despite the initial assumption of the powers that the Turkish armies would hold, it soon became apparent that the Balkan allies would win a quick victory. By May, 1913 Turkey had indeed been virtually forced out of Europe and had been compelled to agree to the cession of all of her territory north of the Enos-Media line. The Porte was left with only the Straits, Constantinople, and a thin edge of surrounding territory. The co-operation that the Balkan governments had shown in fighting the war was not reflected in the making of the peace. The Bulgarian army, because of obvious strategic necessity, had been forced to concentrate its main forces against the Turkish armies marching northward from Constantinople. The Serbian and Greek armies had used the opportunity to occupy the portions of Macedonia that they wanted, and they showed no inclination to leave. Moreover, when in the peace negotiations Austria insisted upon the creation of an independent Albania, Serbia was deprived of territory she had been assigned in the pact with Bulgaria. She naturally then wished a rectification of her claims in Macedonia. In a gross overestimation of their own strength, the Bulgarians attempted to settle the dispute by launching an attack upon their former allies. As a result, Greece and Serbia, joined by Rumania and Turkey, now fought against Bulgaria. In the subsequent peace, Bulgaria, who could not withstand such a combination,

THE BALKANS IN 1914

was forced not only to surrender much of what she had gained in the first war but also to yield southern Dobrudja to Rumania.

As a result of the defeat of Bulgaria, Greece and Serbia received the major share of Macedonia. An independent Albania was also established in concurrence with the wishes of both Austria-Hungary and Italy. The monarchy wished to block Serbian access to the sea; Italy saw the land as a future colony. In October, 1913 the Habsburg government delivered yet another ultimatum to Serbia, whose troops continued to occupy lands assigned to Albania. Serbia and Montenegro were able, by the partitioning of the Sanjak, to obtain a common frontier. The peace also allowed Greece finally to obtain Crete and other Aegean islands. As could be expected, the Second Balkan War broke the Balkan League. In the subsequent years Bulgaria drifted towards the central powers; the states who had benefited by the treaties, Serbia, Greece, and even Rumania, despite her agreements with Austria-Hungary and Germany, tended to join with the entente powers. The expulsion of Turkey from Europe thus in no way ended with the reconciliation of the states who had once formed her old domains.

With the division of Macedonia, and the expulsion of Turkey from Europe, three chief issues remained unresolved: first, the relations of Serbia and Austria-Hungary; second, the Russian demands for a change in the status of the Straits; and, third, the rivalry over the control of the Ottoman government. In 1911 the Russian ambassador at the Porte, N. V. Charykov, again brought up the question of the Straits, but his proposals were not backed by Sazonov once it became apparent that the powers would oppose any changes. In 1913-1914 an incident occurred that involved the question of the control both of the Straits and of the government when the German general, Liman von Sanders, was placed in command of an army corps stationed at Constantinople. The German general's position in the Turkish army was balanced by the appointment of similar British and French advisors in other sections of the Turkish service. However, his presence in the city in command of the forces would give him and, therefore, the German government a strong position in a time of crisis. Although the Russian government had no immediate plans to take the city, its traditional stand had always been to oppose the control of any other power, be it Britain, France, or Germany. The problem was solved by the promotion of the general to a higher grade so that he could no longer be in command of a mere corps. On the eve of the war Russian interests in the Ottoman Empire were thus what they had been throughout the previous century. Russia was quite willing to pick up the Straits if this could be done cheaply, but she would not launch a war for their acquisition. In the empire as a whole, she opposed German control or primary influence in the same way that she had always previously sought to block British domination. The power that held the Straits must either be entirely independent or under Russian domination.

1914

The year 1914 commenced much as any other in peacetime in the past century of Russian diplomatic activity. Certainly, there were few if any indications that not only Russian autocracy but also the kindred dynasties of the alliance of the three northern courts were on the eve of destruction. In general the Russian international position appeared excellent; her military buildup was proceeding with rapidity. As a partner in the Triple Entente, Russia was associated with the stronger of the diplomatic alignments. The basis of the Russian alliance system remained the military pact with France. Although the two powers had few common interests outside of their opposition to Germany, this bond proved sufficient. They also had no serious points in dispute. As long as the conflict with the German powers was maintained, it was certainly the natural strategic alliance for Russia. Since Berlin stood strongly behind Vienna, Russia needed an ally who could put pressure on the German western frontier, or her position in the Near East would soon become untenable. In July, 1912 the alliance was broadened through a naval convention; in 1912 and 1914 Poincaré visited St. Petersburg. Relations with Britain were never so cordial, due principally to the repeated Russian violations of the agreement on Persia, which were caused largely by the familiar failure of the government to control its local agents. However, as long as the German naval program continued, Britain needed Russia. In 1914 a British squadron visited Kronstadt; discussions for a naval convention were underway when war broke out. By 1914 Russia had also, as we have seen, developed friendly relations with Japan and, in the Balkans, with Serbia, Montenegro, Greece, and Rumania.

Although Europe was indeed divided into two camps, there

was little to indicate that these alliance systems would last any longer than their predecessors. What the Germans chose to regard as an iron ring of encirclement was not so firm and tight as they believed. The traditional alliance for Russia had been the one with Prussia; the ties between the dynasties remained fast. There was, moreover, within Russia, despite Panslavist and Neoslavist enthusiasm, a strong current of sympathy for Germany based on the economic bonds that had developed between the countries and, more important, on the fact that so many of the Russian statesmen had been educated in Germany or had personal ties with that country. Despite the reaction against the system of Nicholas I, it was still true that a large proportion of Russian officialdom was of German background. In addition, both Germany and Russia, as well as Austria-Hungary, were still joined together by their adherence to the conservative order, although in varying degrees. All three monarchs were subject to liberal and socialist pressure within their countries, and none could afford a lost war because of their own deteriorating positions. Moreover, aside from the Franco-Russian military pact, the lines of the entente were loose. Britain was tied to France and Russia by colonial and naval agreements, not by political pacts. The points at issue between Germany and the Entente were primarily Alsace-Lorraine, naval competition, and, with Russia, the problem of Austria-Hungary. The first two questions, although extremely important, could with difficulty trigger a war which would simultaneously draw in all the other states. The relations of the three powers, France, Germany, and Britain, were thus much what they had always been in the entire century; there was no indication that a rearrangement of the alliance systems could not be made as they had so often been in the past century.

The danger spot for European peace in 1914 lay in the Balkans because the issues in this area could draw all the powers into a major war. The nineteenth century had been a century of peace in the sense that there had been no conflicts on the scale of the wars of Napoleon. The engagements had been localized and of short duration, or they had occurred on colonial battlefields. In every case diplomacy had remained in control. For instance, before Russia went to war with Turkey in 1877, she took care to make arrangements with Vienna; and she stopped when faced by the danger of a larger conflict. Bismarck, before proceeding against Denmark, Austria, and France, made efforts to ensure that he would only have to deal with one state at a time. In contrast, the political situation in the Balkans and on the Danube, given the European alliance systems, had by 1914 evolved in such a manner that it would have been very difficult to avoid a world war should the question of Austria-Hungary and Serbia turn into a duel for survival.

The recurrent Balkan crises since the time of Peter the Great have been discussed in the preceding pages. Here we have seen that the powers primarily concerned with the fate of the Balkan peoples were Austria and Russia, both Christian powers, allied by a common political ideology, with a basic interest in the defeat of Moslem power. Their quarrels originated over the preservation of the balance of political power between them, but neither had any interest in the fate of the Ottoman Empire aside from its role in the European equilibrium. It was Britain who became in the nineteenth century the chief upholder of Ottoman integrity. It has also been emphasized that this question was the one issue in foreign policy that captured and held the Russian imagination. The hold of the idea of the Byzantine heritage and the ultimate capture of Constantinople was apparent in Russian thinking during the entire period. Emotional and irrational considerations were thus here at work to an extent not true elsewhere. By 1914, however, the Ottoman Empire had been driven from Europe; the Orthodox and Slavic Balkan peoples had been liberated from Moslem domination, and this deed had been accomplished without a major war between the great powers concerned: Russia, Britain, and Austria-Hungary. Moreover, although the Russian government was still interested in the control of the Straits, this question had lost much of its former significance. Russian domination of the area or the closure of the Straits to foreign warships was of major importance when Russia was at odds with the western naval powers. The only way that these states could harm Russia was to sail into the Black Sea and land on her southern coast. However, in 1914 Russia was in agreement with these governments; instead the opposition came from Germany, whose army stood concentrated at the Russian front door.

With the removal of Turkey from Europe, the next state up for partition, should the national idea continue to win victories, was obviously Austria-Hungary. The relation of the South Slav movement to Serbia, the necessity of the maintenance of the Dual Monarchy to Germany, and the Russian attitude toward Belgrade have all been discussed. The situation was made even more critical by the fact that at this time, not only was the Habsburg Monarchy politically weak, but the Russian government itself was in a position where it could not afford another humiliation in foreign policy. In 1905 Russia had been defeated by a despised Asiatic power; in 1908 she had been forced to give way before the strong stand of the central powers. By 1914 the Russian government felt itself militarily better prepared and it was also more certain of the support of its allies. It was nevertheless in no position to enter a major war, nor did it have any foreign policy aims worth such a risk. The destruction of Austria-Hungary or the complete domination of the Balkans was certainly not at this time a goal of immediate Russian policy. Russian real interests lay in the maintenance of peace and the development of her internal resources; her statesmen were well aware of this condition. A chain of events nevertheless occurred that, in fact, led Russian tsardom to gamble its existence for the sake of Serbia.

It is in the context of the mutual interconnection of the problems of Russia's relations to the Balkan Slavs, the South Slav question in the Monarchy, and Germany's dangerous strategic position that the assassination of Franz Ferdinand on June 28 should be viewed. The wisdom in scheduling a visit of the archduke to the Bosnian capital, Sarajevo, on the date of the Serbian national holiday is certainly debatable. The failure of the local authorities to take even elementary security precautions perhaps made them culpable. Nevertheless, the fact remained that the heir to the throne of the Habsburg Empire had been murdered by a member of a secret organization, whose membership included responsible officials in the Serbian government. The goal of the revolutionary organization was the establishment of a Jugoslavia and thus the dissolution of the Monarchy. Serbia was the center of its activities. Under these circumstances both the Austrian foreign minister Berchtold and Conrad von Hötzendorff now determined upon the destruction of Serbia as an independent power. They were at first opposed by the Hungarian premier, Count Stephen Tisza, who was only won over with the promise that no more Slavs would be incorporated into the empire. At the same time the German government was consulted. Although it was not clearly indicated that hostilities would be initiated, the memorandum sent to Berlin did state "the necessity for the Monarchy to destroy with a determined hand the net which its enemies are attempting to throw over its head." Both William II and his chancellor, Theobald von Bethmann-Hollweg gave their approval along with the assurance that the German government would back the Austrian decisions. This "blank check" considerably strengthened the position of the monarchy.

The final step of the issuance of an ultimatum was delayed about three weeks. During this period the Habsburg government investigated the assassination, but it did not enter into correspondence with other courts concerning its possible courses of action. Austria-Hungary thus adopted in this crisis the same methods that she had successfully used in dealing with Serbia over the annexation of Bosnia-Hercegovina. She attempted to limit the affair to a matter between herself and Serbia, and she resorted again to the use of an ultimatum. In following this course of action, the Monarchy chose to play a very dangerous game and one that violated the traditions of the past century. It will be remembered that before annexing Bosnia, Austria-Hungary did consult Russia; in addition, her action at that time involved no more than a change of status in a territory that was already assigned by great power agreement to her sphere in the Balkans. The elimination of Serbia as an independent power and its reduction to a state of vassalage to the monarchy would, in contrast, result in a profound readjustment of the balance in the area, particularly when it is remembered that as a result of the Second Balkan War, Bulgaria had in fact joined the central powers. Control of the Balkans would thus fall to Austria-Hungary; Russia would be separated from her allies by the very combination that contributed to her downfall in the war: the front of Germany, the Dual Monarchy, Bulgaria, and Turkey. In previous Balkan crises, the German, Austrian, and Russian governments had recognized the necessity of maintaining a balance; Russia had always tried to conciliate Austria before moving forward. Now, however, no attempt was made by Vienna to make a deal with St. Petersburg. It is understandable that the central powers would have opposed a conference where they would have been outvoted.

Undoubtedly, the Habsburg government relied much on the effect that they hoped the assassination would have on other governments. On July 24 Berchtold told the Russian councillor of embassy in Vienna, "The pan-Serbian propaganda directly undermines our house, our dynasty . . . The wiping out of this propaganda root and branch is a question of being or not being for Austria-Hungary as a great power." Berchtold added that Russia could "not desire the collapse of Austria-Hungary also in the interest of the preservation of the Monarchical principle." [4] It should also be noted that Russia would never have tolerated the continued existence of a Polish state on her borders that would have maintained relations with her Polish subjects similar to those between Serbia and the Habsburg South Slavs. It was not however to be considerations of this order that were to determine policy. The Austrian ultimatum was the result largely of what that government regarded as the necessities of her internal order; Russia, in contrast, based her decisions on the general international situation and her past influence in the Balkans.

On July 23 the government of Austria-Hungary finally completed and delivered a forty-eight-hour ultimatum to Serbia.

4. Stählin, *Geschichte Russlands*, IV/2, pp. 1036, 1037.

The document, designed to be rejected, called upon Belgrade to suppress all anti-Austrian activities and to allow Habsburg officials to participate in enquiries concerning the assassination. The Serbs accepted most of the conditions but rejected the presence of Austrian officials. On July 28 the Dual Monarchy declared war on Serbia. The Serbian government had, quite naturally, appealed at the beginning of the crisis to the Russian government, which had advised moderation. When the ultimatum was delivered, Russia promised assistance. Once Serbia and Austria-Hungary were at war, the question was whether this conflict could remain localized or whether the alliance systems would draw all of the powers into the battle. Nicholas II, who was in constant correspondence with William II during the last days, attempted at first to order only partial mobilization against Austria-Hungary. Since the Russian army had no plans to deal with this situation, he finally ordered full mobilization on July 30. Because of the Schlieffen plan, which called for a knock-out blow against France before the Russian armies were fully prepared to fight, the German government then mobilized and declared war first on Russia on July 31 and then on France on August 3. On August 4 Britain entered; on August 6 Austria and Russia were also at war.

Thus, after almost two centuries of controversy over the fate of the Balkan peoples, the powers of Europe were drawn into war by this question. Certainly, when entering the conflict none of the three conservative courts wished to or expected to secure the destruction of the others. No precedent for such an occurrence existed; wars in the nineteenth century had been limited in their results. Even the Napoleonic wars had not brought about a real alteration in the European state system, and the governments of the old regime had in general been returned to power. The war of 1914 was to show that the three eastern empires were indeed linked both in regard to their foreign interests and their basic political structure. Within five years the three dynasties were to be replaced, after defeat in war and with the triumph in each nation of revolutionary principles.

The First World War, 1914-1918

Although the story of Russian foreign policy in the century after the Congress of Vienna ends correctly with the outbreak of the First World War, brief mention should be made of the series of negotiations carried on during the war that were designed either to bring allies into the Russian camp or to provide for a division of the spoils in case of victory. These discussions brought out again the many problems still left unsolved, particularly in central and southeastern Europe. At the beginning of the war in August, 1914, all of the major participants expected a short conflict; their military plans were based on this presupposition, which put a strong emphasis on the time factor. By the winter of 1914-1915 each state had seen its hopes for a quick victory defeated; all were faced with a war for which they were not prepared. Under these circumstances it became more important that the nations that were still neutral be won and also that the allies compensate themselves for present losses with hopes of future gains. The governments thus sought to formulate their war aims and to make their claims for the future peace. This definition of goals was easy for no power. The war had begun basically over the South Slav question in the Habsburg Monarchy and the balance of power; only France in Alsace-Lorraine had a concrete territorial aim. Nevertheless the powers did conclude a series of bargains to protect their position for the future. The agreements of major concern to Russia involved primarily the partition of the Ottoman and Habsburg empires.

On September 5, 1914 Russia signed her first war agreement with the allies. In this the three powers agreed not to conclude a separate peace or to set the terms for the peace without consultation. The powers then turned to the task of trying to gain other states to their side. The first whose allegiance was still in question was the Ottoman Empire. In the beginning of August an alliance had been concluded with Germany, but the Turkish government remained divided over the question of entering the war. After negotiations with both sides, the empire finally decided that it could gain more from the central powers. In September the Straits were closed, and in November Turkey was at war with the entente. The entrance of this state had the immediate effect of cutting the best line of communications between Russia and the west. Supplies in sufficient quantities could thus no longer be sent by the allies, but it is indeed a question if, in view of military conditions on the western front, Russia would ever have received adequate war matériel even if this route had been open.

With Turkey now in the enemy camp, it was possible for the allies to bargain with her territory. The first and obvious claim to Ottoman land was the Russian desire to realize their old dream of the annexation of Constantinople and the Turkish Straits. In sharp contrast to her previous stand, Britain was willing to recognize the demand in return for Russian recognition of British control in Egypt. The French were at first hesitant, but finally in March, 1915 the assent of both western powers was given. A year later in the Sykes-Picot Treaty of March, 1916, France and Britain divided Asiatic Turkey. Russia accepted this agreement in return for recognition of her rights in Armenia and a part of Kurdistan. In other agreements the allies made further bargains, and Italy was also assigned a share.

The disposal of the lands under Turkish rule was not difficult since the empire was an enemy and the powers had in the previous years already established spheres of influence over certain areas. The settlements that concerned lands in the Balkans, particularly those under Habsburg rule, proved more complicated since they involved the conflicting claims of friendly powers. The future of Serbia, in particular, was at stake when the French and British governments wished to use South Slav territory to entice Italy into the war. The former German ally proved a tough bargainer; she desired the Tyrol, Istria, the Dalmatian coast, a protectorate over Albania, and a share in any division of Turkey or the colonies made by the allies. The claims to Dalmatia ran, of course, directly counter to those of Serbia and conflicted with the Russian desire to gain Bulgarian support with the promise of a part of Serbian Macedonia, with Serbia compensated from Habsburg lands. In the end the Serbian interests were sacrificed for what the allies thought was the necessity of Italian intervention. In the Treaty of London of April, 1915 Italy was given most of her demands, including Dalmatia.

The entrance into the war of the remaining uncommitted nations, Bulgaria, Rumania, and Greece, resulted from similar sets of agreements. In the negotiations with Bulgaria the central powers had the advantage of being able to promise Sofia Macedonia without selling out an ally. They also added the promise of Rumanian and Greek lands should those states join with the enemy. Bulgaria thus entered the war on the German side in October, 1915. Opposite conditions prevailed in regard to Rumania, whose national claims centered on the Habsburg lands of Transylvania, Bukovina, and the Banat. With the promise of these territories, Rumania joined the allies in August, 1916. The entrance of Greece, which followed a state of civil war and allied intervention in behalf of the party favoring their interests, came after the abdication of the king in June, 1917.

The last major political agreement into which Russia entered was that of February, 1917 with France. Here Russia agreed to allow France to settle her eastern border with Germany in return for the right to determine her own interests on the Russian western frontier. France thus in effect abandoned the Polish cause to Russian solution although the support of Polish nationalism had been in the previous century a main element of French policy. In August, 1914 the Russian government had issued a declaration to the effect that after the war an autonomous Poland would be created from the Polish lands of all of the partitioning powers, united with Russia through the tsar. This re-creation in an enlarged form of Congress Poland was unlikely to arouse much Polish sympathy because of previous experiences with similar assurances.

EUROPE IN WORLD WAR I

European Allied Nations

Central Powers

Neutral Nations

The carrying out of these agreements was, of course, entirely dependent on the achievement of an allied victory. Bearing the main weight of the fluid war in the east, the Russian military situation steadily deteriorated. Although great efforts were made in the field of war production, the Russian armies, after the winter of 1914, suffered increasingly from disastrous shortages. As in all previous Russian campaigns the problems of supply and communications were not well managed. The tragedy of the war front was repeated at home. Certainly, Nicholas II lacked the force of character necessary for a wartime leader. In September, 1915 he made the great mistake of personally assuming the leadership of the army, and he thereby absented himself from the capital. Control of the government then fell into the hands of Empress Alexandra, who in turn was influenced by the incredible adventurer, Gregory Rasputin. The appointment in July, 1916 of Boris Sturmer, who was regarded as a German adherent, to the post of foreign minister added to the disgust and distrust felt toward the tsar's government. The political opposition, well provided with examples of flagrant misgovernment, therefore, grew steadily during the war years. The collapse of the Russian front, both at home and on the battlefield, thus laid the scene for the revolutions of 1917.

The provisional government, established by the first revolution of March, 1917, forced the abdication of the tsar; and it also sought to continue the war despite a virtually hopeless military situation. This effort was ably exploited by the opposition, particularly the Bolsheviks, who made the conclusion of peace one of their main promises. The new Bolshevik government of the October revolution was, therefore, committed to a policy of ending the war. On December 15, 1917 an armistice was signed with the German government, and a period of negotiations was opened. The Bolshevik leaders, using the conference as a world propaganda platform, pressed for the adoption of the socialist formula of no annexations and no indemnities. This slogan had little appeal for the victors; and, after a renewed period of warfare, the revolutionary government finally signed the severe Treaty of Brest-Litovsk on March 3, 1918. This agreement provided for the national dismemberment of the tsarist empire. Georgia, the Ukraine, and Finland gained their independence; the fates of Poland, Lithuania, Latvia, and Estonia were to be decided by the central powers. Kars, Ardahan, and Batum went back to the Ottoman Empire. The Treaty of Brest-Litovsk was subsequently invalidated by the allied victory, but most of its chief provisions were retained in the later treaties. After a prolonged period of civil and foreign war, the Soviet government was forced to recognize the independence of former Russian controlled nationalities. In 1920 treaties were signed with Estonia, Lithuania, Latvia, and Finland; in 1921, after extreme difficulties, the borders were set with Poland. That year an agreement was also signed with Turkey, who kept Kars and Ardahan. In 1922 the political situation in the Middle and Near East was stabilized, although no final treaties were negotiated with China.

By the 1920's the Russian position in Europe had, thus, profoundly altered. The comparison with 1814 is perhaps the most illuminating. Russia under Alexander I had emerged from the Napoleonic wars as the first military nation in Europe and in a position to influence strongly the peace. In 1919 she had no place at the peace table. Because of the extreme nature of the Russian Revolution, she had become in fact an outlaw power in the eyes of the west. She also lost territory in Finland, Poland, and the Baltic region, which rightly or wrongly she had held for more than a century. Her influence in the Near East, once predominant, was reduced to nothing. Moreover, the war and the revolution had drained the country of money and matériel and had resulted in a disastrous reduction of population. In 1814 Alexander I entered Paris at the head of a victorious army; from 1918 to 1920 foreign armies marched through Russian territory.

The war also brought down the Romanov dynasty. In March, 1917 the tsar was forced to abdicate; in August he was sent to Siberia. There in July, 1918 on Bolshevik orders, he and his family were shot in the cellar of a house in which they were imprisoned. The last members of the family thus suffered the very fate that the tsars from Alexander I through Nicholas II himself foresaw and feared should the revolutionary forces in Russia not be confined.

* * * * *

The entire reign of Nicholas II tends to fall under the shade of the final catastrophe. Indeed a temptation exists to view the period in the terms of an inevitable last act of the drama of Russian tsarism. It is not difficult to emphasize the weakness of Nicholas II as a leader of government, the confusion of the administration, and the inability of responsible officials to see with sufficient clarity the probable consequences of the policies adopted. However, these characteristics had been present in previous regimes without severely endangering the state. Although it is true that the ministers of the tsar were not geniuses of statesmanship, they were no worse on the average than those who held similar offices in other countries. The question thus remains why Russia under Nicholas II failed to avoid a war for which she was not prepared and why, once in the fighting, the regime collapsed from the weight of the responsibilities placed upon it. The answer lies perhaps most completely in the fact that the last tsar was forced to pay the costs of a long series of mistakes and that the bill was presented suddenly in 1914-1918 for the entire account. In foreign policy, Sazonov, not Gorchakov, faced the consequences of the unification of Germany and the subsequent transformation of the Dual Monarchy. Nicholas II, not his four predecessors, had to accept the hard reality that the patronage of Balkan nationalism could involve the Russian government in deadly risks. Moreover, the new Russian alliance system, the Triple Entente, whose chief component was the Franco-Russian alliance inherited from Alexander III, had neither the military nor the ideological advantages for the tsarist regime of the old Holy Alliance in its various forms.

More significant was the internal failure. Throughout the entire century Russian military strength was in reality equal to her foreign power commitments. Through wise diplomacy she had usually avoided military conflicts with the great powers, but when her armies did fight, they demonstrated that they were not up to the necessary standard. The military power of any state rests upon its internal order, its wealth, and its organizing abilities. Nicholas II thus also paid for a century of Russian maladministration that had failed to develop an internal system, whether liberal or despotic, that could produce the armies necessary to defend wide boundaries.

Conclusion:

ᒪᕲᒪᕲᒪᕲᒪᕲ

The Nineteenth Century in Russian Diplomacy

Viewed in its entirety and not in the light of the final failures, Russian diplomacy in the century under discussion was, under the circumstances, remarkably successful. Not only were the frontiers of the eighteenth century held, but enormous expanses of territory in Asia were added to the empire. At the same time the Russian government played a major role in European affairs, particularly in the Balkans where the national movements triumphed largely because of Russian aid. The Russian maintenance of her position in Europe and the defense of the extensive frontiers is even more noteworthy when it is remembered how much Russia lagged behind her European competitors in internal development and in those aspects of national life that contribute to military power. In the preceding pages less attention has been paid to economic influences on the formulation of foreign policy than on questions of an ideological nature or those pertaining to national interest. In individual instances, commercial and industrial considerations played usually less of a role than current Soviet historiography assigns to them. On the wide stage, however, over the entire span of the century it was indeed the economic development of the Russian nation that determined and limited Russian commitments in foreign policy. Because of the tremendous improvement in the means of transportation and in weapons of war in the nineteenth century, the military power of a nation came to rest more than previously on the technological level and the industrial development of the state. Since the diplomacy of a government depends upon the army that backs it, Russian foreign policy was always strongly influenced by the consciousness of weakness. Although Russian actions as viewed from London appeared aggressive and expansionistic, the responsible Russian statesmen themselves were, in the majority, defense-minded. Their great fear was, as we have seen, that a hostile coalition of the powers of the technically superior west would invade their country and destroy their government. These fears were not idle speculation. Western armies entered Russia in 1706, 1812, 1855, and again in 1914 and 1941.

Since Russian policy did not rest on strong foundations, the question naturally arises as to why Russia was so successful in defending and extending her lands. The answer can perhaps be at least partially found under three general categories: the flexibility of Russian policy, the division of her potential enemies, and the alliances with Berlin and Vienna. The first consideration, the looseness of policy, is perhaps the most important. Russia, as has been noted, had no great ideas on a wide scale; she did not have ambitious plans or grand designs. The conquest of Constantinople most nearly approached such a conception, but certainly Russian national energies were never concentrated on the attainment of this goal. Instead, Russian objectives remained limited and circumscribed. The government seldom sought to continue ahead when faced with formidable obstacles; it concentrated instead on the filling of power vacuums. When strong opposition was encountered, the Russian government either made an agreement or shifted its attention to another place. With three fields, the Far and Middle East and the Balkans, open to their influence, the Russians were able to change to another area when one became closed to them. Russian statesmen usually did not try to knock down stone walls or take perilous risks. In addition, it has frequently been mentioned in this account how often the foreign ministry failed to control its agents in other countries. Although this situation could be dangerous, it, too, contributed to the flexibility and fluidity of Russian action. When a representative acted against orders but succeeded, the government could accept his gains; when he failed, he could be denounced and his acts disavowed. This method of advance is difficult for other nations to meet since it is hard to determine where a line should be drawn. The British government, in particular, had difficulty meeting this slow pressure and basic lack of responsibility in Russian activities in the colonial areas.

The second consideration, the division of the European states and their concentration upon their mutual antagonisms, has been amply illustrated throughout these pages. The powers of Europe remained so involved in asserting their claims against each other that they did not unite in a combination against the potentially most powerful state, except in the few instances mentioned. France and Britain, the western powers, although united by ideology, were divided by their empires and British fear of French continental hegemony. Austria and Prussia, with similar internal systems, were separated over the issue of supremacy in central Europe. When these problems were settled, France and Britain stood against Austria and Germany. Since Russia lacked great plans and after 1814 did not threaten to conquer Europe, there were few bases on which all of the states could join against her. The eastern question alone offered the possibility of supplying such a motive, and the Russian statesmen were well aware of this danger. Therefore, only in the highly unusual circumstances of 1812 and 1941 did Russia find the continent united against her; and even then, her usual opponent, Britain, at these times stood with her to prevent Europe from falling under the control of a single power.

It is also interesting to note that Russia at this time enjoyed the unique advantage among the continental powers in that none of her great neighbors had claims on, or desired parts of, her national territory. In contrast, the other nations—France, Britain, Prussia-Germany and the Habsburg Empire—all had rich and attractive lands in dispute between them or they quarreled over colonial domains. No major independent state desired a part of Russia; Poland with enormous historical claims on Russian-held territories was in this entire period under foreign domination. The Bessarabian question, in dispute between Russia and Rumania, could not influence the policy of the great powers. Moreover, although Russia in comparison with the European powers in general was a weak and undeveloped state, there was nothing in the Russian lands to attract the booty hunter. Had Russia had the sugar, spice, jewels or silks of the Orient, she might, because of her military weakness, have fallen victim to imperial movements similar to those which brought about European domination in the Americas, Africa, and the Far East. It was only in the twentieth century that Germany could envisage the Ukraine as a grain producing dependency and Russia as a source of raw materials in an open colonial relationship with Berlin. Under the National Socialist regime Germany did indeed regard Russia in the same light that the European powers had looked upon their imperial domains in the nineteenth century. Certainly, this attitude toward Russia was at no time apparent in the century between 1814 and 1914.

The third consideration, the policy of alliance with the conservative courts, was of equal importance to the failure of the potential Russian enemies to combine. For Russia, the principal problem of defense was closely associated with her geography. It has already been mentioned that the center of Russian life and government lay in the general area between St. Petersburg and Moscow, which was not only without natural geographic protection but which lay open to invasion from the west through Poland and Germany. In contrast, the peripheral areas of the state

were at no time vital to its continued existence. Siberia, Central
Asia, the former Polish territories, and even the Ukraine could be
sacrificed in time of war; but the existence of Russia itself would
be endangered should foreign troops control the crucial area for
a protracted period of time. In 1814 Russia achieved in the peace
the maximum protection for the center of the state. Poland was
in fact under Russian control. Central Europe was split between
Prussia, who was a client state, and Austria, who depended upon
Russian backing for her domination in Italy and in the Germanic
Confederation. The great military threat of the day, France, was
defeated and subjected to a military occupation. In the Holy
Alliance and the Quadruple Alliance, Russia joined with the
powers of Europe to preserve the *status quo*. Although the war
combination soon broke, the important association, the alliance
with Vienna and Berlin, remained intact for most of the century.
When Russia and Austria split over eastern questions, the link
with Prussia was always preserved until the dropping of the Reinsurance Treaty by Germany in 1890. The alliance of the three
northern courts and the traditional Russian-Prussian link guaranteed the safety of the Russian western border, the most sensitive
area of the nation. As long as these agreements held and as long
as Prussia herself remained undefeated by another power, Russia
was safe from the threat of a direct invasion by a hostile coalition.

The alliance of the conservative powers had the additional advantage for the participants in that it formed an ideological unit.
The First World War was to justify the belief of the three emperors that their dynasties would stand or fall together. The
adoption of the principle of intervention in the affairs of countries threatened by revolution also contributed to the strengthening of the Russian position before the abandonment of the policy
after 1856. As long as Russia herself retained a conservative system
she had no interest in seeing established on her borders liberal, national states, who would offer a threat to her government and to
her hold on Poland.Throughout the nineteenth century, to the
credit of Russian statesmanship, the relationship between political
ideology and foreign policy was recognized: states with similar

regimes make the best allies and, conversely, nations with revolutionary governments constitute a danger to their neighbor's internal security. The conservative alliance, thus, shielded Russian autocracy as well as the borders of the state.

During the century Russia made two major efforts to find an alternate combination to that with Berlin and Vienna. The first attempt in 1856 of an entente with France, however, did not signify the dropping of the policy of close collaboration with Prussia. The second, caused by the German refusal to renew the Reinsurance Treaty, resulted in the only lasting major realignment of Russian policy in the century and led to disaster. The formation of the Triple Alliance and the Triple Entente by 1914 signified that Russia had no longer a shield of alliances to cover her western front but that instead she found her major national opponent threatening her at her own front door. The entente also put Russia at the mercy of her allies to an extent not possible in the former arrangement. Britain as an alliance partner would be of little aid in the first period of a war because her strength lay in naval power, and, to use an expression current at the time, the British navy does not run on wheels. Although the French army was indeed strong, it was not equal to that of Germany. Moreover, in a war situation the condition could very easily arise in which the western allies would seek to win the war by sacrificing the Russians. If the western states devoted their efforts to a holding operation on their territories, the central powers would at some time be forced to invade Russia. The main German efforts would thus be drawn into and consumed on the battlefields of the east. In two world wars, where Russia joined with the western powers, this condition did in fact exist. The alliance with Paris and London thus opened the Russian lands to the peril of invasion; the alliance with Berlin and Vienna, in contrast, made such a campaign impossible.

The fact that the conservative alignment covered the Russian western frontier for the greater part of the century allowed Russia to move forward on other fronts when the opportunity occurred. In these fields the chief opponent was Britain, and it is the rivalry of these two powers that forms the constant theme of the century. With the possibility of using the center of Europe as a battleground removed, it was very difficult for these two combatants to meet. Britain could not offer dangerous opposition to Russia unless she could obtain a continental ally with an army. The Russian fear of a liberal Prussia in alliance with Britain and supporting the liberation of Poland was, thus, a legitimate concern. Britain could also menace Russia by sailing through the Straits and landing on the Black Sea coast, but the conquest of Moscow from Sebastopol was not a very practical undertaking. An engagement on the Afghan border was similarly difficult. Britain tried to meet the problem by alliance with Japan in Asia and with the bolstering of Turkey in the Near East, but this policy was not completely successful. Because of the geographic relationship, Russia with territory on the periphery of the British Empire was always in a better position to do damage to British interests than her opponent was in to harm her. The relative strength of St. Petersburg explains much of the intense Russophobia that characterized British feeling at various times. Having the unique double standard of the imperial powers, Britain was able to express a great deal of moral indignation over Russian "threats" to India and "aggression" against her overseas possessions. Britain had, of course, no more right in Persia, India, or Afghanistan than did Russia; both held their positions by right of conquest.

Through most of the century the Russo-British antagonism centered at the Straits, where the questions in contest involved not only the control of the waterway but also the domination of the Ottoman government. Russian policy in regard to the Porte, as we have seen, followed the pattern adopted in relations with weaker states or those on the verge of dissolution in other areas. Three courses of action were open: Russia could conquer the territory and destroy the regime in power; she could seek to dominate the entire state by control of the government; or she could come to terms with other states and partition the land. These possibilities also held true in Poland, the Middle East, and the Far East. In the nineteenth century, the first alternative, the outright annexation of the Ottoman Empire, was not a practical possibility because of the opposition of the other powers to such a major change in the European balance of power. Undoubtedly the Russian government would gratefully have accepted Constantinople (and the entire empire for that matter) if it had been presented on a platter, but the prize was not worth the risking of Russia's national existence. As we have seen, the question was repeatedly discussed during the century, but the dangers involved in every instance caused the rejection of the idea. As a result, the remaining two alternatives became the basis of her action. When it was possible for her to dominate in Constantinople, she supported the integrity of the empire. When another power threatened her position, she called for the partition of the empire either on the basis of a division between the great powers or, later, of increased territories and rights for the new Balkan nations.

The significance of the Near East in Russian historical tradition and its effect on policy has also been discussed in the preceding pages. It cannot be too strongly emphasized that here the influence of considerations that had little to do with Russian national interest were as important as those that related to questions of Russian power. Constantinople was not only a strategic piece of real estate, but it was also the former capital of the Byzantine Empire, of which the tsar felt himself the heir and the religious center for the Orthodox faith. To the hold of historical tradition and faith was later added the additional bond of the idea of the brotherhood of the Slavs. These irrational concepts had at all times an immense attraction for the sections of the Russian public that were in a position to influence policy. It was, thus, very difficult for the Russian government to accept compromise solutions in this area.

The question of whether the Russian government in its official aspects was primarily influenced in its actions in the Balkans by ideological or power considerations has been much debated. A clear answer is probably impossible to give because of the numerous contradictions apparent in the Russian actions. It was undoubtedly due to Russian military aid that the small nations were liberated from Ottoman control. Although within Russia the government followed a policy of Russification, nationalism was supported abroad even when certain of its principles conflicted with those of Russian autocracy. Russia in return for her assistance received very little. The Balkan peoples themselves were caught between their need for Russian aid and their dislike of Russian interference in their affairs. Throughout the century Russian policy wavered between the sacrifice of her own interests for the Balkan peoples and the use of these same nations for the attainment of Russian aims. Although the confusion in motivation was always apparent, the Russian government did at all times understand the dangers these issues held for her relations with other powers. It was here that her conservative ally, Austria, could join with her opponent, Britain, to form the base of a dangerous coalition.

In summary, it can therefore be said that in foreign policy the Russian government did attain its major objectives before 1914. Although it was not at all times uniformly successful, the Russian state was adequately defended, and major conflicts, which could involve the existence or the integrity of the empire, were avoided. Russian policy remained responsive and resilient. No attempt was made to inaugurate great programs of conquest; advances were made when the road was clear. The two conflicts Russia lost, the Crimean War and the Russo-Japanese War, were humiliations, but they did not result in a real reduction of national power. Moreover, in foreign affairs Russia learned lessons from her defeats and sought to rectify her mistakes. Therefore, despite the fact that the preceding pages have catalogued a series of errors, culminating in the losses of 1917-1918, the final impression gained from a study of Russian policy in its purely external aspects should be favorable. The nineteenth century thus provided a firm foundation for the further increases in territory and the relative improvement in power status achieved by the Soviet Union by the middle of the twentieth century.

ᒪᒿᒪᒿᒪᒿ

Suggested References

In the compilation of the following list, titles of books in English have been selected which would provide further information
for the general reader on each of the periods of tsarist foreign
policy discussed in the preceding pages. No attempt has been
made to assemble a complete bibliography of all of the excellent
studies available of Russian and general European diplomacy for
the period.

Betley, J. A., *Belgium and Poland in International Relations, 1830-
1831* (The Hague: Mouton, 1960).
Black, C. E., *The Establishment of Constitutional Government in
Bulgaria* (Princeton: Princeton University Press, 1943).
Charykov, N. V., *Glimpses of High Politics* (New York: Macmillan,
1931).
Churchill, R. P., *The Anglo-Russian Convention of 1907* (Cedar
Rapids, Iowa: Torch Press, 1939).
Crawley, C. W., *The Question of Greek Independence* (Cambridge:
Cambridge University Press, 1930).
Cresson, W. P., *The Holy Alliance* (New York: Oxford University
Press, 1922).
Dallin, David J., *The Rise of Russia in Asia* (New Haven, Conn.:
Yale University Press, 1949).
Florinsky, Michael T., *Russia*, 2 vols. (New York: Macmillan, 1960).
Giers, N. K., *The Education of a Russian Statesman: the Memoirs of
N. K. Giers*, eds. Charles and Barbara Jelavich (Berkeley: Uni-
versity of California Press, 1962).
Gleason, John H., *The Genesis of Russophobia in Great Britain*
(Cambridge, Mass.: Harvard University Press, 1950).
Harris, David, *A Diplomatic History of the Balkan Crisis, 1875-1878:
The First Year* (Stanford, Calif.: Stanford University Press,
1936).
Helmreich, E. C., *The Diplomacy of the Balkan Wars* (Cambridge,
Mass.: Harvard University Press, 1938).

296

Izvolsky, A. P., *Recollections of a Foreign Minister* (Garden City, N.Y.: Doubleday, Page, 1921).

Jelavich, Barbara, *Russia and the Rumanian National Cause, 1858-1859* (Bloomington: Indiana University Press, 1959).

Jelavich, Charles, *Tsarist Russia and Balkan Nationalism* (Berkeley: University of California Press, 1958).

Kohn, Hans, *Panslavism* (New York: Vintage Books, 1960).

Korff, S. A., *Russia's Foreign Relations during the Last Half Century* (New York: Macmillan, 1922).

Lang, D. M., *The Last Years of the Georgian Monarchy, 1658-1832* (New York: Columbia University Press, 1957).

Langer, William L., *The Diplomacy of Imperialism, 1890-1902* (New York: Knopf, 1951).

Langer, William L., *European Alliances and Alignments, 1871-1890* (New York: Knopf, 1950).

Langer, William L., *The Franco-Russian Alliance* (Cambridge, Mass.: Harvard University Press, 1930).

Lederer, Ivo (ed.), *Russian Foreign Policy* (New Haven, Conn.: Yale University Press, 1962).

Lenson, George A., *The Russian Push Toward Japan* (Princeton, N.J.: Princeton University Press, 1959).

Lobanov-Rostovsky, A., *Russia and Asia* (Ann Arbor, Mich.: George Wahr, 1951).

Lobanov-Rostovsky, A., *Russia and Europe, 1789-1825* (Durham, N.C.: Duke University Press, 1947).

Lobanov-Rostovsky, A., *Russia and Europe, 1825-1878* (Ann Arbor, Mich.: George Wahr, 1954).

Malozemoff, A., *Russian Far Eastern Policy, 1881-1904* (Berkeley: University of California Press, 1958).

Medlicott, W. N., *The Congress of Berlin and After* (London: Methuen, 1938).

Mosely, Philip E., *Russian Diplomacy and the Opening of the Eastern Question in 1838 and 1839* (Cambridge, Mass.: Harvard University Press, 1934).

Mosse, W. E., *The European Powers and the German Question, 1848-1871* (Cambridge: Cambridge University Press, 1958).

Nicolson, Harold, *The Congress of Vienna, 1812-1822* (New York: Viking Press, 1946).

Petrovich, Michael Boro, *The Emergence of Russian Panslavism, 1856-1870* (New York: New York University Press, 1956).

Pierce, Richard A., *Russian Central Asia, 1867-1917* (Berkeley: University of California Press, 1960).

Puryear, V., *England, Russia and the Straits Question, 1844-1856* (Berkeley: University of California Press, 1931).

Puryear, V., *Napoleon and the Dardanelles* (Berkeley: University of California Press, 1951).

Riasanovsky, Nicholas, *Nicholas I and Official Nationality in Russia*, (Berkeley: University of California Press, 1959).

Romanov, Boris A., *Russia in Manchuria, 1892-1906*, translated by Susan Wilbur Jones (Ann Arbor, Mich.: J. W. Edwards, 1952).

Rosen, R. R., *Forty Years of Diplomacy*, 2 vols. (New York: Knopf, 1922).

Saburov, P. A., *The Saburov Memoirs*, ed. J. Y. Simpson (Cambridge: Cambridge University Press, 1929).

Sazonov, Serge, *Fateful Years* (New York: Stokes, 1928).

Schmitt, Bernadotte E., *The Annexation of Bosnia, 1908-1909* (Cambridge: Cambridge University Press, 1937).

Seton-Watson, Hugh, *The Decline of Imperial Russia, 1855-1914* (New York: Praeger, 1952).

Seton-Watson, R. W., *Britain in Europe, 1789-1914* (Cambridge: Cambridge University Press, 1955).

Stavrianos, L. S., *The Balkans Since 1453* (New York: Rinehart and Company, 1958).

Stojanovic, Mihailo D., *The Great Powers and the Balkans, 1875-1878* (Cambridge: Cambridge University Press, 1939).

Sumner, B. H., *Russia and the Balkans, 1870-1880* (Oxford: Clarendon Press, 1937).

Sumner, B. H., *Tsardom and Imperialism in the Far East and Middle East, 1880-1914* (London: Humphrey Milford, n.d.).

Taylor, A. J. P., *The Struggle for Mastery in Europe, 1848-1918* (Oxford: Clarendon Press, 1954).

Temperley, Harold, *The Crimea* (London: Longmans, 1936).

Vucinich, Wayne, *Serbia between East and West* (Stanford, Calif.: Stanford University Press, 1954).

William II, *The Kaiser's Letters to the Tsar*, ed. N. F. Grant (London: Hodder & Stoughton, 1920).

Witte, S. I., *The Memoirs of Count Witte* (Garden City, N.Y.: Doubleday, 1921).

Zabriskie, Edward H., *American-Russian Rivalry in the Far East, 1895-1914* (Philadelphia: University of Pennsylvania Press, 1946).

Index